'Silke Roth provides us with a candid insight into the life-world of aid workers in humanitarian and development programmes. She connects their personal experiences to the contemporary context of neo-liberal societies and lays bare how the multi-layered and ethnicised hierarchies within "aidland" – notwithstandig the good intentions -reproduce existing global privilege and inequalities. The book addresses (aspiring) aid workers and is both sobering and inspiring, encouraging aid workers to reconsider the boundaries of "aidland", and seek to break the cycles where global inequalities are being produced.'

Dorothea Hilhorst, Wageningen University, The Netherlands

'This is a first rate book. Silke Roth has written the best description to date of contemporary aid workers. Her analysis is rigorous, evidence-based and rich with the testimony of aid workers of all kinds. She has described aid workers to themselves and to others with limpid clarity. At last we have a book on aid from a critical scholar that is accessible and constructive.'

Hugo Slim, University of Oxford, UK

'It is people, both staff and volunteers, who deliver the missions of aid organisations. By exploring the biographies of those working in the sector this book offers insights into factors, and perceptions, of essential interest to practitioners and employers: staff equity, gender issues, career motivation, and the impact of conditions of service.'

Jonathan Potter, Executive Director, People In Aid

'Silke Roth brilliantly analyzes the paradoxes of aid-work. She discusses how aid is structured through North-South inequalities and neoliberal agendas. Despite the commitment and passion of people who are engaged in such work, aid-work does not live up to its promises. A path-breaking book.'

Bandana Purkayastha, University of Connecticut, USA

'This book is an important and wide-ranging contribution to the growing literature on international aid as a form of work. Drawing on research with professionals from both the Global South and North, the book impressively highlights what characterises this work, and how people stay involved despite its often challenging and sometimes dangerous nature.'

Anne-Meike Fechter, University of Sussex, UK

'The best book on the aid world as it is today brought to life through a series of life histories. Written with crystal clear clarity. Well researched and a great read. I will buy a copy for each of my team of tutors and I will recommend it to all of my students.'

Larry Hollingworth, Fordham University, USA

The Paradoxes of Aid Work

This book explores what attracts people to aid work and to what extent the promises of aid work are fulfilled. 'Aidland' is a highly complex and heterogeneous context which includes many different occupations, forms of employment and organizations. Analysing the processes that lead to the involvement in development cooperation, emergency relief and human rights work and tracing the pathways into and through Aidland, the book addresses working and living conditions in Aidland, gender relations and inequality among aid personnel and what impact aid work has on the life-courses of aid workers.

In order to capture the trajectories that lead to Aidland, a biographical perspective is employed which reveals that boundary crossing between development cooperation, emergency relief and human rights is not unusual and that considering these fields as separate spheres might overlook important connections. Rich reflexive data is used to theorize about the often contradictory experiences of people working in aid whose careers are shaped by geo-politics, changing priorities of donors and a changing composition of the aid sector.

Exploring the life worlds of people working in aid, this book contributes to the emerging sociology and anthropology of aid work and will be of interest to professionals and researchers in humanitarian and development studies, sociology, anthropology, political science and international relations, international social work and social psychology.

Silke Roth is Associate Professor of Sociology, University of Southampton, UK.

Routledge Humanitarian Studies Series

Series editors: Alex de Waal and Dorothea Hilhorst
Editorial Board: Mihir Bhatt, Dennis Dijkzeul, Wendy Fenton, Kirsten Johnson, Julia Streets, Peter Walker

The Routledge Humanitarian Studies series in collaboration with the International Humanitarian Studies Association (IHSA) takes a comprehensive approach to the growing field of expertise that is humanitarian studies. This field is concerned with humanitarian crises caused by natural disaster, conflict or political instability and deals with the study of how humanitarian crises evolve, how they affect people and their institutions and societies, and the responses they trigger.

We invite book proposals that address, amongst other topics, questions of aid delivery, institutional aspects of service provision, the dynamics of rebel wars, state building after war, the international architecture of peacekeeping, the ways in which ordinary people continue to make a living throughout crises, and the effect of crises on gender relations.

This interdisciplinary series draws on and is relevant to a range of disciplines, including development studies, international relations, international law, anthropology, peace and conflict studies, public health and migration studies.

Disaster, Conflict and Society in Crises
Everyday politics of crisis response
Edited by Dorothea Hilhorst

Human Security and Natural Disasters
Edited by Christopher Hobson, Paul Bacon and Robin Cameron

Human Security and Japan's Triple Disaster
Responding to the 2011 earthquake, tsunami and Fukushima nuclear crisis
Edited by Paul Bacon and Christopher Hobson

The Paradoxes of Aid Work
Passionate professionals
Silke Roth

The Paradoxes of Aid Work
Passionate professionals

Silke Roth

LONDON AND NEW YORK

First published 2015 by Routledge

2 Park Square, Milton Park, Abingdon, Oxon OX14 4RN
711 Third Avenue, New York, NY 10017, USA

Routledge is an imprint of the Taylor & Francis Group, an informa business

First issued in paperback 2016

Copyright © 2015 Silke Roth

The right of Silke Roth to be identified as author of this work has been asserted by her in accordance with sections 77 and 78 of the Copyright, Designs and Patents Act 1988.

All rights reserved. No part of this book may be reprinted or reproduced or utilized in any form or by any electronic, mechanical, or other means, now known or hereafter invented, including photocopying and recording, or in any information storage or retrieval system, without permission in writing from the publishers.

Notice:

Product or corporate names may be trademarks or registered trademarks, and are used only for identification and explanation without intent to infringe.

British Library Cataloguing-in-Publication Data
A catalogue record for this book is available from the British Library

Library of Congress Cataloging-in-Publication Data
Roth, Silke.
The paradoxes of aid work : passionate professionals / Silke Roth.
pages cm
Includes bibliographical references and index.
1. Social workers--Biography. 2. Social service. 3. Humanitarian assistance. 4. Technical assistance. 5. Economic assistance. I. Title.
HV40.3.R68 2015
361.3092'2--dc23
2014041859

ISBN 978-0-415-74592-5 (hbk)
ISBN 978-1-138-20000-5 (pbk)

Typeset in Goudy
by Taylor & Francis Books

Contents

Acronyms viii

Introduction 1

1 Mapping Aidland 16

2 Theorizing (aid)work 45

3 Entering Aidland 65

4 Living and working in Aidland 83

5 Doing gender in Aidland 111

6 Othering and otherness 128

7 Should I stay or should I go? 148

Conclusions 168

Methods appendix 173
Acknowledgements 180
Bibliography 182
Index 205

Acronyms

ACF	Action Contre La Faim
ADA	Australian Development Agency
AKDN	Aga Khan Development Network
ALNAP	Active Learning Network for Accountability in Humanitarian Action
APDOVE	Association of Protestant Development Organizations in Europe
ATTAC	Association pour la Taxation des Transactions pour l'Aide
CARE	Cooperative for Assistance and Relief Everywhere
CERF	Central Emergency Response Fund
CISDE	Coopération Internationale pour le Développement et la Solidarité
CISOE	Centro Internacional de Pensamiento Social y Economico
DAC	Development Assistance Committee
DFID	Department for International Development
ECHO	European Community Humanitarian Office
ELHRA	Enhancing Learning and Research for Humanitarian Assistance
EPN	Emergency Personnel Network
ERC	Emergency Response Coordinator
EU	European Union
EVAC	EU Aid Volunteers
FAO	Food and Agriculture Organization
GAD	Gender and Development
GDN	Global Development Network
GDP	Gross Domestic Product
GNI	Gross National Income
GNP	Gross National Product
GTZ	Gesellschaft für technische Zusammenarbeit (Society for technical cooperation)
HAP	Humanitarian Accountability Partnership
HDX	Humanitarian Data Exchange

HIV/AIDS	Human immunodeficiency virus/acquired immunodeficiency syndrome
HPG	Humanitarian Policy Group
HPN	Humanitarian Practice Network
HR	Human Resources
IASC	Inter-Agency Standing Committee
ICRC	International Committee of the Red Cross
ICT	Information and Communication Technologies
IFAD	International Fund for Agricultural Development
IGO	Intergovernmental Organization
IHSA	International Humanitarian Studies Association
IMF	International Monetary Fund
INGO	International Non-Governmental Organization
IO	International Organization
IOM	International Organization for Migration
IRC	International Rescue Committee
JPO	Junior Professional Officer
LAT	Living Apart Together
MDM	Médecins du Monde
MP	Member of Parliament
MSF	Médecins Sans Frontières
NGO	Non-Governmental Organization
NOHA	Network on Humanitarian Assistance
OCHA	United Nations Office for the Coordination of Humanitarian Affairs
ODA	Overseas Development Assistance
ODI	Overseas Development Institute
OECD	Organization for Economic Cooperation and Development
OEEC	Organization for European Economic Cooperation
OHCHR	Office of the High Commissioner for Human Rights
OPEC	Organization of the Petroleum Exporting Countries
OSCE	Organization for Security and Co-operation in Europe
PHAP	Professionals in Humanitarian Assistance and Protection
PTSD	Post-Traumatic Stress Disorder
SIDA	Swedish International Development Cooperation Agency
TCI	Third Culture Individuals
TSOL	Total Social Organization of Labour
UK	United Kingdom
UN	United Nations
UNDP	United Nations Development Programme
UNFPA	United Nations Population Fund
UNHCR	United Nations High Commissioner for Refugees
UNICEF	United Nations Children's Fund
UNIFEM	United Nations Women's Fund
UNV	United Nations Volunteers

UNRWA	United Nations Relief and Works Agency for Palestine Refugees
US	United States
USAID	United States Agency for International Development
USG	Under-Secretary General
VSO	Voluntary Services Overseas
WFP	World Food Programme
WHO	World Health Organization
WID	Women in Development

Introduction

This book endeavours to understand what attracts people to aidwork and to what extent the promises of aidwork are fulfilled. I use a biographical approach which allows me to capture the whole field of aid by tracing pathways into and through Aidland. The careers in aid are shaped by geopolitics, changing priorities of donors and a changing composition of the aid sector. Over the past ten years, I have conducted in-depth interviews with people working in aid to understand what drew them to this work, what prepared them to enter the field, what opportunities they found and how they experienced working in aid. For aidworkers from the Global North, in particular those who work as field workers in emergency relief, aidwork is experienced as deeply exhausting and exhilarating, and contrasted with 'normal work' and 'normal life'. Until recently, sociologists neglected the study of aid organizations and the people working in them. This is surprising given that aidwork offers a rich field for the analysis of work, organizations, gender,[1] race[2] and intersectionality,[3] and that it epitomizes some aspects of work in contemporary neoliberal global societies. People working in aid raise important questions with respect to expectations of work and how work relates to values as well as to other aspects of life, leisure and personal relationships. It is of interest with respect to mobility and globalization. Moreover, aidwork is ridden with paradoxes that are grounded in North/South inequalities and tied into neoliberalism. These paradoxes will be explored throughout the book. My perspective is critical, but the criticism is not directed at people working in aid, nor at the commitment to social justice inherent in the aid system. My question is, in fact, whether aid goes far enough and in what way it could go further in order to overcome the paradoxes of aidwork and come closer to making good on its promises.

Aidland encompasses the real and virtual space of aid organizations and aidworkers working in development and humanitarian aid (Apthorpe 2005; 2011a; 2011b). I am interested in the 'real space' and use 'Aidland' for convenience as an umbrella term comprising development cooperation, emergency relief and human rights work, including personnel based in head offices who occasionally visit regional offices and the 'field': regional and field offices of international as well as local organizations. Aidland includes volunteers, consultants, staff on longer or shorter contracts, working in their own country or abroad, in a neighbouring country or on another continent. Aidland is thus a highly complex and heterogeneous context which includes many different occupations, forms of employment and organizations. It is global, including nationals from every country – as donors or expatriates, as recipients of aid or as national staff. In order to acknowledge this heterogeneity and complexity, contradictions and tensions, I argue that it is important to look at Aidland as a whole rather than focusing on specific organizations or sectors. A widely cited study estimates that the number of humanitarian aid personnel working for UN agencies and NGOs increased by 77 per cent between 1997 and 2005 from around 130,000 to approximately 240,000 (Stoddard et al. 2006). Only three years later, in 2008, an estimated 595,000 development and humanitarian workers were working for UN agencies, the Red Cross and Red Crescent movements and major NGOs (Stoddard et al. 2009). Despite this growth, compared to other occupational groups, aidworkers are just a small group. I argue that regardless of the size of this group, they are a significant field to study as they raise important questions concerning meaningful work and the corporatization of activism.

The end of the twentieth century saw a surge in transnational mobilization symbolized by the 'battle of Seattle' in 1999 which brought together a broad coalition of labour, environmental and global justice groups which protested against neoliberal politics. The turn of the century also brought the mobilization of the World Social Forum and ATTAC to discuss and demand more global justice, for example, the Tobin Tax.[4] These broad coalitions were undermined in the aftermath of 9/11 which led to a securitization of protest and silencing of critical voices. This securitization is expressed in the policing and criminalization of critical groups constraining advocacy of groups concerned with global social justice. The rise of the major humanitarian non-governmental organizations (NGOs) pursuing their brand identities to secure donations from individuals as well as government support has been interpreted as a corporatization of activism (Dauvergne and LeBaron 2014). At the same time there is an increasing involvement of celebrities in humanitarianism which serves both the brand of the celebrity as well as the NGOs which draw on star power (Kapoor 2013; Chouliaraki 2013). They demonstrate that development has 'become sexy' (Cameron and Haanstra 2008), and the central role of humanitarian reason (Fassin 2012) in contemporary societies in humanitarianism has to some extent replaced social critique.

Expatriates, locals and beneficiaries

Throughout this book I refer to 'Aidland' and 'people working in aid', thus lumping together vastly different experiences in these two broad categories which gloss over the fact that mandates of organizations active in Aidland differ widely. However, I use these categories not only for pragmatic reasons (it saves me from listing the variety fields in which organizations are active), but also because I argue that despite these differences, taken together these organizations constitute a field of power (Bourdieu 1977; 1990; Bourdieu and Wacquant 1992; Go 2008; Krause 2014) which is shaped by and continues to shape North–South relationships which reflect and result in global inequality. Employing the notion of Aidland allows me to capture a variety of interventions, tensions between different approaches and different relationships. It is important to consider that development and humanitarianism are related and to what extent there is an overlap between these fields and to what extent they are distinct.

My focus is on the individuals working in these organizations, not the organizations themselves. The biographical perspective allows me to capture the tensions that result from different approaches and the affinities to certain types of organizations or interventions. The individuals who participated in this study were admirable, dedicated, humble, highly reflective and sincere. Often torn about their position and the potential contribution that they might be able to make, they were self-critical as well as critical of particular aid organizations and the aid industry as a whole. One response to these doubts was to obtain further education and training. They were also aware and highlighted their privileged position – vis-à-vis those who are not involved in Aidland, vis-à-vis recipients of 'aid' or 'capacity building' – and – in the case of international aidworkers – vis-à-vis national staff. Furthermore, they stressed how much they were in awe of the generosity, happiness and resilience of the disadvantaged, poor and victims of conflict and disasters. However, although they emphasized that they would hope they would work themselves out of a job as their aid was no longer needed (or acknowledged that the diaspora, neighbouring countries or the governments of affected crisis regions themselves provided far more aid than international aid organizations), the vast majority were also interested in continuing to pursue their careers within Aidland.

By tracing the trajectories of people working in aid – entering, living, working, travelling through and leaving Aidland – I am interested in questioning the terms 'expatriates', 'locals' and 'beneficiaries', and in discussing how these groups see each other and relate to one another. The use of the term 'expatriate' is often reserved for those from highly developed, high-income countries, but everybody who is working outside their country of citizenship needs to be considered an 'expatriate' (Crewe and Fernando 2006). Thus 'expatriate' experiences can differ widely not only with respect to access to resources, but also with respect to cultural and regional familiarity and language skills. A white North American woman working in Uganda who depends on translators to engage with national staff and beneficiaries because she does not speak the local language is differently positioned than a Congolese man, who has relatives in Uganda and speaks the local language, working in the same organization. Local populations engage with expatriate aidworkers in diverse ways, as co-workers, clients and household aides. These relationships can secure a sense of meaning, but may also be experienced as frustrating, problematic and dislocating. Furthermore, not only does the term 'expatriate' need to be unpacked; the notion of 'local staff' also needs to be problematized. People who have been hired locally may have moved from another region of the country, and it is therefore more appropriate to refer to 'national staff'. Furthermore, 'national staff' working in supporting roles such as drivers and translators include skilled professionals. Thus the line between support and programme staff may be arbitrary and is more related to region of origin (Global South/Global North) than to skills and knowledge. While the aid industry addresses global inequalities, such inequalities are at the same time perpetuated within Aidland. Thus it is necessary to unpack the racialized meaning of the terms 'expatriate', 'national staff' and 'beneficiary'. Despite – or because – development is a 'racial project'[5] race is rarely openly addressed (White 2002; 2006; Kothari 2006a, 2006b; Crewe and Fernando 2006). This applies not only to development but also to other forms of aid.

Where and what is Aidland?

Development and humanitarianism are usually either discussed separately even though development studies programmes include humanitarianism (and vice versa) or the terms are used interchangeably. The relationship between humanitarianism and development is rarely addressed explicitly (but see Slim 2000; Hilhorst 2002; Barnett 2011). This is problematic because it is important both to acknowledge the difference between long-term projects and short-term interventions, but also to acknowledge the relationship between these different forms of North–South 'cooperation'. In Chapter 1, I will provide a brief overview of the emergence, transformation and interrelation of development and humanitarianism. A historical perspective on the changing structure of the aid system is needed in order to understand the structural conditions which shape living and working in Aidland. Aidland is shaped by colonialism and neo-colonialism, independence and solidarity movements. The role of missionaries and the military in humanitarian endeavours is still reflected in metaphors such as 'field', 'post' and 'mission', which are also used by secular, pacifist, non-governmental organizations (Slim 1996, 2001). A historical perspective on aid relations is needed in order to understand continuities and discontinuities in aid relationships. Chapter 1 provides a backdrop for later chapters, in which I will analyse how the power relations that constitute Aidland shape the relationships between internationals and nationals, men and women working in aid organizations. The overview provided in Chapter 1 includes a shift from development which went out of fashion in the 1980s to humanitarianism. While aid budgets decreased overall, an increasing proportion was allocated to humanitarianism (Fearon 2008). Compared to development, humanitarianism appears flashier, less expensive, better at mobilizing media attention through focusing on need rather than solidarity. The shift of resources and attention from development to humanitarianism at the end of the twentieth century was accompanied by the increasing role of NGOs which is an expression of neoliberalism by transferring responsibilities from the state to the private sector, including civil society (Howell and Pearce 2001; Watkins et al. 2012).[6] Neoliberalism is characterized by marketization and privatization, and has shaped working conditions through managerialism and audit cultures.

How have these changes affected the work and work relations in Aidland? Power relations appear to be more obvious or explicit in development and perhaps more hidden in relief efforts. Furthermore, development and development studies have for a long time been shaped by extensive self-criticism – is that matched by humanitarianism and humanitarian studies and to what extent could lessons learned in development be useful for relief? I argue that in order to understand the careers of aidworkers and the paradoxes they face, it is necessary to acknowledge the changing relationship between development and humanitarianism. Aidland also encompasses peace-building, post-conflict, reconstruction, disaster preparedness and disaster management. The same group of beneficiaries – for example, refugees – may be approached from a human rights, humanitarian or development perspective. Human rights work addresses legal aspects and protection of refugees; humanitarian efforts address shelter, medical services, food and water; while education and training are important for long-term development and resilience. Individuals, organizations and countries may be positioned differently at different points of time with respect to providing or obtaining various types of aid. For example, Nepal for a long time was considered a poor but stable country which was targeted by various development strategies, whereas more recently humanitarian relief and human rights work have become increasingly prominent. These various approaches complement as well as conflict and compete with each other and offer a variety of work opportunities. Moreover, my data show that at the personal level a change from one intervention or organization to another can be a strategy to address the discontent with aid. This study thus configures Aidland as comprising a range of different interventions in the Global South. I understand Aidland as a 'humanitarian arena' (Hilhorst and Serrano 2010) which includes a whole range of services, and acknowledges the continuities and discontinuities between stable and crisis situations. As Smillie and Minear (2004, p. 7) point out: 'Humanitarian action includes providing relief material and protecting human rights, advocacy, education, and reminding parties in conflict of their obligations under humanitarian law.' Aidland and humanitarian interventions thus encompass 'development' and 'relief' which can be complementary as well as contradictory.

'Development' is a complex phenomenon and the meanings of development have changed frequently over the course of the twentieth century. Initially, development referred to modernization and industrialization processes and implied a distinction between the 'developed' Global North and the less, un- or underdeveloped Global South. Progress in the metropole was contrasted with the backwardness of the periphery which justified the intervention of explorers, missionaries and colonial administrators. Trade 'agreements' and the exploitation of former colonies contributed to and enabled modernization processes in European countries and thus contributed to European 'development', or what Petras and Veltmeyer (2002) call 'reverse aid'. Overall, 'development' moved from economic development and growth to human development and well-being, and most recently an emphasis on 'resilience'. Development implies longer-term strategies of improving living conditions through bringing about social and economic change in more or less politically stable environments and with the approval of the host government.

In contrast, humanitarian aid or emergency relief is provided in situations of acute need whether they are an outcome of natural disasters or political conflicts. This includes providing food, medical services, water and shelter for populations who have lost their accommodation and livelihoods. These are – at least theoretically – temporary solutions, although, in reality, relief operations and structures may be in place for a long time. Refugee camps may exist over long periods of time, for which the Palestine refugee problem serves as a good example. The United Nations Relief and Works Agency for Palestine Refugees (UNRWA) was established in 1948 and repeatedly renewed, most recently until June 2017, spanning thus far four generations of refugees. Relief constitutes the earliest phase of assistance, followed by a rehabilitation phase which includes demilitarization and de-mining, the restoration of basic services providing water, energy, education and medical services as well as the reconstruction of houses, roads and economic activities. Rehabilitation thus constitutes a mid-point between immediate emergency relief and long-term development. Furthermore, organizations which focused initially on relief, such as Oxfam or Médecins sans Frontières (MSF), became involved in development cooperation (Oxfam) or in long-term efforts to address specific diseases (MSF). Moreover, multi-mandated organizations are involved in providing emergency relief as well as development cooperation and peace efforts. 'Relief' and 'development' not only constitute different phases and types of intervention; another distinguishing factor is that humanitarian aid is guided by the principle of neutrality – offering aid on the basis of need and without an agenda. However, it is not always clear what constitutes humanitarian and what constitutes development work and, since humanitarian aid is instrumentalized, politicized and manipulated, it is in reality 'hardly neutral' (Donini 2013).

'Aidland' is a geographic space that is constructed through crises and poverty. Countries move in and out of Aidland as both recipients of aid and as donors. However, such a construction of Aidland which is associated with 'distant suffering' (Boltanski 1999) glosses over the fact that Aidland manifests itself in many spaces and contexts – not only in the refugee camps and development projects in the Global South but also in the head offices in Geneva, London, New York or Johannesburg. Aidland may be found in newspaper advertisements or those popping up on computer screens that ask for donations to aid organizations with mouse clicks or direct debits. Moreover, many humanitarian crises are grounded in social, economic and political causes. This applies to conflicts as well as to climate change caused by production methods and lifestyle choices which can contribute to 'natural disasters'. Aidland may be encountered in food, clothing and other consumer goods that have been produced under conditions that exploit workers, their communities and the environment. Visitors from high-income countries pass slums and beggars on the way between the airport and their final destination. Our everyday life is based on these global inequalities, privileging a few and disadvantaging many. Moreover, a focus on distant suffering may contribute to overlooking the needs of those nearby: the homeless person in front of the local railway station, the beggar outside the supermarket in which fair trade goods are sold. The consequences of the global division of labour and racially segregated labour markets are inherent in Aidland. Indeed, Kapoor (2013) argues that (celebrity) humanitarianism perpetuates and legitimizes capitalism.

What is aidwork and who is an aidworker?

Aidwork is not necessarily paid work and not every staff member working for an aid organization necessarily classifies herself or is classified by others as an 'aidworker'. Human rights lawyers and other professionals serving as consultants, staff from head offices visiting country and field office for short spells or those in administrative positions at regional offices, for example, do not consider themselves as 'aidworkers'. Those in support positions like drivers, security guards and translators are also not necessarily perceived as 'aidworkers'. However, these often locally hired staff members are crucial for carrying out aid programmes. Furthermore, in particular with respect to translators, the boundary between supporting programme staff through interpretation services which are involved in assessing needs and helping beneficiaries by providing information and help negotiating application procedures becomes quite blurry. Moreover, just as volunteering can lead to paid positions in aid organizations, so can support work as drivers or translators lead to programme positions. Thus people working in aid encompass paid and unpaid work, working in programme and support positions in a range of different organizations. Paid and unpaid work may be carried out simultaneously or consecutively, and unpaid positions or support positions may be the starting point for a career in Aidland.

Reliable data on people in aid are rarely published. Aid agencies either do not gather or do not publish staff data, so we lack reliable and representative information on the characteristics of people in aid, their age, gender, marital status, qualifications and how long they stay in this kind of work in addition to having 'no idea what size this population is' (Walker and Russ 2010, p. 11). Available data suggest that aid organizations are no longer 'white, middle class and male' (Ojelay-Surtees 2004, p. 58).[7] For example, the British

Department for International Development (DFID), reported an increase of non-white senior staff from 3 per cent in 1999 to 11 per cent in 2004 (Crewe and Fernando 2006, p. 44). Nevertheless, Western expatriates are still over-represented in senior management (Stoddard 2004). A recent study suggests that 46 per cent of country directors are European and 11 per cent are North American (Knox Clarke 2014). The leadership teams are somewhat more diverse (29 per cent European, 25 per cent Asian, 25 per cent African, 9 per cent Latin American Caribbean, 8 per cent North American and 5 per cent Australasian). Western men and women tend to dominate senior management, whereas about 90 per cent of aidworkers are national staff.

The relationship between international and national staff, people working in aid and local populations and beneficiaries is of central importance for the aid industry. After all, the beneficiaries should be the centre of all considerations of providing aid. In a way they are; it only depends on who is defined as beneficiary. Or, put differently, almost everyone involved in the aid sector could be considered a beneficiary – the refugee or poor person who is the target of interventions as well as the local population being offered job opportunities by international aid organizations, local and national governments who are provided with access to resources as well as the international aid organizations and their personnel who find job and project opportunities in regions that are affected by disaster and conflict. But it is necessary to ask who gains what and who has a say in how projects are run. Development studies have for a long time engaged in a debate around understanding the 'power of development' and endeavouring to account for the unequal relationships within aid projects (Crewe and Harrison 1998; Grammig 2002; Hilhorst 2003; Mosse 2005). Given that – at least rhetorically – empowerment has become central within development, this is not surprising. The increasing emphasis on humanitarianism has diverted the attention away from the relationship between aid providers and recipients and focused more on the instant provision of aid (Kapoor 2012). The recent discourse shift towards resilience puts the capacity and empowerment of the local population at the centre. What is unclear is what role international aid organizations play in a project that emphasizes resilience. Is it the withdrawal of international staff? Aid organizations have certainly begun to place more emphasis on perception and in assessing how the international aid community is perceived by the local community and staff (Dijkzeul and Wakenge 2010; Abu-Sada 2012; Hilhorst et al. 2013). Furthermore, 'internationalization' and 'localization' processes are underway. This involves moving head offices to the Global South, for example, South Africa or India (Eyben 2006, 2014) or opening sections in different regions of the world, like Médecins Sans Frontières (Fox 2014).[8] It also includes promoting more staff from the Global South into leadership positions, including regional offices and head offices.

To some extent these developments may be related to the fact that given smaller budgets, aid organizations seek to cut costs by spending less on expatriate salaries, since local staff salaries tend to be significantly lower

(McMaster 2008; Carr et al. 2010; Ridde 2010; McWha 2011; McWha and MacLachlan 2011). In addition, security concerns of aid organizations may involve shifting responsibilities from international to national staff (Fast 2014). These developments coincide with an increase in graduates from humanitarian studies programmes and may make it more difficult for graduates from Western countries who do not yet have field experience to find a job in Aidland. Whether this constitutes a 'crisis of aidwork' or rather a crisis of (Northern) 'aidworkers' is a matter of perspective. If the goal of aid is to enable and empower communities in the Global South, then South–South cooperation and finding a capable workforce in the countries needing help is certainly a welcome development. However, these developments may also contribute to the frustration of graduates from the Global North who fail to find a paid position in Aidland. One solution may be to look for opportunities to 'make a difference' closer to home – in deprived neighbourhoods, with marginalized communities, working with asylum seekers, refugees or racially disadvantaged groups. Thus, not only would a stronger integration of development and humanitarian studies be useful, but also an exchange with social work, third sector and social movement studies.

A biographical approach to aidwork

In this book, I employ a biographical or life-history approach in order to understand the experiences of people working in aid. Biographies of people working in aid shed light on the changing working conditions in Aidland, which are shaped by the interacting processes of professionalization and securitization, but also exploitation and insecurity. The life-history approach illustrates how personal, institutional and national histories are intertwined (Bebbington and Kothari 2006; Andrews 2007; Yarrow 2008). This method is also particularly useful for illustrating how the personal and the professional as well as voluntary social and political activism are interrelated in the lives of people working in aid. The approach captures which personal, educational, professional and political developments led to the involvement in the field of aid and what impact this involvement has on the lives of aid personnel. Furthermore, a life-history approach allows capturing the decision-making processes that led individuals to move from development cooperation to emergency relief (and vice versa). Such a dynamic perspective is missing from studies which focus on only one of these fields. Furthermore, it acknowledges the interconnectedness of paid and unpaid work. A biographical approach thus cuts across different sectors of life and captures the interaction between work and family, social and political involvement.

It would be misleading to assume that biographical interviews can only reveal information about individual motivations and experiences. Meaning construction in qualitative interviews, including biographical interviews, goes well beyond individual experiences (Andrews 2007; for the development context see Hilhorst 2003; Lewis 2008a; for auto-ethnographies see Charles

2007; Eyben 2014). I used a purposive sample that aimed at maximum contrast by including a great variety of people working in aid, which provides insights into decision-making processes and how they are structured by (perceived) opportunities. Biographical interviews are retrospective as well as prospective, which means that they involve an assessment and explanation for past decisions as well as an outlook on future developments. A biographical perspective is also holistic, and, rather than focusing on work or private life, shows how developments and decisions in separate spheres shape each other. How does the decision to take a job affect relationships? What impact does the wish to start a family have on career decisions? Biographical interviews not only reveal the personal, professional and political developments that led people to Aidland, but also how they cross boundaries between countries, work sectors and areas of expertise, and how 'life' and 'work' are intertwined in the lives of people working in aid. Representing different standpoints, my respondents' ability to reflect on their situation provides me with rich reflexive data that allow me to explore the paradoxes of aidwork.

Biographical methods are well established in German sociology, but they have so far found less use in other countries and other disciplines. For example, the life-history approach has so far rarely been used in social policy research (Chamberlayne et al. 2004; Lewis 2008a), but it has found more use in social movement studies, in particular for studying recruitment processes and the biographical consequences of activism (Goldstone and McAdam 2001; Giugni 2004; Miethe and Roth 2005). Some have emphasized the 'biographical availability' of students who are free from professional and family commitments (McAdam 1986; Eddy 2011). However, other studies indicate that the greatest occupational and family demands are no obstacle to getting involved in high-risk activism (Nepstad and Smith 1999). Furthermore, activists tend to remain committed to social change goals and this commitment has significant effects on their work lives and personal relationships (Evans 1979; Andrews 1991; Passy and Giugni 2000; Goldstone and McAdam 2001). The charismatic Bernard Kouchner and other founders of Médecins Sans Frontières (Doctors Without Borders) came from an activist background and had witnessed the student movement of 1968 (Taithe 2004; Redfield 2010; Fox 2014). Drawing on his own biography and recalling his student days in the late 1960s, Vaux (2001) posits that 'aid work in its heyday in the 1980s was an expression of that 1960s radicalism' (p. 11).

In this book, I examine the biographies and careers of people in aid in a life-course perspective. Between 2004 and 2013, I conducted interviews with aid personnel working in development cooperation and emergency relief in smaller and larger NGOs as well as UN agencies.[9] These organizations not only differed with respect to their programmes, but also regarding salaries and benefits, training and career opportunities. The respondents were born between 1937 and 1986 and included women and men from Western Europe, North America, Central and Eastern Europe, Asia, the Middle East, Africa and Latin America. The sample thus includes 'Western' and 'Non-Western',

'Northern' and 'Southern' respondents. I refer to the respondents from Western Europe, North America, Japan, Australia and New Zealand as from the 'Global North' and to the respondents from Eastern Europe, Asia, Africa and Latin America as from the 'Global South', thus juxtaposing donor countries with aid-receiving countries. However, the relationship is of course much more complex and countries such as India are by now aid donors as well as recipients, whereas countries in Eastern Europe were donors prior to the end of the Cold War and are now donor countries again. In contrast to studies on aidworkers that focus either on North/Western expatriates (Cook 2007; Heron 2007; Fechter and Hindman 2011; Mosse 2011) or on local volunteer and staff (Heaton Shrestha 2006; Ahmad 2007; Arvidson 2008), my sample includes both national and international staff. It also reflects the diversity of the aidworker population with respect to organizations and type of contract, which comprises few with permanent contracts with UN agencies or major international NGOs, many short-term consultants based in home countries and a 'social core' of longer-term contract workers who move from one organization to another (Apthorpe 2011b). Respondents worked in a range of different areas (for example, education, medical support, logistics, refugees, human rights) and included paid staff and volunteers, field workers and those working in regional or head offices as well as consultants. Furthermore, respondents differed with respect to marital status. The vast majority of respondents were single and did not have children. However, there were some regional as well as gender differences (which will be discussed in Chapter 5).

The respondents had joined aidwork at various stages of their life-course. Some had started aidwork before they were 20 or after they were 50, about one-third were in their early twenties, more than half were in their late twenties or early thirties and a smaller proportion were in their late thirties or forties when they started working in aid. Respondents were also at different stages in their careers, ranging from veterans who had been working in various organizations for over 20 years, to newcomers who were looking for their first paid position in an aid organization. Only a few respondents had permanent contracts with UN agencies or major international NGOs; many had short-term contracts and moved from one organization to the next and some worked as consultants. About one-third of those I interviewed had been working in various aid organizations for under five years, while two-thirds had been involved for more than five years, and a quarter for more than ten years. I also spoke with a few who had left Aidland after a few years or after a long career in the sector.

The vast majority of the respondents both from the Global North and the Global South came from (upper)-middle-class backgrounds. All respondents were highly educated, all were university graduates, most had postgraduate degrees, many had studied overseas and some were conducting doctoral research. The respondents from the Global North were overwhelmingly white and very few came from a working-class or immigrant background.

Thus, my sample was homogeneous with respect to class, but quite diverse with respect to nationality, age, length of working in aid as well as with respect to organizations and contracts.[10] This diversity allows me to illuminate the living and working experiences of Aidland. They represent people working in different fields and distinctive jobs. Many moved between these fields and organizations and engaged in multiple forms of 'boundary-crossing'. David Lewis (2008b) introduced the notion of boundary-crossing to refer to changes between working for governmental and non-governmental organizations, but I find that it may be employed more widely to capture the move from the private sector to Aidland, between non-governmental and UN organizations, secular and faith-based organizations, development and relief, to give a few examples. For example, several respondents started out as relief workers in a small NGO and then moved to a larger NGO later on. They moved not only between fields and organizations, but also between volunteering and paid work, consultancies and fixed-term positions, head office and field positions. Thus the use of biographical interviews with a diverse set of respondents allows me to compare and contrast the experiences of people working in aid who are situated differently in Aidland. This approach captures how frequent changes were experienced, what influenced the decision-making processes to move to the next position, and how the frequent moves affected personal relationships or what is often referred to as 'work–life balance'. Thus, while the focus of this book is on understanding work motivations and experiences in Aidland, I argue that work cannot be separated from other aspects of life. The life-history method is thus better suited to understanding the pathways through Aidland than static studies focusing on one particular organization or site.

Structure of the book

In a brief historical overview, Chapter 1 addresses how and when various forms of humanitarian aid emerged, who the actors were and which of these actors are still involved and how. I introduce different forms of aidwork as well as organizations engaged in Aidland. Rather than making a strict distinction between 'development' and 'relief', I place different aid and international cooperation strategies on a continuum to highlight the relationship between different forms of assistance and cooperation. The emergence and transformation of aid organizations is closely related to political developments, wars and conflicts, colonialism and independence, and they are to a varying extent characterized by impartiality or solidarity, independence or subcontracting. The broad overview of changes in Aidland provided in this chapter serves as the backdrop for analysing what consequences these developments have for people working in aid.

In Chapter 2, I argue that Aidland provides an excellent lens for understanding work in contemporary neoliberal societies. Sociological perspectives on work, volunteering and social movements help frame the tensions and dilemmas that people working in aid experience. Aidwork includes professional volunteers (or volunteering professionals). There is a close connection between paid and unpaid work which is performed simultaneously or consecutively. Aidwork is at the same time characterized by privilege and precariousness. Jobs are not necessarily well paid and thus require independent means or forgoing financial security. Aidwork is contrasted with 'normal life' and represents an attempt to escape rationalization and disenchantment while undergoing bureaucratization and professionalization processes. The professionalization of Aidland may result in the disciplining of boundary-crossers pursuing boundary-less careers. I argue that aidwork as 'meaningful work' must be understood as a comment and critique of work experiences in the Global North for Northern aidworkers, while it represents an important career opportunity for aidworkers from the Global South.

I turn to the processes of entering Aidland in Chapter 3. Based on the biographical interviews, I distinguish sudden and gradual entries into Aidland at different life-stages. A range of resources mattered for securing the first appointment in Aidland: travel and volunteering experiences, job training and experience, education and language skills. However, which of these resources were needed to secure an appointment varied for national and international staff. Some national staff were overqualified for support positions, while some international staff were hired even though they had neither the job training nor prior experience for the position.

Following the Aidlanders into the field, in Chapter 4 I go on to describe the working conditions in Aidland and how they shape the relationship between the private and public sphere. Work intensity and living situation are shaped by the security situation, the mandate and budget of an organization and the position within the organization. In this chapter, I address the fact that often the most difficult and challenging working conditions were experienced as the most satisfying and that interactions within the expat community could be more stressful than encounters with indigenous rebels.

In Chapter 5 I address how Aidland is gendered; that is, to what extent men and women are differently positioned within Aidland and to what extent a stay in Aidland has dissimilar consequences for men and women. I argue that Aidland simultaneously undermines, challenges and perpetuates conventional assumptions of gender. Moreover, gender intersects with other forms of inequality and thus requires an intersectional perspective which acknowledges that gender relations in Aidland are informed by other aspects of privilege and disadvantage.

I examine the relationships between expatriate and national staff in Chapter 6. I discuss how different groups experience working with each other; I also address whether and how they interact in their leisure. The chapter considers the role of nationality and race (including whiteness) and how they serve to privilege or to conceal certain forms of knowledge and skills. It thus focuses on the diversity of the aidworker population and the paradox that

14 *Introduction*

global inequalities are perpetuated within aid organizations as long as (white) Western expatriates are privileged.

Finally, in Chapter 7, I discuss how the working conditions and paradoxes encountered in Aidland shape people's decision-making concerning staying in an organization (if there is an option) or in a field (opportunities), or in Aidland overall. This includes professional considerations concerning career planning or more general doubts about the impact of aid and the role of expatriate staff in aid organizations as well as personal considerations related to family planning.

My book seeks to demonstrate that a life-course perspective is particularly useful for analysing the paradoxes, ambivalences and contradictions of aidwork. Furthermore, I propose that dialogues between development and humanitarian studies, sociology of work and social movements research are necessary to understand how work opportunities in Aidland structure the biographies and careers of people working in aid. In addition, I argue that multiple forms of privilege and disadvantage need to be approached from an intersectional perspective. My analysis of the reproduction of global inequalities within aid organizations is a contribution to 'connected sociologies' (Bhambra 2014), and highlights how processes in the Global North and the Global South are inextricably intertwined.

Notes

1 I understand gender as a social construct and social institution 'that establishes patterns of expectations for individuals, orders the social processes of everyday life, is built into major social organizations of society, such as the economy, ideology, the family and politics, and is also an entity in and of itself' (Lorber 1994, p. 1).
2 Like gender, race is socially constructed and may be defined as 'a concept which signifies and symbolizes social conflicts and interests by referring to different types of human bodies' (Omi and Winant 1994, p. 55). In the context of aid (and elsewhere), of course not only race, but also citizenship, ethnicity and nationality matter.
3 Intersectionality has become increasingly prominent in gender studies and addresses the fact that multiple systems of privilege and discrimination inform each other (Choo and Ferree 2010).
4 ATTAC stands for Association pour la Taxation des Transactions pour l'Aide aux Citoyens or Association for the Taxation of Financial Transaction for the Aid of Citizens. The organizations demand a tax on foreign financial transaction, such as the Tobin Tax, which would apply to foreign exchange transactions.
5 According to Omi and Winant (1994, p. 56), 'a racial project is simultaneously an interpretation, representation, or explanation of racial dynamics, and an effort to reorganize and redistribute resources along particular racial lines'.
6 Of course, civil society has both the potential to support as well as to challenge neoliberal capitalism (Howell and Pearce 2001).
7 According to an internal report of Oxfam from 1996 cited by Ojelay-Surtees (2004, p. 58): 'Oxfam seeks to employ a certain "type" of person. That is someone who is highly educated, intellectual, speaks the Oxbridge language, has a breadth of managerial and/or technical experience, and who is familiar with a Western style of managing. This type of person tends to be white, middle class and male.'

8 In November 2014, Oxfam International announced that it will move its headquarters from Oxford, UK and split them between Nairobi, Kenya and Bangkok, Thailand over the next few years. Furthermore, the organization announced the addition of affiliate organizations, including Oxfam South Africa and Oxfam Brazil. https://www.devex.com/news/oxfam-to-split-headquarters-welcome-new-associate-members-84918 (accessed 5 December 2014).
9 I provide more information about the sample, the interview process and the evaluation of the interviews in the Methods appendix.
10 The sample is of course not representative, but this is not the focus of qualitative research, which aims at uncovering meaning structures and generating grounded theory.

1 Mapping Aidland

Jean worked for a bilateral development agency in Central Africa from the 1970s until the 1990s. After the Rwandan genocide, he decided to enrol in a humanitarian studies programme and started to specialize in refugee issues. He has worked as consultant and lecturer, focusing in particular on the link between relief and development. Furthermore, he has experience as election observer and as a trained psychologist has selected candidates for overseas missions. In addition, he has volunteered for the Red Cross and held short appointments with various UN agencies and the OSCE.

Jean's brief biography spans several decades and encompasses work experience in relief and development, a long-term appointment in a bilateral aid agency and volunteering for the Red Cross, in addition to consultancies, lecturing and personnel development. The decision to change from development to relief and election observation was influenced by political developments and by personal career decisions. Jean's biography illustrates changes within the aid sector and the variety of work opportunities that Aidland offers, reflecting the different mandates, cultures and histories of aid organizations. This chapter gives a brief historical overview of the emergence and transformation of humanitarianism and development, and covers colonialism, de-colonialization, cold war, new wars and the War on Terror. In the course of the changing social, political and economic relations between the Global North and the Global South, the relationship between humanitarian relief, development and human rights also changed constantly. Furthermore, Aidland includes a range of actors, including faith-based and secular, governmental and non-governmental, international and local organizations which compete and collaborate with one another. The shifting practices and priorities of these organizations shape the job opportunities of people working in aid, whether as volunteers or as paid staff.

Modernization, humanitarianism and development

The roots of Aidland lie in the modernization processes in the Global North which were co-constituted through colonial and imperialist endeavours constructing the 'less developed' Global South as 'other' (Bhambra 2014; Go 2013; Steinmetz 2013). Thus, the less developed South serves at the same time as a contrast to the highly developed North which in turn seeks to 'improve' the South, even though, for example, India played a critical role in the industrialization of English textile production (Go 2013). Aidland is rooted in missionary movements, colonialism and imperialism, and is thus shaped by unequal power relations between North and South. This has long-lasting consequences for North–South relationships in contemporary aid encounters. Postcolonial theories remind us to understand 'the other' as being embedded in and constituting identities and positions, whether these positions and identities are privileged or marginalized.

Humanitarianism and development are rooted in religious as well as imperial traditions, and 'colonialism and human rights have been inter-meshed over the past 200 years' (Taithe 2004, p. 155). Colonialism has been justified by a humanitarian argument: the duty to 'civilize' presumably less enlightened peoples. Humanitarianism is inextricably embedded in colonial governmentality and is one of the roots of modern development discourse (Lester and Dussart 2014). Different types of colonialism may be distinguished which varied in their impact on the economic and political development of the former colonies (Acemoglu et al. 2001; Lange et al. 2006). Colonial institutions, in particular those regulating race and ethnicity, had long-term consequences for social development resulting in ethno-racial stratification between European settlers and colonial administrators, local elites, privileged racial ethnic groups and indigenous populations. These deeply rooted divisions re-emerge in contemporary social conflicts and play an important role in occurrences of violent confrontations, including the genocide in Rwanda in 1994.

Missionaries have been labelled 'handmaidens of colonialism' (Maxwell 2005) and education was primarily a means of evangelism rather than improving living conditions in the colonies. Medical service was even more ambivalent than missionary education, since missionaries and other settlers were not necessarily able to cure diseases that had been brought to the colonies by the colonial settlers (Etherington 2005a). The relationships between Christian missionaries, colonial administrators and settlers and the indigenous populations were complex and contradictory (Stanley 1990; Etherington 2005b). Furthermore, missionary work also offered an alternative to marriage and career opportunities for single, middle-class women who were not allowed to work as doctors or teachers in their home country (Grimshaw and Sherlock 2005). By the late nineteenth century white women outnumbered men in imperial missions, which offered opportunities for single as well as married women. In addition to supporting missionary men, missionary wives were engaged in public activities; for example, running schools or standing in for their absent husbands. Thus Aidland has been gendered from the very beginning, offering white middle-class women from the Global North opportunities to 'stretch and bend' (Ferree 2009) gendered norms.

Haskell (1985a; 1985b) explains the emergence of a new humanitarian sensibility in Europe in the late eighteenth century with a higher level of conscientiousness combined with the confidence of having the capacity to act on behalf of human suffering and injustice. Yet, British industrialists who were active in the abolitionist movement were not necessarily concerned with labour exploitation in their own country (or enterprises), thus distinguishing between the suffering overseas and that in their own communities. This distinction is still relevant today, if fair trade activism that addresses working conditions overseas is not linked to the situation of low-paid workers, including migrants and ethnic minorities in high-income countries. Kapoor (2013) describes the contributions of billionaires such as Bill Gates to philanthropy as 'decaf capitalism' or 'philanthrocapitalism' – giving with one hand but taking with the other by engaging in profit-making, the creation of inequality and the accumulation of wealth.

The battle of Solferino (1859) which led Henry Dunant to initiate the formation of the International Committee of the Red Cross (ICRC), the first Geneva Convention (1864) and the founding of the Salvation Army (1865) represent important steps with respect to human rights and are decisive events for the emergence of the modern concept of humanitarianism (Redfield and Bornstein 2011). In the first half of the twentieth century in response to the First and Second World Wars a number of non-governmental organizations were created in response to poverty and other consequences of wars and other humanitarian crises. The Save the Children Fund was created in response to the First World War. Throughout the twentieth century, humanitarian crises resulted in the creation of organizations including a number of non-governmental humanitarian organizations addressing the needs of refugees, displaced persons and other victims of wars such as the International Rescue Committee (IRC) in 1933, Oxfam in 1942 and CARE in 1945. While these non-governmental organizations were initially involved in relief work, some of them later on included development activities, as I will discuss below.

Thus modernization, development and humanitarianism are inextricably intertwined and reflect unequal power relations between North and South. Benevolent individuals and organizations which sought to address these sources of inequality through acts of charity were acting from a position of privilege which remained unchallenged.

Development post-independence

Some missionary interventions had unintended side effects and missionary education inadvertently undermined colonial rule, as it provided crucial training for the leadership of nationalist movements and was central in the creation of nationalist elites. Overall, the stance of missionaries towards decolonialization has been characterized as 'ambivalent and aloof', and only a few missionaries actively supported African nationalist movements (Maxwell 2005). The reluctance to support nationalist movements was to some extent grounded in self-interest and concerns that the communist and cultural nationalism in China and South Asia might provide a model for anti-colonial movements in other parts of the world. Mission-educated African elites were therefore disappointed to realize that missionary leaders provided little support for equality and social justice, and therefore turned to voluntary organizations, trade unions and political parties as allies (Maxwell 2005). The trajectory of post-independence development and transition to democracy were shaped by legacies of colonial rule (Subramaniam 2006).

Following de-colonialization processes, development assistance was introduced in the late 1940s and led to the transformation of existing organizations, namely former colonial administrations, and the formation of new organizations. Newly established organizations included the Organization for Economic Cooperation and Development (OECD) which was based on the Organization for European Economic Cooperation (OEEC) responsible for the Marshall Plan. The Marshall Plan which had proved successful in rebuilding war-damaged Western Europe offered a model to provide aid to 'developing' countries, the majority former colonies and newly independent states. It was run by the OEEC which was formed of 18 European countries and was established in 1948. Based on the success of the Marshall Plan, the mandate of the OEEC was extended globally, leading to the formation of the OECD with the declared goal to 'contribute to lasting peace through economic collaboration and reconstruction'. The OECD and its Development Assistance Committee (DAC) does not provide funding, but seeks to contribute to economic development through monitoring, providing data and policy recommendations. Like the Marshall Plan, development aid for the newly independent countries had a political agenda reflecting the cold war dichotomy. Thus, in the mid-twentieth century, Europe (and other industrialized countries) provided the model for modernization of the newly independent states who became the targets and recipients of aid, initially in the form of large loans for infrastructure which resulted in a debt crisis. The institutional foundations for an aid system were laid between 1944 and the end of the 1960s, and included the World Bank and International Monetary Fund which were established at Bretton Woods in 1944, as well as bilateral and multilateral organizations. Simon (2009) characterizes the post-Second World War period as the heyday of development.

Bilateral organizations

Many OECD countries established bilateral development organizations, which were part of the foreign policy agenda and trade policies of donor governments. For example, the United States Agency for International Development (USAID) combined various goals, including the promotion of democracy, freedom and human rights, and the creation of job opportunities for Americans while supporting economic growth and development in poor countries (Riddell 2007). Donor countries tended to forge a special relationship with their former colonies. The British aid programme may serve as a good example here. It goes back to the colonial administration which addressed economic development and responded to social unrest to the welfare of subjects in the colonies (Barder 2007). Following independence, Britain provided technical assistance grants and loans (including concessionary loans) to former colonies as well as to other Commonwealth and non-Commonwealth states. The trajectory from colonial rule to contemporary international development is thus characterized by continuities and divergences (Kothari 2006a). Aid organizations experienced tensions between former colonial officers and post-independence development 'experts' who disagreed concerning the importance of in-depth knowledge of the countries obtaining 'aid' (Kothari 2005a). Aid credits and projects were tied to the use of British goods and services, not only pursuing development aims, but also serving British political, industrial and commercial interests (Barder 2007). This practice was not unique to Britain; until recently, most bilateral donors provided tied aid to a greater or lesser extent. For example, it is estimated that Germany obtained returns at 50 per cent or higher (Randel and German 1997, p. 71). In contrast to (West) Germany and Britain, France, which had been Europe's largest donor until 2005, did not have a single comprehensive aid budget or ministry. Instead, a number of ministries, including the Ministry for Economic Affairs, Finance and Industry and the Ministry of Foreign Affairs, were responsible for the allocation of aid, thus indicating policy priorities (Riddell 2007). Sweden, Norway and the Netherlands constitute smaller donors, but exceeded the 0.7 per cent ODA/GNI target of the Millennium Development Goals and are thus deemed generous donors. Among the DAC countries, the bilateral share of overseas development assistance is 70 per cent and about 8 per cent of overseas assistance goes to humanitarian aid.[1] The United States remains the largest donor, with a larger bilateral share (83%) than the DAC average and a higher proportion of humanitarian aid (15%). However, the US have been less generous with respect to the GNP/ODA ratio. In 2012, the ODA/GNI share for the United States was 0.18 per cent compared to a DAC average of 0.28 per cent and thus nowhere near the 0.7 per cent demanded in the Millennium Development Goals. In contrast, the Scandinavian countries which are smaller donors were more generous; for example, Sweden's GNP/ODA ratio was 0.97 in 2012. This means that the United States give a lower proportion of ODA to bilateral organizations than the DAC average and – compared to the GNP – more generous countries such as Sweden. Moreover, in contrast to other donors discussed above, since 1962 Sweden's core objective in providing ODA is not foreign policy and economic interests, but the desire to improve the living conditions of the poor and to support independence movements. The Swedish International Development Cooperation Agency (SIDA) administers Sweden's aid programme, while development policy is the responsibility of the ministry for foreign affairs (Riddell 2007). Australia and New Zealand also established official aid programmes in the 1960s which expanded in the 1970s. While both aid programmes address poverty reduction, they also pursue foreign policy objectives and have primarily targeted the Pacific and some Asian countries, but also gave aid to other regions. The Australian Development Agency (ADA) was founded in 1974 and was renamed several times; the most recent incarnation of the Australian government agency was AusAid (the Australian Agency for International Development) which was integrated into the Department of Foreign Affairs and Trade in 2013. Before AusAid ceased to exist as an independent agency, it had over 1,500 employees.

Bilateral aid agencies offer employment opportunities in country offices as well as the head office. Due to the size and hierarchical structure, these organizations also offer career opportunities and full-time, permanent and pensionable positions (Eyben 2003; Coles 2007). In addition to permanent staff positions, bilateral organizations also offer consultancies (Stirrat 2000). Indeed, employment practices of international aid agencies have shifted to cost-saving short-term appointments which significantly affects the lives of people working in aid (Hindman 2011). Since the 1980s, in the context of neoliberalism and efforts to improve the efficiency of public administration, Western governments have reduced staff in ministries of foreign affairs and development (Borton 2009). This has resulted in new approaches to management and the administration of humanitarian funds which I will discuss further below. First, I will turn to a brief overview of multilateral organizations, in particular UN agencies, which are recipients of bilateral aid which is then further disbursed to implementing non-governmental organizations.

Multilateral organizations

The creation of the United Nations (UN) in 1945 led to the formation of a range of UN agencies which obtain funding from national governments and subcontract bilateral as well as non-governmental organizations. These include the United High Commissioner for Refugees (UNHCR), the World Food Programme (WFP), the United Nations Development Programme (UNDP) and the Office for the Coordination of Humanitarian Affairs (OCHA), to name a few. UN agencies provide a broad range of employment opportunities in head offices and regional offices for permanent staff and consultants, international and regional staff. The UN system includes different categories of staff, interns and volunteers, some of whom are hired locally, others internationally. In each category, several tiers associated with different levels of education and work experience, as well as levels of experience, are distinguished. Professional and higher categories are usually internationally recruited and involve different duty stations throughout a career. General Service and related services as well as National Professional Officers are generally recruited locally, but do not require a particular nationality. In contrast to those on permanent positions who are expected to rotate between various countries and assignments, the work opportunities for staff hired locally are more restricted.[2] UN agencies such as UNDP also offer internships to graduate-level students and volunteer opportunities through UN Volunteers (UNV). The United Nations Volunteers (UNV) offers volunteer opportunities in development assistance, humanitarian and peacekeeping operations. In 2013, UNV comprised nearly 8,000 volunteers.[3]

UN personnel has increased from approximately 500 in the founding year to 75,000 (excluding peace operations, IMF and World Bank) in 2011 (Weiss 2012). Kofi Annan's presidency (1997–2006) introduced comprehensive reforms which included a reduction of posts as well as a phasing out of permanent contracts. Only a very small proportion of staff on fixed-term contracts who meet the 'highest standards of efficiency, competence and integrity' are eligible for continuing contracts (Weiss 2012). Staff on fixed-term contracts are thus under considerable pressure to perform and can hardly expect a lifelong UN position. While these reforms are meant to increase the efficiency of the organization they may have counter-productive effects, as limited lateral and upward mobility can be a disincentive. Furthermore, these policies seem to conflict with the demand of the UN Joint Inspections Unit to address 'work–life' and 'work–family' issues to prevent the resignation of young qualified staff (Weiss 2012).

Gender and development

As a result of several UN World women's conferences,[4] gender has increasingly been addressed in development (Porter and Sweetman 2005) and humanitarianism (Hyndman 1998). Just like 'participation', 'gender mainstreaming' is a 'buzzword' which has been widely adopted throughout the aid world (Cornwall 2007). The introduction of gender mainstreaming demonstrates how women put gender on the agenda and 'transformed international development' (Fraser and Tinker 2004). In 2000, the UN Security Council Resolution 1325 which requires attention to gender in all aspects of gender management, conflict reconstruction and peace-building was adopted (for a critical review see Shepherd 2011).

Gender – mostly understood as referring to women and girls rather than to gender relations – is now firmly established in Aidland and is reflected in donor requirements, project design and hiring decisions. However, this does not necessarily mean that gender mainstreaming is successfully implemented or that gender equality is achieved. Nevertheless, it opens up job and career opportunities for gender specialists and women in Aidland (White 2006; Eyben 2007). Gender equality and gender mainstreaming not only affect the programmes of UN agencies, but also hiring and promotion which is reflected in conscious efforts to bring more women into leadership positions by appointing gender and diversity advisers and creating units addressing the composition of staff. The UN and some NGOs are monitoring the gender distribution within their organizations and have action plans to bring more women into leadership positions. So far the humanitarian sector remains male-dominated at senior management level and male field staff lack understanding of gender issues (Hoare et al. 2012, p. 216). However, a study surveying how gender is included in humanitarian assistance found that 32 per cent of senior management and 43 per cent of mid-level positions were held by women (DARA 2012, p. 51).[5] In this regard the proportion of women in leadership positions is higher than in the private sector and comparable to the third and public sectors in many countries.

Nevertheless, overall, senior positions still tend to be held by men. For example, at the beginning of the millennium none of the 34 special representatives and envoys appointed by the UN Secretary General to conflict regions was a woman (Naraghi 2000 cited in Karam 2000, p. 21). An overview of the gender distribution of all UN staff from the highest level (USG) to general services indicates in 2007 that women represented 44 per cent of all UN staff although men held 75 per cent of the highest ranking positions, while women were slightly overrepresented at the lowest professional level (55%). The UN identified a number of barriers to achieving gender parity at the more senior level which include a lack of qualified female applicants which is associated with lack of outreach as well as a lack of enforcement mechanisms, special measures for achieving a gender balance as well as a lack of flexibility in work arrangements (United Nations General Assembly 2008). However, the underrepresentation of women in senior leadership positions may not be due to a lack of qualified candidates, but because qualified – and in particular overqualified – women may not be hired because they are seen as a threat to men (Tiessen 2004). In 2010, the General Assembly of the United Nations established the United Nations Entity for Gender Equality and Empowerment of Women (also known as UN Women). This newly created entity monitors and reports the participation of men and women at all levels of the UN. A range of UN agencies including UNICEF, WFP, UNFPA, WHO, OHCHR and UNHCR have been led by women.

Women have not only led UN agencies, but also NGOs such as Oxfam and Save the Children. However, there is little available data on gender distribution of volunteers, staff and management positions in aid organizations. Data are either not collected or not published. The percentage of male and female aidworkers varies from study to study, and organization to organization. While a survey of aidworkers in Kosovo found that 51 per cent of the expatriate staff was female (Cardozo and Salama 2002), a study of Spanish development NGOs found that 67 per cent of the volunteers and 80 per cent of the technical assistants were female; however, the directors of the NGOs tended to be male (Dema 2008). Similarly Damman et al. (2014) found that 57 per cent of MSF Holland's employees were female, but only 45 per cent of those promoted to management positions were women. The 'mass presence' of women in NGOs seems to have contributed to an invisibility of gender inequalities (Dema 2008, p. 446) and a glass ceiling for women in development (Sampson and Moore 2008). However, other studies found that women are not only underrepresented among the leadership but among various staff groups as well. A study of NGOs in Malawi found that women represented

26 per cent of all staff for both international and national NGOs (Tiessen 2004). According to this study, in international NGOs, women represented 15 per cent of field staff, 30 per cent of support staff and 30 per cent of management staff. In national NGOs, women represented 26 per cent of field staff, 20 per cent of support staff and 33 per cent of management staff. Regardless of their senior management positions, most of these women were excluded from the decision-making bodies of their organizations (Tiessen 2004). Furthermore, women fieldworkers have been hired in development projects in order to increase women's participation, but tend to be marginalized (O'Reilly 2004, 2006). Thus the results are mixed – on the one hand women appear to have more opportunities than in other sectors of the labour market; on the other hand they are still underrepresented and may even be marginalized if they are in the majority.

In contrast to gender, race, ethnicity and nationality have so far attracted less attention in the context of development and humanitarianism. Development and development discourse have been described as 'colour-blind', hardly addressing race despite its centrality in the development project (White 2002; Goudge 2003; Kothari 2006a; 2006b). Race and nationality structure the opportunities of people working in aid, a fact which is recognized by those privileged by whiteness and those disadvantaged by race and ethnicity. However, openly addressing development as a 'racial project' (Omi and Winant 1994; White 2006) is a taboo; instead 'difference' is euphemistically referred to as 'local', 'indigenous' or 'culture' (White 2006; Crewe and Fernando 2006). Nevertheless, the staff of development organizations became more diverse (Groves and Hinton 2005; Robb 2005; McKinnon 2007). Similarly, in humanitarian organizations the complicated dynamics between expatriate and national staff (Shevchenko and Fox 2008; Redfield 2012) and the overrepresentation of Western expatriates in senior management positions require more attention (Stoddard 2004).

The lost decade

The rise of gender in Aidland since the 1970s intersected with a turn to participation and rural development and the rise of non-governmental organizations. The 1980s debt crisis led to a significant rethinking and restructuring of international development. Multilateral credit institutions such as the International Monetary Fund (IMF) as well as bilateral organizations had provided large credits to newly independent states which led to prestige objects, corruption and debt. Furthermore, the debt of developing countries increased tremendously when Western (commercial) banks gave large credits to developing countries following the increase in oil prices. These credits did not necessarily improve economic development but were used for arms purchases, unsustainable projects or offshore finance. The credits thus benefited leaders of (military) governments (including dictatorships), but did not contribute to the well-being of the wider population which was affected by the consequences of the debt crisis which started in 1982, when Mexico could no longer service its debt and defaulted. In order to prevent defaults from spreading through the developing world, the IMF and World Bank granted structural adjustment loans allowing the repayment of loans (and interest) to commercial banks. These further credits were provided under the condition of implementing structural adjustment policies, i.e. reducing budget deficits through cutting spending on social services such as health and education and privatizing public services. Thus while the credits benefited leaders, the wider population and in particular the poor suffered from structural adjustment policies. Furthermore, aid practices – supplying developing countries with loans or providing technical interventions – tended to serve the interests of the donors rather than to respond to the needs of the poor. At the beginning of the new millennium, the gap between the richest and poorest countries had widened. A broad coalition of development NGOs and other organizations mobilized for debt relief under the banner of Jubilee 2000 (Saunders 2009) or for greater pharmaceutical advocacy (Redfield 2008b), while the UN adopted the Millennium Development Goals.

Practices that were grounded in the economic interests of donors (for example, donating food supplies from domestic food mountains produced by protectionist policies and other in-kind donations) came increasingly under attack. Regardless of the concern with poverty, welfare and inequality, development was increasingly discussed as neocolonial practice encompassing political, economic as well as discursive hegemony (Ferguson 1990; Crush 1995; Escobar 1995) The feminist and postcolonial critique of aid coincided with the rise of neoliberalism and the growing role of NGOs in development, and a shift to participation, empowerment and rural development projects. Neoliberalism is characterized by privatization and emphasizes the role of the market and civil society. It is associated with cuts in aid budgets which affect staff as well as management practices of bilateral aid organizations. Services which were previously provided by state organizations are outsourced to market agencies and non-governmental organizations which bid for contracts. New managerial techniques presumably improve and assure efficiency and accountability.[6] A central tool in this effort to define concrete goals and measure impact is the log-frame which has 'created the project as the unit of humanitarian and development work' (Krause 2014, p. 88) by operationalizing policy goals.

The 1990s were characterized by a further decline in development aid levels and a growing mobilization of civil society groups in North and South. NGOs became the most important constituency in development aid and took on important functions in disintegrating nation states. NGOs are not only seen as more cost-effective, but also closer to constituencies than governmental organizations. NGOs appeared to be the ideal organizational form to implement 'bottom-up' development (Kamat 2004) following the failure of 'top-down' approaches of development which were led by large bureaucratic institutions including governments, bilateral and multilateral organizations.

In a neoliberal perspective, poverty reduction could be achieved through the integration in global markets, democracy and good governance. NGOs took on a central role in implementing projects and mediating between donors and communities.

The rise of NGOs

Staff and budget cuts of bilateral organizations coincided with the growth of NGOs with respect to staff and budgets. These changes are also related to the increasing prominence of humanitarianism. Given that humanitarianism and development are still discussed separately, it is often emphasized that the annual funding for humanitarianism is consistently growing. For example, Maxwell and Walker (2008) report that between 1971 and 2006 humanitarian assistance by bilateral donors grew from $436 million to $9.2 billion (p. 117). This increased further to $13.8 billion (including non-Development Assistance Committee (DAC) donors) in 2011 (Development Initiatives, Global Humanitarian Assistance 2013). However, it needs to be pointed out that humanitarian assistance still only represents a small proportion of overseas assistance. In 2011 to 2012, only 8 per cent of ODA of the DAC countries was allocated to humanitarian relief.[7] Furthermore, it needs to be stressed that the vast majority of NGOs are multi-mandated; that is, they engage in both humanitarian relief as well as in development activities. Thus the growth in humanitarian assistance is associated with a shift from development to humanitarianism on the one hand and an involvement of development NGOs in humanitarianism on the other. These shifts have of course important implications for staff working in both development and humanitarianism. Rather than being limited to short-term emergencies, 'job descriptions now include such broader objectives as protecting human rights, promoting democracy, fostering development, and hastening peace building' (Weiss 2012, p. 159). This means that to some extent a shift from development to humanitarianism is in fact a relabelling of humanitarianism as development (or vice versa) and may be explained by strategies of gaining funding.

In the 1990s, a group of eight federations of international NGOs began to dominate the NGO market which include World Vision International, Oxfam, MSF, CARE, Save the Children, CISDE (a coalition of Catholic development NGOs), APDOVE (an association of European Protestant Development organizations) and Eurostep (a coalition of European secular NGOs) (Donini 1995). Based on a comparison between US, UK and French humanitarian and human rights NGOs, Stroup (2012) argues that national differences in the ethos of these organizations may be found: US NGOs were more professionalized and paid higher salaries than their European counterparts, whereas in the UK and France voluntarism played a stronger role. Furthermore, the main French NGOs which send a large proportion of expatriates overseas emerged around professions, for example, specializing in medicine (MSF, MDM) and nutrition (ACF). In contrast, British NGOs which prefer local staff focused on themes such as poverty (Oxfam), children's rights (Save the Children) and education (ActionAid) (Brauman 2011). In addition, there is a stronger division between development and humanitarian NGOs in France than in the US and the UK (Ryfman 2011). However, British NGOs also experience a tension between relief and development objectives and priorities (Slim 2011). In France as well as in Britain, the formation of development NGOs was informed by colonialism as well as de-colonialization (Ryfman 2011; Slim 2011). Following the formation of MSF, development NGOs in France decreased and lost influence. Financially far more independent from the state than NGOs in Britain or the US, French NGOs in general and MSF in particular are known for being critical of government policies, representing the 'Dunantist' tradition emphasizing independence from government interests (Davey 2012). In contrast, most US NGOs who rely on government funding for their operation stand in the 'Wilsonian' tradition and align themselves with US foreign policy (Stoddard 2003; Tong 2004; Dijkzeul and Moke 2005; Stroup 2012).

Médecins Sans Frontières (MSF) has received much more scholarly attention than other humanitarian (and development) NGOs. In addition to being a very prominent organization which received the Nobel Prize in 1999 and has charismatic leaders, this may be due to the fact that MSF has a research centre which publishes research initiated by MSF, as well as providing scholars with access to the organization (Heyse 2007; Korff 2012; Fassin 2012; Redfield 2013; Fox 2014). MSF attracts not only a huge amount of donations which guarantee its independence, but also a lot interest from people who wish to work for the organization. A number of former volunteers have published memoirs (for example, Olson 1999). MSF is very outspoken of its criticism of the aid system. Founded in 1971, MSF represented a new type of humanitarian organization that felt constrained by humanitarian law, insisting on impartiality and neutrality. Bernard Kouchner, one of the co-founders of MSF, saw parallels between the Holocaust and the situation in Biafra (Terry 2002), which they perceived as genocide. MSF thus rejected an attitude epitomized in the decision of the ICRC not to publicize the knowledge of what had happened in Nazi concentration camps. This decision of the ICRC was grounded in the conviction that its credibility depended on neutrality and discretion. In contrast, MSF felt it necessary to expose what was going on during the Biafran war in addition to providing aid (Rieff 2002). MSF thus makes political choices and has the duty to bear witness (Grossrieder 2003, p. 12; Taithe 2004; Redfield 2006). MSF engages in advocacy work, for example, the Access Campaign which started in 1999 and which calls for lowering the price for HIV/AIDS treatment and research on medicines to treat malaria, and neglected diseases such as sleeping sickness and kala azar (Fox 2014). Thus, the organization combines the provision of quality medical care for people in crisis with bearing witness and drawing attention to abuse and forgotten crises, and criticizing inadequacies of the aid system. Due to the fact that more than 90 per cent of MSF's funding comes from private sources MSF is independent from government support.

Differences between different MSF sections may be noted; for example, MSF-Holland is more comfortable accepting government funding (Sondorp 2011) and conflicts between sections occur (Simeant 2005). Moreover, Stroup (2012, p. 4) argues that 'CARE, Oxfam and MSF resemble other charities from their home countries more than they do humanitarian relief groups around the world', reflecting the regulatory environment (for example, tax advantages), political opportunities, material resources and social networks. Thus, MSF-USA can draw on the generosity of American foundations and MSF-UK receives government support. Both sections are involved in fundraising, advocacy, public education and volunteer recruitment but are not operational like MSF-France, which relies on private donors and the support from other sections (one-third provided by MSF-USA) (Stroup 2012, p. 87). In 2011, MSF-South Africa, MSF-East Africa, MSF-Brazil and MSF-Latin America became members of the MSF Federation contributing to the internationalization of the MSF movement (Fox 2014).

In addition to the major INGOs, there is also a multitude of smaller NGOs. Referring to the influx of NGOs during the post-tsunami response in Sri Lanka, Stirrat (2006) characterizes them as 'small furry animals'.

> in a world of slow-moving dinosaurs. One of the striking features of the relief effort was the presence of a horde of small, often newly formed foreign organizations with little if any experience in disaster relief but motivated by a strong humanitarian impulse that 'something had to be done'.
>
> (Stirrat 2006, p. 14)

Similar to Rwanda before and Haiti after the tsunami, these disasters attracted a multitude of NGOs. These may be either national or international NGOs; they may also include some small organizations, funded and run by individuals, which only serve a single purpose and are only active in one particular country or even village. Such small organizations do not necessarily have to be less professional – for example, a health professional who specializes in a particular disease or health problem may provide highly valuable and efficient care. However, smaller organizations tend to have fewer resources for training or to participate in coordinating meetings; they also offer fewer career opportunities, although this should not constitute a problem for the founders of such organizations. Smaller organizations may be marginalized through professionalization processes.

Faith-based organizations

Faith-based non-governmental organizations have recently attracted more attention (Barnett and Stein 2012), even though religiously motivated organizations were involved in development and humanitarianism long before the structural adjustment programmes and rise of the NGOs in the 1980s and their globalization in the 1990s. Indeed, as noted above, missionaries played an important role in the earliest stages of humanitarianism and development, and churches still play a significant role in aid, both as donors and as local partners of a variety of aid organizations. In addition to the increasing role of NGOs in development and relief, a number of other factors played a role in the proliferation of faith-based organizations: the growth of the Christian right in the US and the growth of political Islam, the rise of identity politics and decline of communism, the emergence of a transnational civil society and the support of diaspora communities for humanitarian and development assistance (Tomalin 2012). It is important to distinguish different types of faith-based organization, not just by religion, but with respect to their religious identity which may be more or less moderate. Indeed, Benedetti (2006) argues that it is better to understand the distinction between secular and faith-based organizations as a continuum rather than as distinct categories. Secular Christian NGOs resemble secular NGOs, include staff that are non-practising Christians and do not distinguish beneficiaries of aid based on religion. In contrast, militant Christian NGOs are characterized by 'high religious pervasiveness'; that is, requiring high religious motivations of their members and spreading the gospel, for example, by distributing bibles in refugee camps (Benedetti 2006, p. 853). World Vision, Tearfund and Medair represent examples of Christian aid organizations of different size and mandate. Evangelical relief and development organizations continued to grow throughout the 1980s, and World Vision started to rely on federal funds and gained consultative status with UN agencies like UNHCR, WFP and UNICEF (King 2012, p. 937). Between 1993 and 2008, the international budget of World Vision grew from $300 million to $2.6 billion, making it one of the largest development and relief agencies. The growth of the organization was accompanied by increased professionalization – which was required to obtain government funds – and partnerships across ecumenical, interreligious and secular divides which allowed the organization to collaborate with UN and other agencies and to operate in a variety of contexts. Faith-based NGOs include some of the largest as well as smaller organizations.

Furthermore, Muslim and other faith-based organizations contribute to the diversification of aid organizations (Benthall 2008; De Cordier 2009; Benthall 2011; Barnett and Stein 2012). Muslim aid agencies may in some respects be understood as a response to Western Christian and secular aid agencies. Like Christianity, Islam has a long tradition of charitable giving, but the emergence of transnational Muslim NGOs is a more recent phenomenon facilitated by increasing oil revenues and the spread of communication technology which supported solidarity efforts for Muslim victims of conflicts and natural disasters (Petersen 2012a). Disasters such as the famine in the Horn of Africa resulted in the creation of Muslim relief organizations operating in Ethiopia, Chad and Somalia in order to counter the aid of Christian and secular Western aid agencies which were feared to be motivated by Christian missionary evangelism. Petersen (2012b) distinguishes four generations of transnational Muslim aid: da'watist NGOs, which emerged at the end of the 1970s and understand aid as 'simultaneously material and spiritual'; jihadist NGOs, which emphasize justice and militancy and were shaped by the war in Afghanistan; solidarity NGOs, which distanced themselves from da'wa and jihad, adopted mainstream humanitarian principles and rejected any involvement in conflict which emerged during the war in Bosnia; and finally secularized Muslim NGOs which are an outcome of the stricter regulations and control following 9/11 and the War on Terror[8] (Petersen 2012b).

Each generation of Muslim aid organization is thus tied to a different political context. The relationship between these different types of transnational Muslim NGOs to other faith-based and secular organizations also varies. Moderate Christian and Islamic NGOs in some respect have more in common with each other than with secular NGOs (Benedetti 2006). Militant Islamic and Christian NGOs find it harder if not impossible to cooperate. Given the increased presence of humanitarian organizations in Muslim contexts, Muslim NGOs may have an advantage of gaining the trust of the local population more easily than Christian and secular organizations (De Cordier 2009). However, in observing the impact of Islamic foundations in Bulgaria, Ghodsee (2005) warns that Muslim aid may contribute to ethnic conflict.

Complex emergencies

The rise of NGOs in the 1990s was not only associated with a critique of existing development aid, but also with an increasing proportion of aid allocated to emergency relief. The end of the Cold War was followed by an increase in complex emergencies in many regions of the world and a virtual cessation of the veto powers of the United States and the Soviet Union in the UN (Wood *et al.* 2001). Due to these developments, humanitarian activities became more frequent and, since 1980, official humanitarian assistance expanded almost four-fold in real terms and by 50 per cent since 1993, with the steepest increase in the early 1990s and the post-2002 period (Riddell 2007, p. 317). The increase of humanitarian emergencies in the 1990s was thus accompanied by a shift in funding from development to relief activities (Fearon 2008). Given the critical assessment of development success (or lack thereof) it was easier to mobilize donations for victims of war or disasters. It is therefore not surprising that some organizations which had initially been active in development assistance shifted their activities to relief activities (Barnett 2011). For example, in 1988 almost three-quarters of the expenditures of the World Food Programme (WFP) were for development activities, whereas ten years later, 78 per cent were allocated to relief activities (Tanguy 2003, p. 221). Between 1990 and 2000 humanitarian aid almost tripled, from US$2.1 to $5.9 billion and the percentage of humanitarian aid of development assistance increased from 6 per cent to 11 per cent between 1989 and

1993. However, despite this increase in humanitarian aid, overall aid flows as well as aid as a proportion of national wealth declined during the 1990s (Macrae *et al.* 2002, p. 15). Between 2000 and 2009, humanitarian aid from government donors (including OECD as well as non-OECD DAC governments) increased from US$6.7 to $11.7 billion (Development Initiatives, Global Humanitarian Assistance 2011, p. 12). In 2010, humanitarian assistance increased to US$12.4 billion (out of a total of official development assistance of US$143 billion). The majority of ODA was provided by the OECD governments. In 2009, US$11.2 billion were given by OECD governments and US$555 million by non-DAC donors. Between 2011 and 2012, the international humanitarian response declined from US$19.4 billion to US$17.9 billion (Development Initiatives, Global Humanitarian Assistance 2013, p. 11).

In addition to the shift from development to relief, an increasing deployment of peacekeeping troops occurred. Peacekeeping involves neutral military forces who are involved in post-conflict tasks, including landmine clearance, refugee repatriation, infrastructure (re)construction and maintaining law and order. Peacekeeping operations include the military, international aid agencies and non-governmental organizations which seek to strengthen civil society, democracy, human rights and economic development. This means that people working in aid interact both with staff and volunteers from other NGOs and aid agencies, and with military forces. It therefore may not always be clear to the local population and beneficiaries whether they interact with military personnel or civilians (de Torrente 2004; Slim 1996).

In order to enhance the provision of humanitarian aid, the cluster approach was adopted enabling the coordination of international humanitarian assistance through the UN's Office for the Coordination of Humanitarian Affairs (OCHA). The humanitarian reform included the creation of the Central Emergency Response Fund (CERF) and the strengthening of the role and capacity of humanitarian coordinators (Holmes 2007; Street 2009). The promise of the cluster approach and the humanitarian reform project was to support the dialogue among a broad range of actors, including UN agencies, local and international NGOs (Holmes 2007, p. 5). However, the coordination efforts have been criticized for marginalizing local actors, being dominated by the UN and resulting in collective positions, thus undermining independent operations (Dederian *et al.* 2007; Street 2009; Stumpenhorst *et al.* 2011).

9/11 and the Global War on Terror

The peace-keeping operations and humanitarian interventions in the 1990s had already brought military and civilian actors into contact with each other: a trend which intensified after 9/11 and the start of the Global War on Terror. After 2001, 'weak and failing' states increasingly became the focus of aid, justified by the argument that a lack of security presented an obstacle to achieving the Millennium Development Goals. The integration of development, foreign policy and military concern resulted in a whole range of initiatives, including the development of new governance and justice systems, training for police and armed forces, and the reintegration of fighters into society and the economy (Barder 2007). This was achieved through consultancies and programmes rather than financial support. In addition, resources were given to humanitarian assistance. These developments meant that the focus of aid moved to conflict and post-conflict regions. In the UK, DFID expanded its support to insecure countries and development projects, which began to outweigh humanitarian expenditures in secure environments (National Audit Office 2008, p. 5). In the new millennium, the allocation of aid became increasingly determined by security interests (Bradbury and Kleinman 2010); in 2010 65 per cent of humanitarian assistance went to conflict-affected and post-conflict areas (Development Initiatives, Global Humanitarian Assistance 2011, p. 6). In 2009 the top recipients of humanitarian assistance were Sudan, Pakistan, Afghanistan and Bangladesh (Global Humanitarian Assistance 2011, p. 29). Almost 70 per cent of humanitarian aid was long term; many of the countries which receive long-term humanitarian aid also receive peace-keeping funds. Not only humanitarian, but also development assistance increased in insecure areas.

The complex emergencies of the 1990s led to the increasing awareness that neutrality, which in the Dunantist tradition is seen as a pre-condition for humanitarian aid, might neither be possible nor desirable. Humanitarian organizations have not only been instrumentalized by the parties involved in the conflict but also by donor countries (Schade 2007), probably most famously in the 'hearts and minds' approach during the war in Afghanistan when Colin Powell referred to NGOs as 'force multipliers' (Powell 2001). Moreover, humanitarian space was eroded when aid personnel sought military protection, used military resources such as planes and other means of transportation and received government grants, while military personnel were engaged in relief and reconstruction work providing logistical as well as security support (Weiss and Collins 2000; Smyser 2003). Furthermore, more and more long-term development assistance is provided in areas which are also recipients of humanitarian assistance.

Through these developments, aidwork increasingly became 'dangerous business' (Thomas 2005). Of course, people working in aid are based in insecure environments and are thus confronted with environmental threats. Moreover, attacks on aidworkers are not a new phenomenon. Relief workers have disappeared or died during missions throughout the twentieth century (Fast 2014, ch. 3). However, attacks on aidworkers, including kidnapping and killing, has steadily increased since the 1990s and even more so since 2001. Such intentional violence against aid personnel constitutes 'performative acts', eliciting worldwide media attention and sending the message about the level of insecurity and disregard of humanitarian principles (Hammond 2008).

The growing numbers of reported attacks on aidworkers reflect the increase of risks as well as the growth of people working in aid. The distribution of victims of attacks on aidworkers highlights the importance of NGOs as employers. Almost half of the victims were working for international NGOs, whereas less than a quarter were working for UN agencies, and about 6 per cent of those attacked were working for the Red Cross/Red Crescent. Larger organizations also have more resources than smaller organizations (Stoddard et al. 2006). Different types of organizations attract different types of risk related to the environment in which employers are working, their mandate and their relationship to local communities and authorities. Thus, the type of organization and work contract matter tremendously for the security of people working in aid (Van Brabant 2000).

Between 1997 and 2013, a total of 3,115 victims of attacks have been recorded, the great majority of the victims (82%) national staff members. National and international staff faced different types of risks. National staff were more likely to be killed (40 per cent national staff, 29 per cent international staff) or wounded (37 per cent national staff, 24 per cent international staff), while a higher proportion of international staff were kidnapped (47 per cent, compared to 23 per cent national staff). Furthermore, between 1997 and 2013, the number of attacks on national staff increased, while it decreased for international staff (see Table 1.1). Even though national staff were much more likely to be victims of attack, security measures so far are primarily targeted at international staff (Stoddard et al. 2006).

Table 1.1 Attacks on aidworkers

Year	National staff	International staff	Total
1997	43 (59%)	30 (41%)	73
1998	46 (68%)	22 (32%)	68
1999	43 (63%)	25 (37%)	68
2000	70 (77%)	21 (23%)	91
2001	62 (69%)	28 (31%)	90
2002	68 (80%)	17 (20%)	85
2003	116 (81%)	27 (19%)	143
2004	110 (83%)	24 (17%)	134
2005	158 (91%)	15 (9%)	173
2006	214 (89%)	26 (11%)	240
2007	186 (85%)	34 (15%)	220
2008	227 (82%)	51 (18%)	278
2009	221 (75%)	75 (25%)	296
2010	208 (85%)	37 (15%)	245
2011	280 (91%)	29 (9%)	309
2012	227 (82%)	49 (18%)	276
2013	275 (82%)	60 (18%)	335
Total	2545 (82%)	570 (18%)	3115

Source: www.aidworkersecurity.org (accessed 21 January 2014).

The increased risk that people working in aid are confronted with affected the security management of aid organizations (Duffield 1997; 2010; Van Brabant 2001; 2010). In particular, the attacks on the UN and the ICRC in Baghdad in 2003 resulted in a growing interest in security and the creation of new structures. In December 2004, the UN General Assembly created the Department of Safety and Security, while international aid organizations started to develop security systems and to employ security advisers (Bruderlein and Gassmann 2006). The fact that security measures are primarily directed at international staff in combination with a strategy to 'stay and deliver' and 'localization' (i.e. the transfer of tasks from international to national staff) emphasizes the inequality of national and international staff. Moreover, Fast (2014) argues that individuals and organizations working in aid need to pay far more attention to internal factors – that is, how their behaviour and programmes contribute to the insecurity of aid. Security measures that distance aidworkers from the population can be counterproductive by undermining trust and contributing to increasing separation and inequality. She therefore warns that a professionalization of security measures can jeopardize the humanitarian project.

Professionalization processes

Security is not the only area affected by professionalization and standardization processes which are shaping the working conditions of people working in aid. The transformation of NGOs into 'complex transnational bureaucracies' includes the adoption of strategic planning and strategic management, the adoption of internal staff guidelines, recruiting staffers with a background, the professionalization of human resources departments and paid staff becoming more of a standard (Ryfman 2011; Slim 2011; Stroup 2012). These changes are associated with a loss of autonomy of country operation and a shift to newly regional management structures 'with a new breed of NGO manager that emerged who oversees programme planning and reporting systems and rolls out new initiatives across the organization instead of simply administering projects' (Slim 2011, p. 37). For example, a former head of human resources found 'no fundamental difference whether the business is a corporation or a humanitarian organization like CARE' with respect to managing organizational staff (Stroup 2012, p. 91). As I will discuss in the following chapters, my data suggest that some leave the business sector in order to find more meaningful work in humanitarian and development organizations. However, Simeant (2005) compares the internationalization of NGOs to the expansion of multinational corporations.

The growth of the humanitarian aid industry including an increase in budgets, agencies and personnel led to a critical evaluation of the impact of aid as well as a debate about the need for the professionalization, accountability and coordination of aid efforts. A discussion of the professionalization of humanitarian aid had already begun in the late 1980s (Minear 1988), but the

Rwanda Crisis of 1994 had revealed massive shortcomings in aid delivery and resulted in a critical evaluation of emergency assistance in this case. This debate had wide-reaching consequences for the aid world in terms of developing and disseminating standards for the delivery of humanitarian assistance (Buchanan-Smith 2003). A number of networks and organizations have emerged which serve as platforms for debating and critically reflecting the aims, conditions and obstacles of carrying out humanitarian aid such as the Active Learning Network for Accountability in Humanitarian Action (ALNAP), the Humanitarian Practice Network (HPN), Enhancing Learning and Research for Humanitarian Assistance (ELHRA), the International Humanitarian Studies Association (IHSA), Professionals in Humanitarian Assistance and Protection (PHAP) and People in Aid, to name just a few initiatives (Walker 2004; Walker and Russ 2011). These organizations are engaged in debates about the professionalization of the sector, surveying challenges and providing practitioners with support which includes online and offline reports and events. The development of standards and codes of conduct is important with respect to mobilizing resources – obtaining funding and donations as well as recruiting qualified staff.

Efforts to draft a code of conduct had already started in the early 1990s initiated by the International Federation of Red Cross and Red Crescent societies and the Steering Committee for Humanitarian Response (Walker 2005).[9] In addition to emphasizing the fundamental humanitarian principles (impartiality, neutrality and independence), the code also stressed respect for local cultures, inclusion of local capacities and beneficiaries, the reduction of further vulnerabilities, accountability towards 'beneficiaries' as well as donors, and the dignified representation of aid recipients (Hilhorst 2005, p. 354). The code was quickly adopted, in particular by Western INGOs, reflecting the fact that it was written from the perspective of and biased towards Western INGOs and thus less relevant to local NGOs (Hilhorst 2005, p. 367).

Furthermore, the *Sphere* project, which started in 1997, aimed at improving the quality and accountability of aid agencies. The first edition of the *Sphere Handbook* was published in 2000 and was subsequently evaluated and revised. The newly developed standards were disseminated through training courses, some of them university based. Although the handbook was comprehensive and detailed, a number of concerns have been raised. In particular, it has been questioned to what extent universal principles may be adapted to local principles and practices in the field, or reflect the priorities of technical professionals of highly developed countries. Concerns include that the standards may constrain creativity and improvising skills, marginalize and weaken local organizations or be politically abused (Hilhorst 2002; Hilhorst and Schmiemann 2002; Dufour et al. 2004; Tong 2004; Vaux 2006). MSF, for instance, was critical of the introduction of standards concerning the delivery of aid. However, as Redfield (2008b) discusses, the organization had already started to develop 'modular, standardized kits' in the middle of the 1980s, thus representing 'materialized memory'. This is of great use given the high turnover in humanitarian assistance, but at the same time standardized kits are highly contradictory. They are the exact opposite of 'local knowledge', and yet they were developed by drawing on 'local knowledge' in a variety of contexts and thus provide a connection between various crises in which MSF gained experience.[10] After an initial emphasis on standardization, MSF now employs a 'post-Fordist' approach, characterized by outsourcing and flexibility which involves purchasing a greater variety of materials from local sources (Redfield 2008).

In addition, a code of best practice managing aid personnel and organizations supporting the management of humanitarian organizations was introduced in 1997 (Davidson and Raynard 2001; Walker and Russ 2010). However, while the organizations engaged in promoting codes and standards highlight their contributions to a promotion of 'best practice', there is so far little evidence of the impact of these initiatives upon performance (Crack 2014). Moreover, the proliferation of standards[11] may even be counter-productive if reporting is experienced as an additional task which absorbs resources of aid organizations and the energy of fieldworkers, and perhaps discourages openness about problems, as this might jeopardize certification proceedings. Thus, as long as the introduction of standards is based on peer regulation and lacks independent assessments, the most significant impact may be the creation of new job opportunities for accountability managers (Crack 2014).

A qualified workforce in the aid industry is of interest not only for job satisfaction and career building of individual aidworkers, but also for employers of aidworkers, donors and clients or beneficiaries (Richardson 2006). Organizations seeking to promote the professionalization of aidwork such as People in Aid emphasize good leadership skills, the ability to write grant proposals and reports and to represent the organization.[12] One important aspect of the professionalization of aidwork concerns the debate around the creation of professional pathways. Furthermore, training represents a non-financial incentive that may contribute to employee motivation and lower staff turnover (Loquercio et al. 2006). However, aid organizations do not necessarily have the resources to provide staff and volunteers with training opportunities. While some larger organizations can pay for the participation in shorter or longer training or university courses, smaller organizations are less able to support their staff and volunteers. Thus aidworkers themselves take on the responsibility to obtain further skills and knowledge, either as training on the job or through participating in university programmes or training courses. This debate around professionalization very rarely addresses the relationship between development studies and humanitarian studies, even though an early survey of 'humanitarian development studies' (Gonzalez et al. 1999, p. 23) notes close links between (1) poverty and development, (2) migration, multiculturality and ethnic conflict, (3) human rights, (4) peace studies, and (5) humanitarian crises. Nevertheless, development studies and humanitarian studies are usually discussed separately and the relationship (and overlap) between the two fields remains unaddressed. This may be explained by the competition for funding and students. Furthermore, a closer cooperation between development and humanitarian studies may reveal that some of the new insights of humanitarian studies (for example, the promises of and obstacles to participatory approaches) have been long debated in development studies. It would therefore be beneficial to consider the relationship between these fields and how they complement each other.

The origins of development studies in the UK reflect the colonial legacy and resulted in specialized multi-disciplinary centres which include development economics, the sociology of development, anthropology and development, and development geography. The first development studies programmes in the UK emerged in the 1940s. Following independence, former British colonial administrators became teachers in development studies programmes or expatriate consultants working for non-governmental, bilateral and multilateral organizations (Cooke 2003; Kothari 2006a). About 40 universities in the UK offer courses in international development and disseminate approaches such as participatory development and sustainable livelihood. Given that the vast majority of people working in development are graduates, universities (supported by bilateral organizations) thus play a significant role in shaping the development approaches of aid practitioners (Muir 2003). In contrast to the multidisciplinary study centres in the UK, it is typical for North America and Western Europe that development studies are part of traditional social science disciplines (sociology, anthropology, economics, etc.) or area studies (Kothari 2005b).

Since the 1990s, a number of universities in North America and Western Europe have established humanitarian studies courses which respond to the demands of the professionalization of the humanitarian sector. Like development studies, humanitarian development studies in Europe reveal national differences which reflect educational traditions (Gonzalez *et al.* 1999). University programmes preparing for humanitarian development studies are either subject specific (agriculture, forestry, medicine, engineering, economics) or multidisciplinary. The latter, focusing on emergency relief, peace-building or human rights, are more recent developments. In 1993, the Network on Humanitarian Assistance (NOHA), an inter-university multidisciplinary European Master's degree in international humanitarian action, was formed with support from the EU (Walker and Russ 2010). Two surveys of humanitarian studies programmes (which included some development programmes) found that the majority of these programmes were based at North American and European universities, while only very few are offered in Africa, Australia and Asia (Rainhorn *et al.* 2010; Walker and Russ 2010).[13] However, Master's programmes in low(er)-income countries may be under-represented in these surveys. Furthermore, postgraduate degrees offered at Asian or African universities tend to offer less prestige than those offered at universities in Europe and North America and thus may jeopardize recruitment and promotion in prominent NGOs and UN agencies. The vast majority of courses surveyed by Rainhorn *et al.* (2010) and Walker and Russ (2010) are offered in English-speaking countries. The Masters-level programmes cover a wide range of subjects, including law, international studies, nutrition, health, disaster management, conflict resolution, security and peace studies, peacekeeping, migration, logistics, journalism and development as well as general programmes in humanitarian studies.

A core curriculum which may be beneficial for the career planning of aid professionals as well as the organizations hiring them (and the donors funding these organizations) is missing thus far (Walker and Russ 2010). Some of these programmes are conceptualized as a combination of modules that may be taken at various points of time, thus allowing students to enrol in a course for a few weeks or months rather than for an entire year or longer. This enables particularly those who are employed to participate in such courses during their holiday or a paid or unpaid leave of absence. Qualifications may be obtained in the form of certificates and diplomas and – depending on the programme – a combination of such certificates may be converted into a Master's degree. Initially, these humanitarian studies programmes sought to recruit practitioners with job experience, including medical personnel who had not yet worked overseas or former military personnel. Increasingly, they are also including undergraduate students without previous job experience as well as people who are interested in a career change; for example, people with a background in human resources, management, communication and public relations. In addition to these Master's programmes, a range of short-term courses lasting between a day and several months are available at a much broader range of locations, including African and Asian (see overview in Walker and Russ 2010). Furthermore, international humanitarian organizations are engaged in distance learning which will most likely become increasingly important (Bollettino and Bruderlein 2008).

Thus, a multitude of university- and non-university-based training programmes are available. However, a survey of humanitarian NGOs revealed that applicants did not demonstrate any major gaps in academic knowledge but instead lacked experience to deal with stress and to apply techniques and methods in the field (Gonzalez et al. 1999). The authors of the study are sceptical as to whether university education may be able to remedy this situation. The ECHO has addressed this problem by creating a volunteer programme (EVAC) which allows for gaining field experience. Furthermore, some NGOs provide placements (Walker and Russ 2011). However, overall, on-the-job training – either un- or low paid as volunteer for an aid organization – or work experience in a 'regular' career in the private or public sector remain central for the involvement in aid, as I will show in the following chapters.

Buzzwords and fuzzwords

As already outlined above, Aidland experienced frequent shifts which shape the agenda though not necessarily the practices of aid organizations. This includes an emphasis on participation, empowerment, gender mainstreaming, sustainability, peace-building, human rights, internationalization and diversity (Cornwall and Brock 2005; Cornwall 2007). Cooke (2003) compares participatory approaches to indirect rule during colonialism. Another shift in discourse concerning international interventions and the relationship between human rights, humanitarianism and development occurred in the 2000s with the rising prominence of the concept 'resilience'. With respect to human security, resilience may be understood as 'post-interventionist'; that is, the emphasis is put on empowerment and capacity-building rather than protection, intervention and direct provision from external forces (Chandler 2012). However, 'post-interventionist' or preventive approaches can still deploy military means, as the bombing of Libya demonstrated (Chandler 2012, p. 221). The difference between the humanitarian and military interventions in Bosnia, Kosovo, Afghanistan and Iraq and the bombing of Libya was that, in the latter case, Western forces did not take responsibility for the outcome of the intervention or make any transformative promises (ibid.). Thus, on the one hand, post-interventionist approaches may only differ with respect to a lack of accountability; on the other hand, little is said about how 'resilience' may be accomplished and what this means for (Western) aid agencies. To what extent can power be shared if the partners differ with respect to power and resources? If vulnerable communities are to be empowered without outside intervention, what space does this leave for volunteers and staff of the plethora of aid agencies if resilience is defined as 'the capacity of affected communities to recover with little or no external assistance' (Manyena 2006, p. 433)? If resilience is understood as outcome, the emphasis lies on supplied aid characteristic for humanitarianism. However, if resilience is understood as a process, it involves community involvement (ibid., p. 438), more typical for participatory approaches in development. However, while the resilience paradigm places a lot of emphasis on empowerment and the role communities play in helping themselves, the role of international aid agencies and people working in aid becomes more opaque and is not necessarily addressed. How does the 'dispersal of power' and 'Western facilitation' (Chandler 2012, p. 223) work, and what questions does it raise for accountability towards donors? Strategies to achieve resilience include human resource development, physical capacity (transport, computer), operational systems and communication for sustainability and action research, advocacy and lesson sharing as strategies to achieve resilience (Tadele and Manyena 2009, p. 319). The emphasis is thus put on coaching and formal training, providing means of transportation and communication and the monitoring of practices. However, this does not address who is developing the training material and the criteria employed to evaluate and monitor group processes. To what extent does the empowerment allow vulnerable communities to speak up and negotiate with donor agencies and Western 'experts'? The focus on resilience certainly demands addressing the relationship among relief, human rights and development and the relationship among local, national and international actors. O'Dempsey (2009) therefore calls for 'fair training' and the establishment of a fair training network to strengthen local capacity.

'New' donors

Richard Manning (2006), Chair of the OECD's DAC, has pointed out that the 1990s during which DAC countries provided 95 per cent of all international aid represented the exception, rather than the norm. Throughout the Cold War, the former Soviet Union and her allies provided about 10 per cent of aid. Furthermore, India, other Commonwealth countries and China provided technical assistance from the 1950s, while the first Middle East fund was established in Kuwait in 1961 and the OPEC countries provided 30 per cent of international aid worldwide in 1978. Manning (2006) therefore recommends referring to 'non-DAC' donors rather than to 'newly emerging' donors.

Non-DAC donors such as China, India and other 'Southern' states challenge the very idea of development as a Western postcolonial concept and possibly contribute to the deconstruction of the Western development paradigm (Six 2009). This group of donors holds a dual position – as developing countries as well as developing partners – and acts in an interest-oriented manner as well as displaying Third World Solidarity and thus may offer a 'chance for real progress towards serious partnership' (Six 2009, p. 1109). Historically, India has supported African national liberation movements and the anti-apartheid movement in South Africa. China's relationship with Africa is characterized by self-interest and economic cooperation (trade). The rise of postcolonial states as donors may contribute to an 'erosion of dominance of Western countries in framing the terms and content of development debates' (Six 2009, p. 1116). In addition to the internationalization of the work of some Southern NGOs, a transfer from 'South' to 'North' may also be observed, for example, when Oxfam brings in a community worker from India to work on a UK housing estate (Thekaekara in Lewis 2006). Furthermore, the increasing involvement of non-Western donors is not restricted to development assistance. Between 2009 and 2010 the contributions from non-OECD member governments to humanitarian pooled funds increased from US$4 million to US$98 million (Development Initiatives, Global Humanitarian Assistance 2011, p. 7). Furthermore, between 2005 and 2010 the Indian government spent US$6.2 billion on emergencies in its own country, far more humanitarian assistance than India received from international donors (US$315 million) (ibid., p. 6). While traditional Western donors distinguish humanitarian assistance from other forms of overseas aid, including development aid or peace-keeping, non-Western donors do not make a distinction between short-term and long-term aid (Binder et al. 2010).

Furthermore, in addition to the aid budgets of bilateral, multilateral and non-governmental organizations, remittances from diasporas play a major role in overseas assistance (Driffield and Jones 2013). Finally, it should not be forgotten that the vast majority of survivors of conflicts and disasters – about 90 per cent – survive through their own efforts rather than due to international interventions (Minear 2002; Apthorpe 2012). Poor African states open their borders to victims of wars and hunger regardless of the state of their fragile economies (Farah 2003). In fact, examples from Rwanda, Somalia, Jordan, Montenegro, Albania and Macedonia indicate that 'local resources are often mobilized more quickly, prove more appropriate and cost-effective, and have greater staying power than those brought in by external actors' (Weiss and Collins 2000, p. 68). Another example of regional assistance would be the aid provided by Turkey to refugees from Syria in the context of the civil war which began in 2012 and other regional crises.

Media representations and celebrity involvement in development and humanitarianism

In contrast to the relatively minor role that international aid and expatriate aidworkers play in the support of victims of poverty, conflict and disasters, Western aid organizations and aidworkers dominate the Western media which play a central role in providing information about humanitarian crises and poverty as well as the work of humanitarian and development organizations. Media attention is a critical resource for aid organizations which seek to mobilize resources in the form of individual donors as well as bilateral and multilateral donors. Media coverage of poverty, disaster and conflict is subjected to the economy of the media. The media need images; some aid organizations therefore facilitate access to crisis situations and invest in bringing journalists to the story. At the same time, critical reporting can harm aid organizations which therefore seek to control how they are presented. Media coverage is thus crucial for framing crises as requiring the action of governments, multilateral organizations, non-governmental organizations or individuals as donors of various types of resources. Furthermore, media coverage as well as annual reports contribute to the accountability of aid organizations to their donors. In addition to the traditional media, aid organizations make use of digital and social media to elicit donations. Media coverage thus plays a crucial role in the mobilization of solidarity with 'distant strangers' (Boltanski 1999). Compassion and solidarity may be distinguished from pity and distance, although pity may lead to compassion. Furthermore, the 'communication of solidarity' has shifted from an ethics of pity to an ethics of irony (Chouliaraki 2013).

The increased media attention since the 1990s may to some extent be explained by media events such as BandAid and LifeAid and celebrity involvement. Various waves of celebrity activism may be distinguished. The first and second waves in the 1960s concerned the US civil rights movement, followed by the opposition to the Vietnam War and military draft. The third wave starting in the 1970s differed from the earlier waves because celebrities now took on leadership roles rather than simply participating and by the response to global concerns with various live concerts which became more widespread after the Live Aid concerts of 1985. The shift from 'Band-Aid' to 'Brand Aid' which links consumerism, celebrities and good causes represents a fourth wave (Richey and Ponte 2011, pp. 32–33). At the same time, business involvement in aid may be observed which is motivated by investigating the image of corporations, attracting and retaining staff, philanthropic motives of business leaders and to a lesser extent gaining knowledge and access to new markets (Binder and Witte 2007, pp. 14–15). Interestingly, the 'brand aid' and 'business involvement' in the humanitarian sector coincides with the untying of aid in development. Thus, commercial interests do not disappear from Aidland but reflect a shift from protectionist to neoliberal principles.[14]

Aid organizations have become increasingly professional with respect to marketing, fundraising and branding. The communication of aid organizations is increasingly characterized by branding, seeking to gain donor loyalty and following the logic of the market. Efforts to sell development through media spectacles can lead to a depoliticization of aid. On the other hand, broad coalitions of aid organizations have jointly pursued campaigns like the Make Poverty History and Jubilee Debt Campaign and thus bring development issues on to the public agendas. While development has faced a lot of criticism and (new) social movements have lost some momentum at the end of the twentieth century, humanitarian aidworkers – in particular MSF – have become the 'last heroes' (Boltanski 1999; Fassin 2012). Branding and the use of new media play a central role in solidarity activism which requires little time and effort. However, while the click of a mouse to sign a petition or make a donation requires little time and effort, such online involvement can be less satisfying than actual participation which enables Aidland to be experienced. Thus, the presentation of an aid organization not only attracts donors but also potential volunteers and staff. Development has become 'sexy', the 'pornography of poverty' has been replaced by a shift of attention 'to the identity of the "self" by targeting the libido' (Cameron and Haanstra 2008, p. 1476). This is achieved through the good-looking, competent, beneficent Northern donors (and celebrities) who have the agency and knowledge to come to the rescue of people from the Global South which tend to be represented as incompetent and in need of aid. Moreover, 'liberated' women from developed countries are juxtaposed with 'oppressed' women in less developed countries, thus perpetuating the colonial perception of gender relations in the Global North. 'Doing development' thus becomes attractive for young global citizens from the Global North and has given rise to a whole gap-year industry (Simpson 2004; Vrasti 2013).

Conclusions

The transformations of Aidland are shaping the conditions of people working in aid. This includes a growing importance of humanitarian relief (even though the majority of aid is still allocated to development), reforms of the UN system and bilateral organizations, and the increasing role of faith-based and other non-governmental organizations. Combined, these changes have resulted in more short-term, project-based positions in crisis regions. This emphasis on emergency and exception brings about more insecurity for those working in aid and may reduce opportunities for engaging with inequality among national and international staff, aidworkers and other beneficiaries. Paradoxically, the 'state of emergency' (Calhoun 2010) goes hand in hand with the institutionalization of the aid system. These institutionalization processes include the increased emphasis on professionalization, standardization and branding. Careers are thus based in a never-ending string of crises that are caused by political conflicts, poverty and climate change which are grounded in political and social relations. While, at least theoretically, development cooperation should be temporary and humanitarian assistance exceptional, in reality, both forms of assistance have become long term and institutionalized. The provision of aid which has been given for centuries is shaped by altruistic as well as selfish motives – at the individual, organizational, national and international levels. There is no shortage of critical evaluations of what development cooperation and humanitarian relief can or cannot achieve. The critical engagement with aid has resulted in new approaches in development and professionalization processes in humanitarian assistance. In addition, non-DAC donors introduce new voices and practices, and challenge the conventional distinction between development and humanitarian aid. Whether a crisis of aid can be stated or not, it is accompanied by growing aid budgets and significant media coverage of aid organizations and their operations eliciting compassion with 'distant strangers'. In the following chapters, I will analyse how those working in aid organizations experience and deal with the inequality and limited change that shapes North–South relations and how changing working conditions shape their career planning.

Notes

1 See OECD-DAC; www.oedc.or/dac/stats (last accessed 26 July 2014).
2 For more detailed information see https://careers.un.org.
3 See www.unv.org.
4 In 1975, the first UN world conference on the status of women took place in Mexico City. Key objectives of the conference included the elimination of gender discrimination and the integration and full participation of women in development. The Women in Development (WID) approach was associated with efforts to integrate women into productive activities. In the 1980s, WID was replaced by the Gender and Development (GAD) approach which emphasized 'agency'. The Third World Women's conference in Nairobi (1985) emphasized women's inequality in social and political participation and decision-making. This was further broadened in 1995 at the Fourth World Women's conference when gender mainstreaming was adopted.
5 However, DARA (2012) does not provide any information concerning sampling and response rate; due to the fact that the study focused on gender, women may

be over-represented. DARA is a non-profit organization which produces the Humanitarian Response Index (www.daraint.org).
6 Although associated with neoliberalism, administrative reform and results-based management in the public sector has a long history in the twentieth century and earlier (Krause 2014).
7 OECD-DAC; www.oecd.org/dac/stats (last accessed 26 July 2014).
8 The impact of 9/11 and the War on Terror upon aid organizations will be discussed below.
9 This section draws on Roth (2012).
10 See also Scott-Smith (2014) for a critical assessment of supplementary feeding.
11 HAP and People in Aid discuss the integration of their peer regulation schemes in the 'Core Humanitarian Standard' (http://www.hapinternationalor/what-we-do/hap-standard/the-core-humanitarian-standard.aspx).
12 Reporting from meetings of human resources managers of aid organizations, Jonathan Potter, Executive Director of People in Aid, claimed: '[At EPN Rome] [the] Good Samaritan disappeared, redundant from increasing professionalism. At EPN Nairobi, [the] cowboy made way for someone with enhanced powers of emotional intelligence. In Bangkok, multitasking Rambo was unwanted. Angels of mercy and do-gooders have been criticised, leaving the more conventional development worker, project worker, aidworker' (People in Aid newsletter, October 2007, p. 1).
13 A lack of entry- and mid-level qualifications has also been noted and far fewer university courses are offered for undergraduate students.
14 Furthermore, some aid organizations engage in business partnerships (Andonova and Carbonnier 2014) and business actors are involved in armed conflict (Slim 2012).

2 Theorizing (aid)work

> Well, it is very interesting. It is very fulfilling, or can be very fulfilling if you do a good job, you get to see lots of places and things that you would not normally see. It is the opposite of a boring nine-to-five job. The money can be very good, and I mean there is a lot of freedom involved, I mean you both, yes, the idea of going from one contract to the other while it can be a bit stressful, it is actually quite liberating, you are not stuck into routines and particularly if you are well paid, that you have, you know, you buy freedom because you work for a period. And there is a sense of comradeship, I mean you make good friends.
>
> European Human Rights Worker, 2004

> I feel that most of the young people who are getting into this field are doing it because it is trendy, because it is sexy to be somewhere else in Africa or South America, taking pictures with little naked kids.
>
> Latin American Human Rights Worker, 2006

These quotes illustrate the 'mixed motivations' (Fechter 2012) of people working in aid and combine a whole range of – but not nearly all – aspects that attract people to work in aid organizations. In this chapter I discuss the continuities and discontinuities between aidwork and other forms of work in contemporary neoliberal societies in the Global North and the Global South. What, if anything, is distinctive about aidwork? One of the recurrent themes in the interviews was that respondents distinguished working and living in Aidland from 'normal life' or 'real life'. My respondents conceptualized their involvement in the aid sector as separate and exceptional, even if it was carried out over long periods of time.[1] This distinction was more pronounced in the interviews by international aidworkers from high-income countries. However, respondents who worked in their own countries who usually came from an (upper)-middle-class background also noted the difference of working with vulnerable communities in their home town or other regions of the country as distinct from the careers of their peers. Respondents explained that they chose aidwork as an alternative to 'normal' work, including the proverbial 'boring nine-to-five jobs'.

I argue that Aidland provides opportunities for educated middle classes, global professionals who are pursuing self-realization as well as personal and professional ambitions with the aim of making 'a difference' and contributing to social change. Privilege and self-interest, however, does not make them cynical mercenaries or 'Lords of Poverty' famously described by the often quoted Hancock (1989); quite the reverse: the desire to 'give something back' was frequently noted in the interviews, with respondents feeling themselves to be driven by the 'helping imperative' (Heron 2007). Furthermore, while the lifestyle of aidworkers can be comfortable, it can also be characterized by multiple risks and precariousness. Aidwork includes a whole range of different working conditions which are accompanied in differences in salaries and lifestyle. Aidland represents a global work culture which is not bound to specific countries and – like other work cultures – is stratified. People working in aid pursue their ambitions in a neoliberal economic environment in a sector that is constituted by historical contradictions, geopolitical conflict and global crises. In particular, it is of interest what impact the recent professionalization processes outlined in the previous chapter have upon the character of aidwork. This chapter puts aidwork in a broader theoretical context, highlights a variety of dimensions of aidwork, and addresses tensions between altruism and idealism on the one hand and professionalization on the other hand.

What is (aid)work?

'Work' is still predominantly associated with paid employment, although due to long-standing feminist (and other) critiques it is now acknowledged that work comprises a broad range of both paid and unpaid activities in the private and public spheres (for an overview, see Budd 2011). Furthermore, what is considered work often depends on the context: the same activity, for example, sport or arts, may be performed professionally or as a leisure activity (Pahl 1988). A broad conception of work which includes un- and low-paid work seems especially appropriate in the context of aidwork which is characterized by a broad range of work forms – rarely permanent and usually fixed term, including stipends for volunteers and contracts for consultants (Fechter 2011; Shutt 2012). Furthermore, some staff members of aid organizations volunteer formally or informally in the communities in which they are based in addition to their paid work. The 'total social organization of labour' (TSOL) approach (Glucksmann 1995; 2005; Taylor 2004; 2005) acknowledges the interconnectedness of paid and unpaid work which may be carried out simultaneously or consecutively. Aidwork which includes volunteering and unpaid internships is also related to political and social engagement which is grounded in solidarity, social, political or religious convictions. Just as (unpaid) volunteers and activists can become paid staff members of social movement and third sector organizations, unpaid involvement in a range of contexts can lead to paid positions in aid organizations. Thus I use the term 'work' to include both paid and unpaid positions.

Even though there is substantial overlap between the NGO literature and third sector literature, these two bodies of research constitute 'separate spheres' (Lewis 1999; 2014). However, it is helpful to draw on studies of the non-profit sector which, like NGOs, comprises unpaid volunteers as well as paid staff. Traditionally, the literature on the workforce of voluntary organizations focused primarily on volunteers (Wilson 2012), while employment in the non-profit sector has only recently attracted attention (McDermott et al. 2012). Compared to private and public sectors, the non-profit sector offers lower pay, fewer benefits, has a lower unionization rate and offers fewer career opportunities (Cunningham et al. 2013). The workforce is predominantly female, white, middle class and educated, and more women take on positions as managers and professionals than in the private and public sectors (Lee and Wilkins 2011; Faulk et al. 2013). With respect to gender and class, this also seems to apply to aid organizations; a recent study found 40 per cent of women among team members and senior management (Knox Clarke 2014, p. 12). Furthermore, like the workforce in the non-profit sector, aidworkers are motivated by values, doing something for others and having more responsibilities and challenges than in other sectors (De Cooman et al. 2011; Stride and Higgs 2014). The gender pay gap in the non-profit sector is lower than in the private sector; men have to accept the lower salaries typical for 'women's' work (Faulk et al. 2013). The higher proportion of women among the non-profit sector workforce at all levels may on the one hand be explained by their values; on the other hand it could be that the non-profit sector offers opportunities not available in the private and public sectors. I suggest that this also applies to the aid sector.

In the context of aidwork, international volunteering and the gap-year industry are of particular interest. Volunteer tourism has become a popular phenomenon and seems to contribute more to honing entrepreneurship and competition among volunteers than contributing to improving the living conditions in the Global South (Vrasti 2013). Indeed, international youth volunteering provides a training ground for global corporate work (Jones 2011) and thus moves away from being a radical activity (Simpson 2005). Rather than promoting global citizenship and tolerance, international gap years have been co-opted by neoliberalism (Lyons et al. 2012). However, some argue that although international volunteering may not help the communities that are supposed to 'benefit' from it, it forces volunteers to reflect on their actions, practices and behaviour, and contributes to a cosmopolitan outlook (Devereux 2008; Mangold 2012). Volunteer tourism and the gap-year industry pose challenges for the aid industry: while professional aid organizations seek to distance themselves from inefficient and potentially harmful interventions, aid organizations are nonetheless interested in recruiting volunteers and staff with field experience. Gap-year participation can lead to an interest in aidwork and can represent the first work experience in the Global South. The EU Aid Volunteer Initiative, developed by the European Community Humanitarian Office (ECHO), provides volunteer opportunities and seeks to support professionalization processes in the aid sector.[2]

In addition to various forms of volunteering, participation in social movements also plays a role in someone becoming an aidworker. Perhaps most famously, the early leaders of Médecins Sans Frontières had been involved in the new social movements of the 1960s. Moreover, MSF considers itself to be a *movement* rather than an organization (Redfield 2013; Fox 2014). However, prior (and parallel) social movement engagement is not restricted to MSF members, but applies to staff and volunteers in a range of development organizations (see e.g. Passy and Giugni 2000; Vaux 2001; Hilhorst 2003). Furthermore, a self-identification of NGO workers as activists is not limited to those from the Global North, as Yarrow (2008) demonstrates with respect to Ghanaian founders of national NGOs. Recruitment into and sustainability of high- or low-risk activism, patterns of participation and the biographical consequences of movement participation, for example, with respect to career choice and marriage, are of great interest to scholars of social movements (Corrigal-Brown 2012). The notion of 'biographical availability' (McAdam 1986; Eddy 2011) is highly relevant for the recruitment and careers of people working in aid, which is how participation in high-risk activism fits into the life-course. Perhaps counter-intuitively, having family and work commitments does not necessarily restrict participation in high-risk activism (Nepstad and Smith 1999), as I will show in the following chapters. However, involvement seems to have biographical consequences (McAdam 1999), as a high proportion of aidworkers, in particular women, appear to be single and without children.

Social movement scholars present critical perspectives on professionalization processes and warn that staff-driven organizations undermine volunteer engagement and de-radicalize social movement organizations (Skocpol 2003; Walker et al. 2011; Dauvergne and LeBaron 2014). However, non-governmental organizations may be both 'insiders' who provide services as well as 'outsiders' who criticize and challenge their opponents (Tarrow 2005; Saunders 2009). For example, in 2014 Oxfam UK was outspoken about the consequences of the austerity measures of the UK government on poverty in Britain which was met by the complaint of a Conservative MP to the Charity Commission which oversees third sector organizations (see also Slim 2011 and Stroup 2012 for an adversarial position of humanitarian organizations). Furthermore, the few existing studies of work experiences and work relations in social movement organizations highlight tensions in value-driven organizations which experience resource shortages, status differences and conflicts, and competition with other organizations (Ferree and Yancey 1995; Kleinman 1996; Newman 2012). This is relevant for staff of aid organizations which are competing for funding and donations.

One of the indicators of the increasing professionalization of humanitarian NGOs are rising salaries of executive staff. Although even if the salaries of executive staff of some larger INGOs are comparable to the private sector, this does not mean that all people working in aid are paid staff, nor that the salaries of all those who are paid are comparable to the private sector. Moreover, while executive salaries of large INGOs in the US tend to be relatively high, they tend to be lower in Britain and France (Stroup 2012). Furthermore, volunteers play a more important role in France and Britain compared to the US. NGO and other aid staff who made a career change from the private, public or third sector to aid organizations are not necessarily interested in obtaining the same financial rewards in the aid sector. Thus, while these professionals certainly bring skills and expertise, their motivation to enter the aid sector tends to be intrinsically motivated and they accept forgoing financial rewards (Frantz 2005).

Thus, the professionalized aid sector includes a wide range of different employment opportunities; while some are well paid and offer career opportunities, overall, many job opportunities are characterized by insecurity if not precariousness (Shutt 2012). Although some larger NGOs, bilateral organizations and UN agencies offer a few well-paid positions, job security and career opportunities within the organizations, overall pay and career opportunities are limited. In the course of the UN reform, permanent positions have been reduced (Weiss 2012). Bilateral organizations have also seen staff reductions and a shift to fixed-term positions and consultancies (Hindman 2011; Eyben 2014, ch. 8). The prevalence of short-term appointments is accompanied by high levels of staff turnover. As we will see in the following chapters, volunteering still plays an important role in aid organizations. In particular, at the beginning of an aidworker's career, volunteering provides the needed field experience which may then lead to a paid position in the sector. My data suggest that self-realization rather than career opportunities attracts the vast majority of aid professionals, some of them leaving well-paid careers and accepting lower-paid and insecure jobs.

Salaries for national staff tend to be lower than for international staff (Carr et al. 2010; Shutt 2012); furthermore, remuneration plays a different role in the recruitment of national and international staff. Jobs in international aid organizations can provide lucrative work opportunities for national staff. In contrast, international staff who have previously been employed in other labour markets are more likely to experience a loss of income due to the fact that volunteering and unpaid internships constitute a prerequisite for securing a paid position in Aidland. Given the prevalence of short-term jobs with little job security, aidworkers from the Global North thus seem to be motivated by 'post-material values' (Inglehart 1977) rather than by financial incentives. For international staff, being able to forgo a well-paid, secure job in the public, private or third sector in order to pursue aidwork may either be possible because they have limited financial responsibilities or because they have independent means. In this regard, international aidworkers may be compared to creative workers who are able to pursue precarious and unpredictable careers while relying on financial resources from parents or partners (Wolkowitz 2009). In addition, aid organizations often provide travel and accommodation for those working in field offices, so as long as there are no other financial obligations, for example, supporting dependants or paying rent or a mortgage, it is possible to live on a small allowance, and even modest incomes allow for a comfortable lifestyle in low-income economies (Fechter 2012). Intermittent high(er)-paid consultancies or other fixed-term appointments allow money to be set aside for those periods without an income or for making investments in order to secure an income for retirement. Thus alternating periods with high(er) and low or no income are not untypical for people working in Aidland. The salaries of those based in head offices in high(er)-income countries are comparable with other third sector jobs (Stroup 2012; Krause 2014). Given that head offices tend to be based in expensive cities like London, Paris, Geneva or New York, my data suggest that these salaries do not allow for sumptuous lifestyles unless there are additional sources of income.

The experience of volunteers and other aid personnel from the Global North who spend time in rural and remote areas in basic living conditions which include limited access to water, electricity and information technologies may be compared to 'slow culture' (Osbaldiston 2013). Slow culture is a reaction to stressful and high-speed life in a consumer culture which is experienced as stressful. This lifestyle movement is a response to the overconsumption and lack of work–life balance typical for 'fast capitalism' (Agger 2004), and involves a turn to meaningfulness and care (Parkins and Craig 2006) and conscious consumption (Schor 2008). Slow culture encourages reflection and the questioning of assumptions and practices of everyday life, and the global impact they have with respect to the environment as well as global justice. Respondents recalled their shock on returning to affluent societies of the Global North and being confronted with seemingly endless consumer choices and waste, or feeling guilty for using potable water to fill a bathtub. In contrast to protest movements, 'slow culture' is a form of political action that rather than primarily addressing corporations, governments or international organizations instead targets the behaviour and conscience of the general public. Aidwork contributes to global justice through interventions and offers opportunities to live in low-carbon economies and thus temporarily withdraw from highly evolved consumption culture. In addition, faith-based involvement in aidwork represents another aspect of the rejection of material values. The contrast between slow living in low-carbon economies and the stressful, complex and fast-paced working conditions which I will discuss further below represents one of the paradoxes of Aidland.

Aidwork thus encompasses un-, low- and well-paid positions and living conditions that range from basic and constrained to comfortable and luxurious. Aidworker careers often start out with unpaid internships and volunteer positions, with paid work and formal as well as informal volunteering sometimes being carried out simultaneously. Work, whether it is paid or not, that involves social interaction, helping others, independence, intellectual stimulation and creative expression enables self-actualization (Dik and Hansen 2008). A calling is not restricted to paid work but may be pursued by those who volunteer and who are voluntarily unemployed (Torrey and Duffy 2012).

Aidwork as a calling and vocation

Aidwork may be considered as a calling or vocation and is a good example of interests, religion and spirituality influencing career choice and self-definition (Dik and Hansen 2008; Dik and Duffy 2009). Meaningful work and altruistic goals can give life sense, and contribute to well-being and psychological success (Morse and Weiss 1955; Dawson 2005; Hall and Chandler 2005; Steger et al. 2010). Whether aidwork is carried out in faith-based or secular organizations, it constitutes meaningful work which is grounded in social justice (development), saving and protecting lives (humanitarianism) and human rights. Indeed, religious beliefs play a crucial role in the emergence of humanitarianism which has transcendental elements even if carried out by secular aid organizations (Barnett 2011, p. 20). Humanitarian reason may be understood as a secularized religious concept (Fassin 2012). Initially associated with religion, vocation became a secularized concept, though it was still associated with selfless service and devotion to a higher goal, and intertwined with the emergence of capitalism. In capitalist societies, 'unproductive' work became marginalized and devalued while secular vocation provided opportunities for self-realization and individualization (Dawson 2005). In particular, those working in helping professions such as teachers, nurses or social workers tend to be drawn to their jobs through their values and motivations, although public sector cuts and increased bureaucracy and managerialism that have changed working conditions in the social sector can undermine self-development and well-being (Rees 1999; Ferguson 2007). For example, across the Global North medical personnel are experiencing emotional exhaustion, a sense of depersonalization, a lack of personal accomplishment and occupational dissatisfaction due to stressful working conditions. Some medical personnel reacted to burnout by getting involved in overseas volunteering and benefited from the feeling of making a difference and being appreciated. In fact, participation in short-term medical missions has increased since the 1980s and contributed to a personal renewal for healthcare professionals who engage in volunteer service in developing countries (Campbell et al. 2009). Furthermore, the direct or vicarious experience of critical life events can initiate a sense of calling or vocation for some (Dik and Duffy 2009, p. 439). For example, anecdotal evidence suggests that a large number of people respond to highly visible disasters (e.g. the 9/11 terrorist attack, Asian tsunami and Hurricane Katrina) by leaving their current jobs, temporarily or permanently, to come to the aid of victims (Eidelson et al. 2003). As I will show in Chapter 3, the dissatisfaction with changing working conditions caused some respondents from the Global North to look for work in Aidland which was perceived as more meaningful. Aidwork (and other helping professions, for that matter) is characterized by a complex relationship between the well-being and suffering of self and others.[3]

Aidwork thus constitutes a vocation, attracting individuals who have altruistic values and motivations who want to make a difference and seek work contexts in which they are challenged. Altruistic values, the wish to help others who are in need and saving the world may also be intertwined with self-realization and the wish to be authentic (Thunman 2012). Aidwork is shaped by a tension between altruism and self-interest which do not have to be mutually exclusive (de Jong 2011). As my data demonstrate, the desire to contribute to improving and saving the lives of others may be combined with a challenging and fulfilling career. Some enter the field hoping that their work should make their involvement superfluous; that is, that if successful, they would work themselves out of a job. It seems paradoxical to pursue a career which has the goal to erase its need which would be the case if aid organizations were indeed successful in ending poverty and suffering. In this regard, it may be useful to make the distinction between organizations which seek to bring about radical structural change and service providers who improve the lives of individuals but overall sustain rather than challenge unequal global relations.

Managerialism and professionalization

In the past decades, the need for professionalization has found considerable interest in the aid sector. Professionalization processes concern the sector as a whole, aid organizations as well as the people working in aid. These aspects are of course closely related; professional aid organizations seek to hire professionals who guarantee that the sector works properly and thus deserve further financial support. Professionalization includes a number of factors such as the growing budgets of NGOs, an emphasis on fundraising and branding, a shift from volunteers to paid professionals, the recruitment of professionals with previous careers in the private sector and salaries that can be compared to the private sector. However, while these developments are often repeated in the literature, they are rarely unpacked and differentiated. This is related to the fact that humanitarianism and development are frequently discussed separately, and thus appear as somewhat parallel universes in the literature. Studies that emphasize the growth of humanitarian budgets rarely address that overall they only constitute a small proportion of ODA. The vast majority of ODA still goes to development and the vast majority of organizations involved in humanitarian assistance are multi-mandated; thus they are involved in a range of activities. This means that the growth of the humanitarian sector to some extent reflects a shift from development to humanitarianism – both for aid organizations and for aid professionals. Development organizations have for a long time employed professional staff working in bilateral and multilateral organizations and more recently in non-governmental organizations. Thus, the increasing budget of a few large NGOs needs to be related to a move away from bilateral and multilateral organizations to non-governmental organizations (Watkins et al. 2012). Furthermore, not just NGOs but also bilateral and multilateral organizations employ neoliberal employment practices which are characterized by shorter work contracts (Hindman 2011). NGOs engage in subcontracting and fundraising, and – in order to be successful in establishing themselves as distinctive from other aid organizations – in branding. Thus some professionalization processes (for example, the shift from volunteers to paid staff) affect NGOs more than other organizations. On the other hand, the introduction of standards and codes affects all aid organizations. They need to demonstrate that they work efficiently, are accountable to donors and beneficiaries, and remain true to their principles.

Aid organizations draw on a wide range of professionals trained in a whole range of disciplines – medicine, law, engineering, economics and management – to name just a few. Furthermore, many volunteers are professionals – doctors, engineers, logisticians, nurses – and apply professional skills while being low or unpaid, sometimes over long time periods working as 'volunteering professionals' or 'professional volunteers'. Thus there is a tension between a notion of 'professional standards' and a concept of professions which has been associated with boundary setting, power and expertise. A profession which successfully establishes itself can claim jurisdiction over practices and processes, including recruitment (Abbott 1988). Thus, one central aspect of the professionalization debate concerns consistent occupational standards and the adoption of core humanitarian competencies. Given the complexity and demands of the aid world, Slim (1995) identifies a range of key skills – in addition to the qualifications in a particular field – required by aidworkers in working in highly politicized contexts: 'informed political analysis, negotiation skills, conflict analysis management and resolution, propaganda monitoring and humanitarian information broadcasting, broader understanding of vulnerability to include notions of political, ethnic, gender and class-based vulnerability; human rights monitoring and reporting, military liaison; and personal security and staff welfare' as well as moral skills (Slim 1995, p. 110). Similarly, Walker (2004) acknowledges that the knowledge and skills of humanitarian professionals are far-reaching – from medicine and engineering to law and politics. He develops a model including various components: values, knowledge and systems, an acknowledgement that these need to exist in the person and in the organization of practitioners, a research and education system which provides an ever-learning foundation for the practitioners, and a dynamic and respectful relationship with the clients for whom the profession is providing a service (Walker 2004). Given such a broad range of necessary competencies, it may be better to speak about a whole range of different aid professionals (logisticians, medical staff, management staff, etc.) rather than *the* humanitarian professional in order to highlight the multiplicity of necessary training and experience. Furthermore, as long as there are little representative data on the composition of people working in aid, it is difficult to say whether aidworkers and aid professionals today are more or less 'professional' than previous generations of aidworkers.

The debate around professionalization has so far focused more on the introduction of codes of conduct and training programmes, and far less around the actual qualifications that people working in aid have or lack.

The introduction of codes of conducts and standards is actually at odds with the autonomy that is characteristic for professions and professionals (Krause 2014). Standardization is thus related to de-professionalization and it may be better to talk about managerialism rather than professionalization of the aid sector. It is therefore not surprising that MSF, an organization founded by professionals and well known for its independence, is a strong critic of the *Sphere* standards (Dufour et al. 2004). It remains to be seen what long-term consequences the increased importance of standards and training has for aid practices and aid relationships. Harrell-Bond (2002) is sceptical about whether education may 'directly impact on behaviour in the field' (p. 71). In addition, depending on how skills are defined and how and where they are obtained, professionalization processes may have an exclusionary effect (Walker 2004). In particular, if staff from the Global South do not have access to training opportunities, professionalization processes may reinforce global inequalities (Roth 2012). Overseas volunteering experience can contribute to a person being accepted into an elite university, and having a degree from an elite university can help a graduate find a leadership position in an aid organization. Rather than joining the diplomatic corps,[4] those who have the necessary cultural, social and economic capital enter Aidland. Aid organizations require international experience that at least initially is acquired while earning little or no pay. My data suggest that the recruitment processes into Aidland thus seem to favour the (upper)-middle class, while working-class and ethnic minorities tend to get involved in their own communities either as volunteers or in helping professions. However, some of my respondents who started out as local staff members and were working in their own communities in programmes of international aid organizations later embarked upon international careers.

Mobility and flexibility

Given that aidwork includes a multitude of professions and is open to generalists (Frantz 2005), it epitomizes neoliberal work practices which are characterized by constant boundary-crossing, rather than the pursuit of a career for life (Walkerdine 2006). In this respect, aidwork represents an extreme case of a project-based search for meaning in paid and unpaid work which requires mobility and flexibility. This means that subjectivities are constituted in the permanent adaptation to new contexts resulting in 'resilience', 'flexibility' and 'transferable skills', typical for people working in aid as I will show in the following chapters. Careers that are changed by constant shifts (and the ability to cope with the anxieties that these changes might produce) may be characterized as 'protean careers' (Hall 2004) which are self-driven or 'boundaryless careers' (Gorman and Sandefur 2011; Inkson et al. 2012).

These careers are not based in lifelong professional affiliation but involve new patterns of occupational affiliation, interruptions and non-professional entry points (Gorman and Sandefur 2011). Such an understanding of career is very useful for an analysis of the employment patterns in Aidland, where staff and volunteers move frequently from one organization to the next. Typical for contemporary societies, these new career forms are no longer organization-based, but the course of the career seems to lie in the interests, drives and motivations of self-realizing individuals with an intrinsic work motivation (Dik and Duffy 2009, p. 435).

Boundary-crossing includes changes between paid and unpaid work as well as between different sectors of the labour market or different professions and occupations. The boundary-less careers of people in aid include volunteering in various stages of the life-course, during youth, in the form of a gap year before or after going to university, during a sabbatical in mid-age or in retirement. Volunteering can encompass a few hours a week or a few weeks or months a year. It provides work experience as well as a contrast and balance to employment. Moreover, boundary-crossing involves switching between the public and the third sector, either simultaneously or consecutively (Lewis 2008b). In addition, some of my respondents transferred skills from the private sector or the military to Aidland. Moving between organizations, such as the public or private sector to the third sector or from a non-governmental organization to an international organization, thus involves various types of 'boundary-crossing'. This gives rise to new questions: How well can the skills from one sector be transferred to another sector? What is the difference between running a project in South Sudan or in a deprived neighbourhood in Europe or North America? To what extent does social work constitute aidwork, and vice versa? Events like Hurricane Katrina[5] bring Aidland 'back home' for aidworkers from the Global North.

Mobility and flexibility encompass both the content of the work such as a change in assignment, organization or responsibility and the location where the work is carried out. Moving from one site, country or continent to another is an inherent characteristic of aidwork regardless of the type of contract; for example, working for different organizations on fixed-term contracts or consultancies, or being employed by an organization on a (more) permanent position for a long(er) period of time. Usually, mobility is required at all levels of aid organizations, from appointments in field, country and regional offices to positions in head office. John Urry (2007) argues that a focus on mobilities – of people, objects and ideas – is crucial in order to understand today's globalized world. He distinguishes five analytically separate but interacting forms of mobility: bodily mobility, the movement of objects as well as imaginary, virtual and communicative journeys. All these forms of mobility play a central role in Aidland (Roth 2010). Voluntary as well as paid aidwork require not just physical and professional mobility which have already been discussed above but also mental mobility, that of being able to negotiate unfamiliar cultures and living conditions. Physical, mental and professional mobilities are maintained through imaginary, virtual and communicative journeys (Urry 2007). Transnational mobility is associated with cosmopolitanism, a state of mind characterized by openness to the world and cultural differences. Global business elites, refugees and expatriates have been represented as 'archetypal cosmopolitans' (Srkribis et al. 2004), while transnational activists in global social movements represent 'rooted cosmopolitans' (Tarrow 2005). Aid people with their interest and concern for people living in other cultures may epitomize cosmopolitanism, although Rajak and Stirrat (2011) characterize the cosmopolitanism of the aid world as parochial. Mobility and a detached relationship to local populations are invoked in a number of metaphors that have been applied to people working in aid, such as development 'pilgrims' and 'nomads' (Eyben 2007), or 'disaster gypsies' and 'disaster tourists' (Norris 2007). This distinction between two types representing postmodernity and globalization – the 'tourist' and the 'vagabond' (Bauman 1998) – are useful for characterizing encounters in Aidland. International aidworkers represent the type of the 'tourist', who has resources and chooses to travel, or in the case of an expatriate aidworker decides which assignment to take on and where to move next. In contrast, refugee populations whose choices are much more constrained represent the type of 'the vagabond'. International mobility is enabled and constrained by citizenship and access to visas and work permits.

International aidworkers are of course not the only group of highly mobile professionals (Hannerz 1996; 2004; Kreutzer and Roth 2006) experiencing various forms of mobility and who tend to be 'dis-embedded' or 'multi-rooted' (Nowicka 2006). Business expatriates and migrants also have to be able to negotiate unfamiliar culture and foreign languages, to familiarize themselves with different regulations, practices and organizational cultures, and to adapt their professional skills to their environment (Nowicka and Kaweh 2009). Objects brought from home or obtained while overseas and shipped back home emphasize continuity and discontinuity between different life spheres. Virtual and communicative journeys using new and old media play a crucial role in maintaining relationships and sharing experiences across distance. International aidworkers, however, represent an extreme case of contemporary forms of mobilities. Although they share characteristics both with business expatriates and third sector workers working in their countries of origin, they differ from both groups due to a lack of separation between their personal and professional lives (Fechter 2012). They may also experience the distinction between their lives in Aidland and in their country of origin as more significant than other chronically mobile groups and have difficulties in bridging these separate spheres, due to being directly exposed to inequality, poverty and need.

Mobility shapes the relationship between work and private life or work–life balance and makes it difficult to establish and maintain relationships. Long-distance relationships are typical for dual-careers couples and contemporary employment conditions which include short-term contracts and frequent job changes combined with moving or commuting between potentially very distant locations. Aidwork thus illuminates one of the core characteristics of contemporary societies which are shaped by frequent travel (Cresswell 2006; Urry 2007) and 'living-apart-together' (Roseneil 2006; van der Klis 2008; Duncan and Phillips 2010) for personal and professional reasons. The fluid and patchwork careers that are characterized by interruptions represent a typical pattern for men and women working in aid. These intermittent work patterns provide opportunities for new forms of sharing care work and – theoretically – allow couples who are working in aid to alternate as follower and leader (Fechter 2013). In the following chapters I will discuss to what extent Aidland actually allows people to experiment with new forms of the division of labour, challenging gender norms. A study of 'patchwork career men' (Halrynjo 2009) who have turned away from conventional careers as well as from commitment to caring and the family, indicates that they have found self-realization and satisfaction in social life and leisure activities (Halrynjo 2009, p. 116). Similarly, as my data suggest, men and women working in aid also abandon conventional careers and many of my respondents were single and without children, and thus eschewed dominant schemas for fulfilment and self-realization.

Self-realization, burnout and personal growth

The continual border-crossing typical for neoliberal work practices which require flexibility and mobility can produce anxieties and have a severe impact upon mental health (Walkerdine 2006, p. 23). Aidwork raises important questions about the complex relationship between self-realization, burnout and personal growth. Contemporary societies are characterized by reflexive modernization (Beck et al. 1994) which involves an ethics of individual self-fulfilment, self-identity and continuous reflexive interaction with the wider social environment. In particular, creative work combines the self-actualization typical for late modern societies and the competitive, deregulated working environment typical for neoliberal societies, given that it is prone to self-exploitation and rarely enables a living to be earned, and so thus becomes a 'labour of love' (McRobbie 2002; Hesmondhalgh 2010; Banks and Milestone 2011). Like creative work, aidwork places a high value on an 'identity project which is generally associated with an active subject who is free to make choices albeit with constraints' (Taylor and Littleton 2012, p. 33). This biographical project of self-realization or individualization needs to be understood as a part of the technologies of self-regulation typical for contemporary societies (Rose 1989). Aidwork requires an ability for self-government, as it demands a high degree of flexibility, adaptability and autonomy. In this sense, aidwork simultaneously epitomizes characteristics of work in contemporary societies and may be understood as an escape from the constraints of advanced capitalist societies.

The way in which identities and self-realization are related to work has also changed in contemporary late modern societies. Project-based work which is grounded in personal involvement, autonomy and individualization and characterized by blurring boundaries between public and private is typical for the 'new spirit of capitalism' (Boltanski and Chiapello 2005). As I will show in the following chapters, the lack of a separation between work and the private sphere is one of the challenges for people working in aid. Given the centrality of projects in humanitarianism and development (Krause 2014), Aidland epitomizes project-based relations which are typical for late modern societies. Projects are characterized by a fluid and highly intense focus on mutual recognition which replaces concrete responsibilities typical for structures and positions. This shift from responsibility to recognition is accompanied by forms of productivity that demand high commitment and authenticity (Ekman 2013). Efforts of self-realization are associated with intensifying norms about autonomy, self-development and intimacy in late modern society (Rose 1989; Illouz 2008; Ehrenberg 2009). Due to the emphasis on self-management in such work contexts, organizational dysfunctions are experienced and identified as responsibilities of individual employees rather than as collective and structural issues. Consequently, personal strategies rather than structure reform are employed to cope with stress or insecure working conditions (Ekman 2013). This is highly relevant for aidwork characterized by high turnover, which can be both the cause and result of stressful working relations.

The notion that working life should encompass passion, challenges and meaningfulness and thus enable a person to realize their personal potential is particularly strong for Generation Y[6] (Parment 2011). This means that once a job is no longer experienced as offering these opportunities, but considered as 'ordinary work' which is predictable rather than challenging, it is time to move on (Ekman 2013, p. 1167). My data show that people working in aid frequently moved from one organization or assignment to the next when they no longer felt challenged. The role that work plays for self-realization also shapes the relationship between managers and employees in which both parties seek validation and recognition which results in 'grandiose mirroring' and alternatively intensive work and time off rather than moderate work, resulting in 'fluid, narcissistic mutual recognition' which displaces concrete responsibility (Ekman 2013, p. 1178). Working hard and autonomously, taking on a lot of responsibility, and demanding and limitless work, is experienced as exhilarating by employees who explain their desire to work a lot by being 'addicts', 'adrenaline junkies' and 'getting high' on inventing and launching new projects (Thunman 2012). My respondents used similar terms to express their pleasure in doing aidwork.

Sharing common values, belonging to networks of solidarity and being recognized by others is an important course of unconditional self-realization (Honneth 1996). However, ironically (or tragically), the new 'institutionalized norm' of self-realization in and through work (Hartmann and Honneth 2006) has resulted in new modes of repression and exploitation, and is associated with an increase in burnout (Thunman 2012). Burnout is characterized by exhaustion, a tendency towards cynicism, detachment from the job, and a sense of ineffectiveness and failure (Maslach *et al.* 1996; 2001). While burnout was initially observed and studied in human services and healthcare, it is now found in most occupations and has negative consequences for mental health, including anxiety, depression and loss of self-esteem. Burnout is caused by a high workload and a lack of support, feedback, information and control. Work becomes unfulfilling and meaningless when energy, involvement and efficacy are missing. The work environment plays a significant role in enabling engagement and preventing burnout with respect to workload, control, reward and recognition, community, fairness and values (Chirkowska-Smolak 2012, p. 77).

Authenticity, flexibility and ongoing 'subjectivation of work' are mentally exhausting; self-realization thus results in exploitation rather than empowerment, leading to an expansion of psychic illnesses including depression (Hartmann and Honneth 2006). The emancipatory potential of self-realization is lost when flexibility is a necessary response to precarious working conditions 'so that people are explicitly or implicitly urged to keep their options regarding their own decisions and goals open all the time' (Honneth 2004, p. 474). Such a transformation of the ideals of an experimental process of self-discovery into compulsions and expectations can lead to 'existential loneliness' and 'fatigue symptoms' (Thunman 2012, p. 55). Self-realization, once seen as an alternative to alienating working conditions, may result in burnout which can be 'considered as a social pathology of today's self-realization norms' (Thunman 2012, p. 56). The requirement to self-realize and create an original biography then gives 'individuals only the alternative of simulating authenticity or of fleeing into a full-blown depression, of staging personal originality for strategic reasons or of pathologically shutting down' (Honneth 2004, p. 475). However, challenging working conditions may also be experienced as contributing to personal growth (Linley and Joseph 2004). Moreover, the pessimistic view outlined above overlooks the possibility of collective self-realization through collective action which may be experienced in social movements (Rheingans and Hollands 2012) – and aidwork, as I would suggest. The humanitarian movement offers a solution to the dilemma of being caught 'between the egoistic ideal of self-realization and an altruistic commitment to a cause which enables one to "realize oneself" through action' (Fassin 2012, p. 9). The relationship between self-realization and well-being is thus highly ambivalent and contradictory: pursuing meaningful work and contributing to the common good and the welfare of others contributes to well-being, but the requirement to self-realize in contemporary societies may be experienced as stressful and result in burnout and depression.

Aidwork thus presents an excellent case to unravel the contradictory relationship between self-realization, burnout and personal growth that characterizes work in contemporary neoliberal societies. While meaningful work contributes to well-being, a permanent search for meaning is also exhausting. Aidwork can be a reaction to working conditions in neoliberal societies and at the same time epitomizes the search for meaning, short-term project-based work and a lack of work–life balance. The suffering of (distant) others is also a precondition for getting involved in this kind of work. Traumatic experiences, vicarious or otherwise, as well as precarious and insecure working conditions within Aidland can contribute to the burnout of people working in aid.

Voluntary risk taking, negative capability and the helping imperative

Aidland seems to attract individuals who do not feel challenged in their 'normal' work lives and therefore leave their previous careers behind. Elsewhere (Roth 2014) I have argued that aidwork may be seen as a response to and escape from routinized work patterns. At the same time it epitomizes the requirement of individualized risk taking and self-government typical for late modern societies. Given the increasing number of attacks on aid personnel which I discussed in the preceding chapter, aidwork clearly represents edgework which has been defined as voluntary risk taking that involves 'a clearly observable threat to one's physical or mental well-being or one's sense of an ordered existence' (Lyng 1990, p. 857). Aidwork involves physical threats, but given short contracts and precarious careers, risks also include job insecurity and de-skilling as well as challenges to family life and an individual's capacity to maintain stable relationships.

Given these risks and insecurities, people working in aid need 'negative capability' (Cornish 2011; Ruch 2014). This concept, coined by Keats, and referring to 'capable of being in uncertainties, mysteries, doubts without any irritable reaching after fact and reason' (cited in Cornish 2011, p. 136), has recently found use in social work studies to account for the fact that the practice of social work requires coping with uncertainty and change, and thus needs reflective practice and emotional intelligence. The notion of 'negative capability' draws attention to the importance of open-mindedness, attention to diversity and the suspension of ego. Professionalism and 'not knowing' are thus not mutually exclusive but improve the relationship between social worker and service user (Cornish 2011). These insights from social work studies are very useful for the reflection on aid relationships. Working in aid is in many ways a humbling experience and satisfaction lies in having contributed to positive (or prevented negative) developments – though in often limited ways.[7] Slim (1997) also employed the concept of negative capability and points to the ability of relief workers to be 'present in the worst of human situations; to be faced with the hardest of choices, and yet still to respect and protect human life in a way which constantly challenges evil without colluding in it' (p. 257). Like professionals in other helping professions, people working in aid would benefit from supervision which would enable them to reflect on the difficulties and dilemmas that constitute aidwork and on the power relations between aid provider and aid recipients, national and international staff. Fechter (2012) points out that 'development ethics' are only now emerging (see also Hunt et al. 2014; Slim 2014). So far, the reflection on aid relationships as well as support for aid professionals has been limited to immersion programmes and debriefings. In order to overcome the social dominance which is inherent in aid relationships, personal, organizational as well as community work is needed (MacLachlan et al. 2010). Thus, aidworkers require self-knowledge (Gilbert 2005) and a self-examination of their motives (Green 2012).

Grounded in altruistic impulses, the 'helping imperative' (Heron 2007) encompasses paternalistic (or maternalistic) elements and an unquestioned belief in the entitlement to achieve self-realization through helping 'others'. Aidwork requires reflecting on inequalities which are challenged or perpetuated within aid organizations; this includes racialized inequalities. Hunter (2010) discusses the shift from 'whiteness through *saving the colonized other* to whiteness as constituted through *saving the white racist self*' (p. 470) in the context of a 'diversity proud organization', the National Health Service in England. Given that aidwork addresses gender inequality, racism and its consequences and human rights violations, it is of course also of great interest how aid organizations deal with diversity and how they manage an inclusive workforce. Aidwork appears to open up careers for women and gender specialists in particular since gender became mainstreamed into development (White 2006; Eyben 2007). The comparatively high proportion of women in leadership positions may also be explained by the fact that a range of helping professions (such as social work or nursing) are female-dominated, and the comparatively lower pay in third-sector organizations and NGOs. It may also be an effect of the 'glass cliff' which refers to the phenomenon that women tend to be chosen as leaders in crisis contexts (Bruckmüller and Branscombe 2010). In contrast to gender, and paradoxically in the context of North–South collaboration, less integration has been achieved with respect to bringing national staff into leadership positions. However, given the silence and taboo of addressing race in the context of development (White 2002; Kothari 2006a; 2006b), this is perhaps not surprising. While about 90 per cent of aidworkers are national staff, 40 per cent of those in leadership positions are international staff members (Knox Clarke 2014). Furthermore, significant pay differences between national and international staff exist and contribute to tensions between national and international staff (Carr et al. 2010; Ridde 2010; McWha 2011). In addition, Aidland is also characterized by 'heteroprofessionalism' (Mizzi 2013), marginalizing homosexual aidworkers and reasserting 'heteromasculinist dominance'. While employment laws in many Western workplaces prevent discrimination on the basis of sexual orientation, homosexual aidworkers experience problems with contract renewal in homophobic regions. A 'pervasiveness of heteronormativity and institutional heterosexism in development' has been noted (Lind and Share 2003; Jolly 2011). Thus homosexual aidworkers experience the fear of losing opportunities, being isolated and feeling undervalued or othered which affects job satisfaction and work quality. 'Agencies need to realize that institutionally sanctioned heteronormativity incites homophobic encounters' (Mizzi 2013, p. 1620). Thus, while aid organizations address human rights violations, gender, race and other forms of inequality, these are not necessarily addressed within aid organizations.

Conclusions

Aidwork has always been part of modernizing processes, whether it was carried out by missionaries, colonial administrators or volunteers, and more recently by aid professionals. It is thus and always has been part of the everyday processes of social, political and economic change. I argue, moreover, that aidwork is simultaneously an expression of as well as a response to working and living conditions in contemporary neoliberal societies. However, 'if humanitarianism is revered because it represents a sanctuary from the everyday world of a liberal, market-oriented world, then the intrusion of everyday practices of measurement, a language of results and outcomes, and a conversation about accountability all risk creating disenchantment within the humanitarian world' (Barnett and Stein 2012, p. 18). If working conditions in aid organizations are shaped by the same mechanisms – managerialism and audit cultures – that characterize workplaces in late modern societies, does aidwork still offer an alternative and escape from disenchanted contemporary societies? And would it be possible to re-enchant work in late modern societies? Can working in a hospital or homeless shelter in a high-income country be compared to work contexts that are more directly affected by global disaster, neocolonialism, North–South relations and grinding poverty? If people want to make a difference, does it matter whether they do that in their own country and community or elsewhere? How do these motivations and the nationality of aid personnel shape the relationship between aid providers and aid recipients? These are important questions when we consider that the vast majority of the aidworker population are national staff and if we consider those working in aid organizations as beneficiaries.

Aidwork in many respects epitomizes the requirements from workers in contemporary societies and is an expression of the 'new spirit of capitalism' as well as 'humanitarian reason'. Aidworkers have an 'entrepreneurial self'. Whether aidwork is carried out in faith-based or secular organizations, it constitutes meaningful work, provides opportunities for self-realization, may be experienced as a vocation and, through the (vicarious) experience of trauma, can lead to personal growth. Aidwork invites us to challenge and further develop paradigms of the sociology of work. First, the sociology of work has typically focused on employment, while advocacy, activism and volunteering have been rarely analysed from this perspective. Unpaid internships, short-term contracts and limited career opportunities are common in the sector and often a requirement for entering Aidland. In other words, aidwork can be precarious employment and privilege of those who have independent means, i.e. who can afford to forgo a regular income. However, not every aidworker has savings or can count on an inheritance, and in particular for those who come from an activist background, the job insecurity associated with short-term and low-paid jobs in NGOs represents a sacrifice. Aidwork thus reflects 'post-material values' (Inglehart 1977); that is, rather than demanding better conditions (higher wages, pension, housing, etc.) the focus lies on the public good (human rights, environmental change). Aidwork includes professional volunteers (or volunteering professionals). There is a close connection between paid and unpaid work which is performed simultaneously or consecutively. Paradoxically, it is a privilege to participate in low or unpaid precarious aidwork. Aidwork requires capital to which those from the upper-middle class have access, and it appears to be an elite profession that is not necessarily well paid (gentlemen volunteers). Second, given intermittent work patterns, aidwork is characterized by both high intensity and by breaks in between assignments. For aidworkers from the Global North, living and working conditions in rural and remote areas may be understood as a form of 'slow living' which involves a distance from consumer culture and a search for authenticity. Paradoxically, international aidworkers distance themselves from tourists and tourism while at the same time engaging in some form of aid tourism. Third, aidwork raises important questions concerning the meaning of work and may be considered a vocation and a means to self-actualization. It enables one to explore the complex and contradictory relationship between self-realization, trauma and personal growth. Aidworkers are directly confronted with trauma when they are witness to conflicts and disaster or are victims of attacks and kidnapping, and indirectly when they listen to and interact with victims of various forms of violence. Paradoxically, the encounter with suffering can contribute to the well-being of people working in aid. Fourth, aidwork is characterized by a high degree of mobility and flexibility, not only geographical, but also with respect to the length of contracts, work areas and careers. This is reflected in boundary-crossing as well as boundary-less careers; that is, careers which are not tied to a particular organization or profession. Paradoxically, the professionalization of aidwork may result in disciplining boundary-crossers. Fifth, given the increasing number of attacks on aid personnel, aidwork may be considered edgework or voluntary risk taking which is a response to alienating and highly regulated working conditions. Paradoxically, people working in aid are voluntary risk takers who are increasingly confronted with security measures which may take the edge off edgework. Sixth, aidwork is characterized by a tension between altruism and self-interest typical for helping (and disabling) professions (Illich 1977). Paradoxically, those who engage in aidwork experience well-being gained through confronting the suffering of others which they try to alleviate or which demonstrates their own privileged position. Finally, aidwork and Aidland are characterized by branding, marketing and professionalization. To what extent do these tendencies (branding, marketing, professionalization) undermine other characteristics (post-materialism, edgework, voluntarism) of aidwork? These tensions will be explored in the remainder of this book.

Notes

1. Scholars of aid relationships have highlighted exceptionalism (Calhoun 2010; Fassin 2012) as well as politics and practices and the continuity between normality and crisis (Hilhorst 2013).
2. For further information about the programme see euaidvolunteers.vsointernational.org/about.
3. Ivan Illich (1977) coined the term 'disabling professions': 'Professions could not become dominant and disabling unless people were already experiencing as a lack that which the expert imputes to them as a need. ... Need, used as a noun became the fodder on which professions were fattened into dominance. Poverty was modernized. The poor became the "needy"' (Illich 1977, pp. 22f.). Of course, the multitude of professions in Aidland are not the only ones based on needs. Dentists, social workers, therapists and teachers are responding to a demand for the relief of suffering or need for education. People working in aid are thus not the only ones confronted with a never-ending supply of 'need'. However, as discussed in the previous chapter, strategies vary with respect to the emphasis they put on the provision of knowledge of experts from high(er) developed countries, and the building capacity and strengthening resilience of communities in low(er) developed countries.
4. Ward (2010), a former foreign officer and senior vice president of World Vision, proposes that humanitarian NGOs should adopt the hiring and promotion practices of the foreign service, although he acknowledges that the limited budgets of NGOs may not allow this.
5. Hurricane Katrina occurred in August 2005 and was one of the deadliest hurricanes in the history of the United States. The affected areas included the Bahamas and Cuba, Louisiana, Mississippi, Alabama, Florida and Texas as well as eastern parts of North America. A wide range of countries, including China, Cuba, France, India, Iran and Russia, offered assistance (which was not necessarily accepted) putting the US in the unusual role of aid recipient (Kelman 2007).
6. The millennial generation born between the early 1980s and the early 2000s are referred to as 'Generation Y' following Generation X born between the early 1960s and the early 1980s.
7. The futility of aid is also captured in MSF's project 'My Sweet La Mancha', referring to Don Quixote's quest.

3 Entering Aidland

> I was definitely thinking along development lines, I had never been in a war situation, or in an emergency situation at all. And one of the jobs I applied for was working with education for [NGO]. It was more of a New York-based position in their headquarters, and I didn't get that. And then they called me a few days later and said, 'Would you like to go to Albania?' [Laughs] 'And you can have the job if you can go in about two days.' [Laughs] And I could, because I didn't have another job at that time. And I was really interested in the issue and so I got on a plane a couple of days later and went over to Albania for [NGO] for six months.
>
> North American NGO worker, August 2004

> And then I went to [African] University where I did a Bachelor degree in public health. And from there I had a chance to work for the Ministry of Health for two years before coming to [North America] for a Master's degree in public health [at a prestigious university]. Then afterwards when I went back [to African country], I was sent to the university as a teaching assistant. So I was hoping to start a teaching career, but unfortunately the [conflict] stopped the whole thing. So that's basically the way I got to be involved in the humanitarian aid. So I left my teaching career, when I started, I worked for a [small European NGO as national staff member]. I worked for them for one year. … Then immediately afterwards I joined [large faith-based NGO] as international staff.
>
> African NGO worker, June 2005

These two quotes illustrate the characteristics of aidwork which include boundary-crossing and boundary-less careers, flexibility and mobility very well. However, the quotes also reveal significant differences: whereas the North American aidworker was free to accept the offer, the African aidworker was pushed into the aid system when his career was interrupted by a violent conflict affecting his country. Many positions are fixed-term and project-based and once an organization has obtained a grant it needs to advertise and fill these positions quickly. This requires flexibility both from the side of the organization which may not find the ideal candidate, that is, a candidate who has the necessary technical skills as well as language skills, overseas experience and knowledge of the region of assignment, as well as from the perspective of the candidate who has to decide at short notice whether or not to accept a position. Furthermore, conflicts and disasters interrupt careers, and international aid organizations offer job opportunities for national staff.

This chapter is organized around three sections. First, I will address the situation or context in which respondents became interested in aidwork and which occurs in different life-stages. I distinguish three patterns: some were attracted to overseas aidwork early on in their childhood and youth, others gradually developed an interest in the course of their career or their political and social engagement, and in some cases they had experienced a crisis or epiphany that caused them to re-evaluate their life choices (Roth 2006). Despite a variety of backgrounds and careers, a unifying element in the careers and biographies of people working in aid is liminality, a transition from one life-stage to another or a straddling of different cultures. In the second part of this chapter I will address the qualifications and experiences that were brought to Aidland. In some cases, a specific job training or university course was chosen explicitly to pursue a career in Aidland, in other cases previous job experiences and qualifications could be converted and transferred to work in aid organizations. This transfer of skills and experiences characterizes boundary-less careers and boundary-crossing. Finally, I will discuss the experience of finding the first assignment in Aidland. In many cases, the entry was associated with carrying out unpaid work and volunteering. In addition, a high degree of flexibility was needed in leaving for the first assignment within a few days or weeks and accepting assignments in a region an individual had hoped to avoid or one to which they had not planned to go.

Liminality

Liminality is a useful concept for understanding the circumstances in which people decide to become involved in aidwork; it is one of the stages of the process of passing from one identity to another (Van Gennep 1960). The liminal person is in an inter-structural position, for example, between youth and adulthood, or in some other transition (Turner 1987). Liminality encompasses a reconstruction of identity which includes liminal practices such as experimentation, reflection and recognition (Beech 2011, p. 286). The concept of liminality applies to entering Aidland, but the position of being 'betwixt and between' (Turner 1987) also applies to living and working conditions as well as to the decision about whether to stay in or leave Aidland. In short, aidwork is characterized by an ongoing destabilization and questioning of the self from the moment of deciding to enter Aidland (Smirl 2012).

Transnational experience

Of course, youth, in particular for the Western middle class, is a period of openness, uncertainty and transition, and graduates have to make decisions about apprenticeships, training and university programmes, and careers in general. In addition, since the 1990s, gap years between school or university or between university and first job have become increasingly institutionalized and professionalized among Western middle-class youth (Simpson 2005; Vrasti 2013). Spending some time abroad participating in a gap-year experience is one strategy of those who after finishing school 'did not know what to do with my life', as one of my respondents put it. The gap-year industry offers volunteer opportunities in the Global South (Lyons et al. 2012; Vrasti 2013) which provided some of my respondents with their first work experiences in development and was the starting point for their careers in Aidland. Take, for example, a North American respondent who did not know what career to pursue after graduating from college. After working for several years, he felt that it was time to look for more meaningful work.

> So at that point, I said, 'I don't want to be a carpenter all my life, I want to do something more socially significant.' And I began to look at different opportunities, around the world. And I took a job as a volunteer with [NGO], working in [Latin America]. And I went down there and I worked with [NGO] for almost one year.

After this volunteering experience, he participated in the Peace Corps which he combined with being enrolled in a postgraduate programme on international management focusing on NGO management and sustainable development. After graduating, he found his first short-term staff position for an NGO which was followed by positions in UN agencies. His interest in development thus emerged gradually in the context of overseas volunteering. Other respondents also discovered their interest in becoming involved in aidwork during overseas stays. Some who had lacked enthusiasm and focus during their university studies decided to participate in a student exchange through which they became aware of internships and volunteer opportunities in development organizations and increased their 'transnational human capital' (Gerhard and Hans 2013). These overseas experiences led to a reorientation and interest in overseas engagement which they then pursued with a focus on development studies in their undergraduate and Master's degrees.

Inexplicable attraction

Some respondents admitted that despite their early interest in working for an aid organization, or a desire to get involved in development or relief, they did not initially have a clear understanding of what that would entail or why exactly they were interested in doing this kind of work. A European woman tried to explain why she had applied to work for a humanitarian organization after graduating from university in the 1990s. 'Why? I had no clue. Actually, it was nice, those guys [aidworkers] I was just looking at them like heroes and I wanted to be part of the nice story.' At that time, 'celebrity humanitarianism' (Kapoor 2013) had increasingly popularized the idea of getting involved in humanitarian action. Although preceded by other entertainers, Bob Geldof and Bono were pioneers of staging charity rock concerts as media events. In addition, MSF's receipt of the Nobel Prize in 1999 resulted in media attention for humanitarian organizations. Aidwork became an expression of global citizenship, cosmopolitanism and globalization.

Respondents were not just attracted to aidwork, but also to Africa in particular. Some (white) European and North American respondents explained that they felt a deep and inexplicable attraction to Africa that they had experienced throughout their lives. A North American man in his twenties tried to understand and explain this attraction:

> I do think about it more deeply and try to figure out where it came from, and then my conclusion is that like because I fall into the category, that a lot of people do, where there is just this big void in thinking about Africa, like because it is not in the educational system here and I did not have any contact with Africans in [American Midwest], and it was like kind of this big empty spot and in a way it is almost kind of colonial the way this happens [laughs], but it attracted me, I wanted to learn more about it. So I think that is the root of my interest internationally, and especially in Africa.

Several women from Western Europe felt that 'Africa was in their blood', thus emphasizing how their interest in working on the continent was beyond their control and innate. Some of these respondents linked their interest to Africa and getting involved in aidwork to childhood memories. Some were inspired by missionaries whom they had encountered in their village or parish, while others had learned about missionary activities through magazines of faith-based organizations. In addition, some of the respondents had met overseas visitors from developing countries as farm workers or exchange students in their parental homes. Although they did not talk about having direct contact with these foreign visitors, they were impressed by them during their childhood and youth, and they served as role models for going overseas. Others were inspired through the media and recalled seeing images in the news of starving children in Biafra or Ethiopia and wanted 'to send chocolate' or 'bring water in a jerry can'. A number of respondents thus developed an interest in overseas aidwork quite early on in their lives without having a clear vision of starting a career in development or humanitarian assistance.

Political and religious values

Another group came to the aid sector motivated by political commitment, solidarity 'with the underdog', wanting to contribute to social justice and to help the less fortunate. Political interest and activism encompassed questions of social inequality and injustice both in their own country as well as in other countries. Many described feelings of guilt of being privileged that motivated them to become involved in volunteering and politics; some activists had experienced discrimination themselves. Several of the politically active respondents were children of immigrants and had spent part of their childhood and youth moving from one country to another. Some had experienced financial constraints as their parents worked in low-paid positions though enabling their children to attend good schools and obtain a university education. They had thus not only had experiences as ethnic minorities or foreigners, but also of class inequalities, and had first-hand experiences of racial and class discrimination. Some had even experienced police violence and arrests while they were engaged in protest activities. This group of respondents experienced and reacted to inequality and injustice through paid and unpaid work both in their home country as well as overseas. Their experience of liminality encompassed being simultaneously cultural in- and outsiders of different cultures, having moved from one country to another. Furthermore, the respondents with a working-class background had experienced upward mobility, since their parents had insisted on giving them educational opportunities.

This is be nicely illustrated with the biography of a North American woman who had grown up in Europe where she was influenced by the leftist movements of the 1970s. When she came to North America as a teenager, she was disappointed to find that her North American peers were not interested in political movements. In North America, she became involved in a Christian youth group which allowed her to work for social justice; she also worked in a voluntary capacity with physically and mentally handicapped people. She described her political orientation as 'left-leaning or progressive' and therefore believed that charity was not enough to bring about social change. After graduating from university, she could not find a paid job which would have allowed her to implement her political views; she therefore became a social worker, even though she felt ambivalent about charities. In her free time she was involved in the peace movement and worked with Chilean refugees, which enabled her to pursue her political commitment. Her life history represents a good example for seeking meaning and self-realization in volunteering and activism as well as paid employment. In the early 1980s, she took an extended period of unpaid leave and visited Latin America for the first time. Her father was very disappointed that she decided 'to live in a slum' in order to work with a national NGO in Latin America rather than pursue a well-paying career after her university studies. Upon her return to North America she got involved in a Latin American solidarity group while continuing to work as a social worker.

> So I was always more involved in development NGOs, more around non-emergency. If anything I actually used to find, I used to think that you know charity was kind of, very, almost objectionable and felt that

we needed to look at structures, relations between North and South, questions of investments, trade, debt, etc.

Her initial involvement in development work was an outcome of her political commitment which was formed during her participation in the church youth group. Several years later she took on a paid position in the European head office of a faith-based relief organization and made frequent trips to Africa. For other respondents, religious values were more important than political commitment. Several respondents came from a religious background and the commitment to help the less fortunate played a role, although it was also a situation to test their faith and to 'trust God more', as one of the respondents put it.

Crisis and re-evaluation of life

The experience of various crisis situations, including personal crises such as divorce or the breakup of a relationship, health issues, the death of a parent and dissatisfaction with work as well as political crises, war and conflict, played a role in turning to aid organizations. These crisis situations represented a turning point and caused respondents to re-evaluate their lives, and to conclude that the work they had been pursuing thus far had not been fulfilling or meaningful, prompting them to explore becoming aidworkers. Thus, work opportunities in their countries of origin could not satisfy their desire for self-realization, whereas aidwork promised fulfilment through pursuing altruistic values and conducting challenging work.

Several respondents explained that the death of one or both parents caused them to evaluate their lives which led to a career change. Being confronted with the limit of life, they were interested in finding more meaningful work and returned to earlier interests which they had abandoned in the course of their lives. For example, one respondent, who had initially been interested in the diplomatic service and had pursued a career as an investment banker, realized that

> I made a career, I was moving up, there are some things about that I saw that I did not like, and I was sort of put in some ethical choices which I did not really like. But the main point is this was not what I felt like doing. This was not my main field of interest. And I also recognized that I never really did it with any degree of passion other than a sense of wanting to do things properly at work. I did find it interesting because in any case there was a lot to learn in terms of how people work, I learned to appreciate efficiency of operations.

Although he was successful and found his work interesting, this respondent did not experience it as a calling. Financially secure and highly educated, he left his career in banking, and after studying International Affairs drew on networks made during compulsory military service to find work in the humanitarian arena. Other respondents also expressed dissatisfaction with their careers which they described as well paid but meaningless. As I discussed in the previous chapter, work plays a crucial role in self-realization. A North American woman in her thirties explained:

> I sort of had that, 'Aha moment', you know, that gestalt moment where you say, I can't believe I grew up to sell plastic module conveyor belts; it just seemed very empty, it seemed very frivolous. I did not like what I was becoming, because I was making a lot of money, and I just felt that I was becoming very superficial as a person. And I felt that what I was doing wasn't making a difference in the world. I felt that what I was doing was very shallow.

However, it was not just the fact that she experienced her work as meaningless. She was also aware that her career opportunities within the organization were limited. Furthermore, she remembered her childhood dream 'to be like Audrey Hepburn' whom she considered a role model. She explained that working as a humanitarian 'was just the image that I had in terms of a great job'. Leaving her corporate career in North America meant a significant loss of income and status as the daughter of working-class immigrants who had supported her education was a difficult decision to take. Similarly, a former journalist abandoned her successful career because she felt that covering humanitarian crises in the media was not enough.

> Because of my work I knew a lot of disasters and refugees and I have always left these places with this kind of sentiment, with this kind of feeling inside me that I would. So when years were passing by, this feeling was becoming big, like I was not feeling very comfortable really with what I was doing, like with my filming, it was nothing to change situations, or to help, or that I was leaving people behind. And there was always like this kind of dilemma inside myself, when I was back in [European country of origin], like, I could have stayed and helped and do other things.

Regardless of the importance of media coverage for mobilizing private and public donations and international interventions, she felt that her work as a journalist was not enough to address suffering. Rather than report on and frame the issue in national and international media, she wanted to be directly involved in humanitarian action and interact directly with people in need instead of documenting their situation or providing NGOs with media access. She felt that her role as an observer was not enough to address (distant) suffering. Rather than supporting overseas aid organizations through donations or advocacy work and supporting people in their own country or communities, for example, refugees or asylum seekers, homeless or poor people who would benefit from the help of volunteers, advocates or professionals, respondents left their previous careers in order to get involved in international aidwork.

For some female respondents the involvement in aid was a result of a career interruption either in order to start a family or to follow a partner who had moved for his career. In this reorientation phase, they remembered an earlier interest in humanitarianism or discovered it for the first time. These women were able to draw on skills and work experience in the private and public sectors, for example, to make use of experience in marketing for a position as director of communication or build on experience dealing with government agencies when interacting with various bi- and multilateral organizations and other donors. While transferring skills was easy, it was a challenge to gain access and establish networks to find consultancies or paid positions in aid.

Respondents from lower-income countries were also motivated by the desire to help others, to pursue meaningful work, and develop, hone and use professional training and skills in their work. An African woman who worked as a national staff member for an international NGO explained what she liked about aid work:

> But what keeps you in it, well the first time I saw someone that was on the verge of dying walk by me, and then several months later, that same person walked by completely full of life, because of the work that you are doing. Not necessarily directly, but maybe indirectly, it makes you realize you have a great sense of job satisfaction [laughs]. The work that you do is saving lives. You know, society is going to tell you, you know, it is based on money, yeah, that's not what I am about. So that's what's kept me, to me to change lives, to save lives.

However, there are two important differences between national and international staff. First, even if national staff did not share the social class, ethnic or religious background of the constituencies they served, they worked in their own country and thus were familiar with local customs. Of course, given class, religious and ethnic differences, sharing the nationality does not mean necessarily sharing the culture of beneficiaries (Slim 1995; Eyben 2011). Indeed, expatriate aidworkers may have more interest in ethnic diversity than the urban middle class of host countries (Heaton Shrestha 2006; Scott-Smith 2014). However, national staff were differently positioned vis-à-vis beneficiaries than international volunteers and staff. In contrast to their international colleagues, they were also more likely to live with their families. Second, jobs offered or sponsored by international aid organizations opened up opportunities in government agencies, university departments, national or international NGOs. This included professional and skilled positions that enabled national staff to draw on their undergraduate and postgraduate studies and work experiences in areas such as medicine, statistics, accounting or community development.

International aid agencies often, however, sought support staff (drivers, translators) who spoke English and were thus able to support international staff who did not speak the local language. Thus English speakers could choose between aid agencies which would offer higher salaries than the local labour market (cf. Baker 2010). Language skills could provide entry, and some of those starting out as translators were able to move into programme positions, taking on more responsibilities and eventually pursuing an expatriate career. Such job opportunities were particularly important for internally displaced people and refugees. Respondents emphasized the fact that they saw these jobs not just as an opportunity to make a living, but that they were committed to humanitarianism, development and human rights work. Overall, the desire to do meaningful work and contribute to the well-being of others was highlighted by the respondents. This desire could emerge at various life-stages and related to dissatisfaction with working conditions, political, social and religious commitment, or personal crises.

My data suggest that paid or unpaid, and regardless of region of origin, respondents were drawn to aid organizations because they felt that these organizations offered them more opportunities for self-realization by making a difference than had the sectors in which they had worked before. Quite a number of respondents had also had an early interest in overseas aid since their childhood and youth, and chose training programmes accordingly.

Qualifications

The heterogeneity of the aid sector includes many professions, ranging from engineering to medical personnel, logisticians to managers. Furthermore, professionalization efforts in the humanitarian sector have resulted in codes of practice, standards and university degrees in humanitarian studies. What qualifications did respondents bring to their first assignments and how did these qualifications matter for their first job? My data suggest that both national and international staff engaged in boundary-crossing, but in different ways.

Language skills

Language skills certainly had different relevance for national and international staff, native and non-native speakers of English. For national staff, the ability to speak the language which was used by international aid organizations was crucial and more important than their job training and university skills. As already mentioned above, language skills provided national staff with job opportunities. Regardless of their education and job experience, in particular in crisis situations, they might start out in support positions as drivers and translators before moving into programme positions. The example of an Eastern European man in his forties who had two university degrees, one in engineering and one in media studies, and who had worked in the media before he started to work as an interpreter in a humanitarian organization, is not unusual. After starting out as a translator, he took on additional responsibilities and moved from a national to an expatriate position within the organization. Initially, he had changed to the aid organization because it offered better job opportunities, but he also emphasized that it was important for him that work was interesting and a means of self-realization.

> So I mean, I was always working for the personal realization, personal expression. Let's say it like that. So I am doing my job, I am trying to express myself, okay.

Overall, English was the lingua franca even in MSF (Fox 2014) and the ability to speak a second (or more) language(s) was much more important for those who were not native speakers of English. The latter did not need to learn another language in order to secure a job, as they could rely on the language skills of their co-workers and interpreters. Europeans who were non-native speakers of English spoke at least one other language (English), and some spoke several languages (usually French and Spanish) in addition to their native language. In my sample, only a few native speakers of English spoke one or more additional languages.[1] Respondents from higher-income countries rarely spoke African, Arabic or Asian languages whereas it was not unusual for national staff to speak several European and non-European languages. However, these language skills were taken for granted by expatriates and aid organizations from (English-speaking) high-income countries and thus made invisible.

Education and work experience

Like language skills, university training also seemed to matter more for national staff than for expatriate staff. National staff with the necessary language skills could find employment related to their university studies and work experience. Based on their qualifications they could secure internships and paid employment with NGOs, UN agencies and bilateral organizations, although they sometimes had to defend their decision to work in aid rather than pursue a more conventional career in engineering or medicine. For example, an Indian respondent chose to pursue a two-year diploma in rural development against the advice of his friends and family who would have preferred him to have chosen a more conventional middle-class career. Having grown up in a middle-class family in a city, he enjoyed staying in villages and gaining practical and experiential knowledge in addition to academic training.

After completing his studies, he began to work for an international NGO which obtained funds through a UN agency. The fact that he enjoyed a good salary convinced his friends and family that he had made the right choice. He stayed with the same organization for many years, since it combined development with relief and gave him an opportunity to serve the same community. He derived satisfaction from the fact that his involvement in development presented a career opportunity for himself, while at the same time improving conditions in his community and the state from which he came.

Whereas national staff found appointments related to their university training, this was less the case for the expatriate aidworkers, even if they had chosen a particular topic such as medicine, nursing, nutrition or a specialization in development studies in order to get involved in overseas aid. In particular those who knew early on that they wanted to go into aid picked very specific courses and training which would prepare them for their chosen careers – or so they assumed. A European woman had chosen to pursue a university degree focusing on nutrition. However, during her first humanitarian assignment she realized that 'what I was taught at university was not necessarily always fitting actually with what was really needed in the field'. Not only was the university-acquired training and knowledge not always applicable, but university studies also did not automatically help respondents from the Global North secure their first appointment. A North American woman in her thirties who had focused on development issues in her study of management and economics believed that these qualifications actually hindered her in finding a job. 'There was this big, big taboo around management people and business administration and economics doing work in development; it was really frowned upon.' This was the case even though she had completed her degree in the early years of the twenty-first century, well into the debate of the professionalization of the aid sector. This demonstrates that NGOs varied in terms of their openness to applicants with a background in economics and management. Furthermore, once she had found a position in development, she was not able to apply her skills because of the attitude of the director of the local NGO in India for which she was working. 'The director asked me to do some project proposals for him, but because I was a woman, he did not want to talk money with me. So I worked on this proposal without a budget [laughs] – it was quite frustrating.' Thus, some female respondents from high-income countries felt that their university degrees did not necessarily help them to secure their first position, in contrast to male respondents who found that their university-based research training did help them to obtain positions with bilateral agencies or NGOs.

Work experience, however – whether paid or unpaid, in the private, public or third sectors – played a central role in securing the first position within aid. A wide range of skills obtained in the private sector could be transferred to Aidland, including work in communications and public relations. For example, a European woman who had dreamed of a diplomatic career before she became a journalist and had good contacts with the Red Cross was asked to cover for a press officer going on maternity leave. Because 'even though you don't have a Red Cross experience, you have a good education, and so on. We need somebody who knows journalists, and who knows the media really well.' She decided to take this opportunity 'in two seconds' and knew that she was doing the right thing; she said that she had 'never been so sure in my life' as when she made this decision. Furthermore, job experiences in fields such as logistics, banking or marketing could be transferred. Respondents also included former teachers and lawyers who got involved in training or human rights work.

Lack of qualifications and experience

Overall, national and international staff brought a broad range of training, skills and experience to their first jobs in Aidland, although a few respondents from the Global North stated that they did not have prior qualifications or training related to their first assignment when they first started working overseas. For example, a European woman had worked in the head office for several years. In order to take the fixed-term position as logistician, she was asked to give up her permanent position in the head office. While her work at the head office made her familiar with the activities of the organization, she had no prior experience in logistics. She answered my question about where she had obtained the qualifications for her first job as a logistician in an African country in the following way:

> That's a good question. I did not have any qualification. I think to be honest I largely got the job because the organization knew me. I had worked there for four years. So largely it was on the basis of what they had seen how I went over my job in the UK. They knew that I was organized and efficient and etc. etc., so I think that they recognized that I had some of the core skills which is probably why I managed to get the position without any logistics qualification.

She was aware that the African staff with whom she worked were much more qualified than she was.[2] Similarly, another European woman in her thirties recalled that when she arrived in Africa, the finance officer had left and she had to take on this responsibility. She recalled that she was told:

> 'You have done maths, so you must be good at finance.' And I said, 'Well, I have no idea, but I guess so' ... I didn't have a clue what I was doing. ... The finance role, I just made up systems and when they worked, I kept them and when they weren't I changed them for something else.

The organization, which needed to fill the position quickly, trusted that she was able to carry out the role without formal qualifications and she learned by trial and error. Later on, working for another aid organization, she needed a formal qualification in order to assume the position as finance officer. While she was enrolled in a degree programme, the organization employed her as a consultant because she had the necessary skills, just not the certificate. During the accounting programme, she was surprised and assured that a lot of what she had learned by 'trial and error' was consistent with what she was taught. This practice of appointing someone as a consultant offered organizations the chance to hire promising applicants who lacked specific qualifications and provided opportunities for applicants at the beginning of their careers.

These examples demonstrate that the need to fill positions at short notice can result in a discrepancy between the skills required for a position and the skills and experiences that applicants bring to the assignments. Several aspects need to be emphasized: overall, the applicants had significant training and experience – but not necessarily in the field in which they had started to work. One of the core abilities for working in Aidland is being able to transfer the skills obtained in one area to another. Thus aidwork provides an excellent example for boundary-less careers and boundary-crossing, concepts that were introduced in the previous chapter. Boundary-crossing varied somewhat for national and international staff. Furthermore, there are significant North–South differences. For national staff, boundary-crossing could involve a down-skilling in the case of multilingual, university-trained professionals who accepted jobs as drivers or as translators because these posts offered higher wages than professional positions in the domestic labour market: thus contributing to the much lamented brain drain; that is, national staff leaving the private or public sector of their country of origin to join international aid organizations. For international staff from the Global North, it could involve up-skilling in terms of being hired to work in programme and leadership positions without prior work experience or training related to the position. Furthermore, the patchwork careers of people working in aid also include periods of additional formal training in order to enhance their skills, networks and employability, as will be discussed in Chapter 7. In addition to formal training and work experience, for some Christian organizations missionary training was relevant. Furthermore, volunteering experience played a central role, as I will discuss below. This suggests that overall professionalization processes thus far do not represent obstacles for those without previous work experience in aid organizations.

Getting the first job

Several respondents reported that they contacted well-known organizations, including the ICRC, NGOs such as MSF, or UN agencies in order to receive advice about how to go about securing a job for these organizations. Often, these enquiries were not answered. Aid organizations are in the paradoxical situation of being on the one hand confronted with a recruitment pool that is greater than career openings, while at the same time finding it difficult to find skilled and experienced staff (Ryfman 2011). Overall, respondents who were very specific about a particular organization, position or field they wished to work for reported more difficulties entering the field. Even applicants who were well qualified and experienced had difficulty finding a position quickly.

Volunteering

Especially for those without any employment experience, volunteering played a central role in getting involved in aidwork. In particular, international staff tended to be engaged in volunteering before they obtained their first paid position, and some even remained volunteers for a number of years. My data suggest that in many cases, volunteering was intrinsic, started early on in life, during childhood and youth, and was related to religious beliefs or political convictions. This may be illustrated by taking the example of a young man from Latin America who recalled that he started to volunteer with the Red Cross in his country while he was pursuing his undergraduate and later his graduate studies. He was involved in rescue work as well as work with street children and the homeless.

> I was just sitting there at the entrance, I had my Red Cross uniform and everything, I would just sit there and they would just come and sit and talk to me. At the beginning, I thought it would be very difficult to talk to them, but I just said, 'Hello, how are you?' And they would just come and say, 'Hey man, I am good, I am fine.' They would start and tell me all their lives, it was very interesting. So at the same time ... it was enriching for me, maybe a little bit useful for them, because they had someone to talk to, and listen.

His voluntary work with homeless people inspired him to evaluate policies addressing homelessness in his Master's thesis. In his case, his voluntary involvement in the Red Cross was intrinsic; he was not involved in order to gain work experience. However, it helped him to secure jobs later on, as it demonstrated his humanitarian disposition. National as well as international staff stressed that helping others was part of their upbringing and that they had been involved in food or clothes delivery, language teaching, or helping the elderly or the handicapped. This concern with helping others informed their job choices later on and provided them with important work experience. Intrinsic motivation to volunteer was linked to an upbringing in a family or community that placed a lot of emphasis on helping others. Those who began to volunteer during their school or university studies maintained it until professional commitments, including the involvement in aidwork, made it no longer possible. Such an intrinsic approach may be distinguished from an instrumental approach when volunteering and internship opportunities were consciously pursued in order to enhance employability. Furthermore, a range of university programmes required unpaid internships. These internships led a range of respondents to their first work experience with NGOs and UN agencies. The university thus provided access to aid agencies. In both cases – intrinsic or instrumental – the work was unpaid, enabled overseas and work experience to be gained, as well as building up networks, all of which could potentially lead to a paid position in an aid organization.

Persistence and initiative

As discussed in Chapter 2, protean careers (Hall 2004) are characterized by self-directedness which applies very much to aidworkers' careers. A number of respondents described how they took the initiative to approach aid organizations. When they realized that their application or enquiry letters were not going to be answered, they went directly to the organizations. An Asian woman who had grown up in Europe recalled:

> I actually walked into the UN and I said 'Do you need anybody to help you out for free?' [Laughs] And they kind of looked at me very strangely and I then sent in my CV and three months later I got a phone call. I went for a first interview and then a second interview, and I started an internship programme. I was so excited about this. I had absolutely no money and I think my parents were thrilled that I was doing something apparently respectable. I began to do waitressing in the evenings to pay my rent and I stayed for a year and a half and I think they were the best years of my life at that time. I learned so much.

Her account combines a number of elements that appear crucial for the first position – own initiative, the readiness and ability to work for free as well as the flexibility to accept a position when it is offered. Despite the long working hours – doing an unpaid internship while earning a living as a waitress – she emphasizes how much she learned which made this period 'the best time' of her life. She was not the only one who described knocking on the doors of aid agencies, both at head offices as well as regional or field offices. This not only included Northern aid organizations, but also making contact with local NGOs in the Global South. CV in hand, they secured an interview and subsequently were hired by the organizations. Acting on their own initiative was particularly important for those who lacked volunteering experience and networks.

Networks

The role of networks which could be built up through volunteering experience and internships, studies and work experience, as well as through travelling, cannot be overestimated. Chance encounters and overseas experience (for example, during a gap year or while working as a business expatriate) could lead to the first encounters with aid organizations. This is nicely illustrated by a North American woman who felt that the local NGO in India within which she was volunteering did not offer her the work experience she had hoped to gain. She therefore left the NGO earlier than expected and travelled through India in early 2005, not long after the devastating tsunami.

> On the bus that was taking me to the beach I met some aidworkers, some Canadian aidworkers, who helped me [laughs] to find my way, and my apartment, my hotel and we got to talking. And they were working

for this Canadian organization, [NGO]. So they were working in the South of India in an orphanage, they basically told me 'We have no work for you, but the organization we are volunteering with, they wanted us to go to Sri Lanka too. So what we recommend is that you just go to Sri Lanka, we'll put you in touch with these guys. And if that does not work out, just knock on doors like we did and say that you work for room and board, like we did. And if there is room and board, they will do it.'

She followed this advice, found a position with an NGO and from that moment felt that 'everything fell into place'. Another respondent had attended an elite school in Latin America which offered work placements in marginalized places in the country. He knew peers who had participated in one of these programmes and enquired about these opportunities. His friends knew about an internship with a UN agency and encouraged him to apply. A phone call later, he was able to secure the internship which was his entry into the UN system. This respondent was fully aware of his privileged position, having had the opportunity to attend a school that would provide him with networking opportunities. At the same time, he had been volunteering throughout his studies which enhanced his job chances. Although some mentioned finding out about opportunities through friends, acquaintances or teachers, overall there was a strong emphasis on merit. Respondents strongly emphasized their own initiative and their qualifications, thus distancing themselves from any notion of nepotism. The networks were important in order to learn about the position or to find out how to access aid organizations, but they had to prove their capability. One respondent, for example, proudly recalled that she was one of 3,700 individuals who had fulfilled the criteria for a UN position and that due to her performance in written exams, tests and interviews she was the one 'selected from the whole Americas'. Overall, respondents highlighted that although in some cases it was a lucky coincidence that they had learned about an opportunity, what was most important was that they were highly committed and capable, and could draw on extensive (paid and unpaid) work experience.

Flexibility

Finally, one of the most important aspects of securing the first position is to be ready to accept a position – including unpaid internships – at very short notice, often within days. Suddenly an opening becomes available or one moves up in a waiting list because someone dropped out or had to be replaced. This high degree of flexibility means that applicants are either in a state of limbo, between jobs, waiting for something to open up, or they have had to leave their workplace. One respondent described that when quitting a job to start her first assignment with an aid agency, she had left the key to the office under the doormat of her previous employer because she had no time to hand it over in person. This also means that friends and family are left within a few days. The flexibility often means packing bags and making arrangements for leaving the country and accepting assignments in other fields or other continents. Respondents who felt that they were well prepared to work in Latin America found their first job in Africa, those who were hoping to work in Africa found an assignment in the Middle East – and vice versa. Thus, during the first assignment, the skills and experiences people bring to the assignment are not necessarily those most needed for the job. People working in aid may thus be over- as well as underqualified for their first assignment. What matters is what they make of this first chance and whether they feel that they want to carry on.

Conclusions

Aidland is a heterogeneous context with a wide range of entry points which require general skills, including overseas experience and language skills, the ability to write grant proposals and to interact with the media, as well as specialized skills. Aidland thus offers a broad diversity of work opportunities in different types of organizations, fields and locations. Professionalization processes in the aid sector so far do not seem to undermine the attraction of promising meaningful work and thus an opportunity for self-realization which is grounded in 'making a difference'. The introduction of codes of practice, standards and new humanitarian degrees so far does not seem to limit the access for newcomers to the field. On the contrary, humanitarian studies programmes certainly serve as recruiters to the sector. Due to the fact that the aid sector is characterized by high turnover, project-based work and – of course – emergencies, organizations need to hire or replace personnel quickly and therefore have to make compromises as far as job experience and training are concerned. The recruitment processes in the aid sector are characterized by contradictions. On the one hand, it can be very difficult to get the first position even for very well-educated people. On the other hand, people are frequently assigned to positions without previous experience in this sector. Most importantly, the first position requires flexibility and perseverance, and the willingness to accept a position which may be the opposite of the desired place and form of assignment. Being thrown in at the deep end, newcomers then have the chance to prove themselves in the job.

Finding the first assignment in Aidland is certainly a challenging experience, and in many cases if a chance occurs it has to be taken – more often than not despite a mismatch in experience and expectations. This means that entering the aid sector requires enormous flexibility, idealism and readiness to accept insecurity; given that many respondents enter the sector in their twenties, youth often seems to be a condition of employment. For some, the involvement in aidwork starts out in childhood and youth, and is grounded in early volunteering, participation in solidarity movements and overseas experiences. However, my data suggest that entering Aidland is by no means restricted to young people, but may also occur in mid-life and involve a shift from a 'regular' corporate career or a career in a helping profession in the public or non-profit sector from domestic to overseas engagement. Regardless of age, for those entering Aidland, boundary-crossing and sector-switching, the ability to transfer skills obtained in paid and unpaid work in a variety of settings in the private, public and third sector is needed.

My data suggest certain generational differences. Some of the older respondents were initially involved in development before they shifted to humanitarianism. In contrast, younger respondents were exposed to media coverage of humanitarian aid organizations, volunteering opportunities and humanitarian studies programmes while attending school or university. Regardless of generation and country of origin, those who emphasized that their motivation was to help others, regardless of whether it was in their own community or overseas, faith-based or not, appeared to have fewer difficulties in securing a job than those who were primarily motivated by a desire to find an interesting job overseas. However, in most cases the motivation was a mixture of altruism and adventure. After all, there are other opportunities to work overseas, for example, in tourism or travel industries, or in transnational corporations. For some respondents from the Global North, a career in Aidland compensated for the failure to pursue a diplomatic career. The entry into Aidland appears to be most difficult for those who have not yet gained any field experience and who lack the intrinsic rewards of those who volunteered or who were politically involved in communities. For national staff working for international aid organizations, a job opportunity may arise which offers better pay and working conditions than in the national labour market. However, they were faced with limited career opportunities compared to international staff from the Global North.

The personal and professional developments that led respondents to Aidland illuminate the desire for meaningful work and the relationship between paid and unpaid work which were discussed in Chapter 2. Once people have entered Aidland, the different paths that lead there seem to be less relevant, though different orientations which shape preferences for organizational cultures, types of contract and field of expertise remain. The decision to enter Aidland is shaped by biography, family and work history, and is structured by the recruitment processes of aid organizations and the resources of future aidworkers. So, how is work experienced, what is exciting, what is exhausting, how do people cope? The next chapter addresses the living and working conditions in Aidland.

Notes

1 Of course, this may be the result of my sampling strategy and my own limited language skills. See Methods appendix.
2 These differences in qualifications and positions within aid organizations and the relationship between national and international staff will be further discussed in Chapter 6.

4 Living and working in Aidland

And it is just such an amazing job, I mean seriously, you get to go where very few people go, you get to see how life really is. ... I mean personally it is a fantastic journey as well, you get to discover your own limits, what you are capable of, which I never thought I was capable of, when I started out. Like security management, like starting from scratch. We are given so much responsibility so quickly, something you never get to do in normal life, well I mean in Western life. And it was just a wonderful learning experience, at every level and it is so genuine. And it is so authentic, and you are meeting people, and when you are having bad experiences, these are authentically bad experiences that you can learn from. Yeah, I love the connection with people. I love, it sounds almost like religious, but I really do believe in humanitarian principles, in humanity, and neutrality, independence and impartiality ... All the rest, all the comfort is just not worth it. That's what I love. But also the criticism is there.

North American woman, February 2013

The continuity like for me is, even [home country] is a developing country ... my previous work was like humanitarian because I worked with the most vulnerable groups of [home country]. Even if it is not like humanitarian activities. I think that it, maybe it [influenced] my thoughts to be flexible to be close to the vulnerable, ... and maybe to understand their needs and their issues. So, I did not see very much there is a change in what I did in [home country] and what I did in the Congo. ... I can see that the level of the standard of living in these areas [in my home country] are the same as I saw in the Congo, so it is not too much change for me, but it is just what I am used to.

African woman, February 2013

The passionate statement in the first quote sums up a whole range of aspects that make humanitarians enthusiastic about their work – the opportunity to learn and travel, being given responsibility early on, the challenging interactions – but it also shows that the belief in the work is mixed with doubt. Moreover, in this statement the involvement in aid is contrasted with 'normal life' and experienced as 'genuine' and 'authentic'. In particular for respondents from the Global North, Aidland is conceptualized as an exceptional space which at the same time feels more real than the life which respondents had left behind and thus fulfils the promise of self-realization and personal growth that attracted respondents to this kind of work and lifestyle. In contrast, the quote from an interview with a respondent from the Global South highlights the continuities and similarity of experiences of working with vulnerable groups in her country of origin and in another African country. This chapter explores the varying living and working conditions that are related to different environments, organizations, posts and tasks which make up the highly heterogeneous space of Aidland introduced in Chapter 1. It focuses on how work in Aidland is organized and experienced, focusing primarily on the situation in field, country and regional offices. Flexibility and mobility continue to matter after the first assignment. My data suggest that work dominates everything and shapes living arrangements and relationships, particularly for those working in field positions. This raises questions about 'work–life balance' or the relationship between professional and personal lives and how sustainable this kind of lifestyle is. First, I will discuss the experience of working conditions, then I will move on to sexual and romantic relationships; finally I will turn to the continuity and discontinuity between work and life in Aidland and at home.

It was the best of times, it was the worst of times

Work can play a central role in self-realization and demanding and limitless work is experienced as exhilarating (Thunman 2012; Ekman 2013). Challenging and intensive work is characterized by a high degree of autonomy and responsibility which can be a source of job satisfaction, self-realization and personal growth. It is therefore not surprising that throughout the interviews the most challenging and difficult living and working conditions were also described as 'the best time of my life'. So what are the challenges associated with work in Aidland? They include the organization of work which is characterized by a high turnover, limited resources, competition and lack of coordination between organizations, strained work relations and security incidents. Part of the job satisfaction is to get things done under these difficult circumstances. Another central source of satisfaction in this work context is being able to make a difference in the lives of beneficiaries. In addition, in particular for the expatriates, it was important that humanitarian work was carried out at sites off the tourist trail (though sometimes within reach of tourist destinations).

Preparation, power and promotion

As we have seen in Chapter 3, even though people in aid tend to be highly educated and to have considerable work experience, the first job in Aidland is often characterized by a mismatch between the qualifications and experience required for the position and the education and job history of the applicant.

Limited preparation applies not only to the first position but is something that continues to shape appointments in Aidland. High turnover, an absence of briefing and handover procedures, and limited coordination among aid organizations contribute to a challenging work environment, and may be stressful for both national and international staff.

Often provided with limited briefing, aidworkers have to figure out the situation upon arrival in the field (Loquercio et al. 2006). While some respondents were satisfied by access to training and information material, a number of interviewees were quite critical with respect to the lack of support, in particular missing an induction or proper handover. A European woman who had worked for various UN agencies and other international organizations described the briefing and debriefing she had experienced in various UN agencies and other international organizations as 'by and large it is lousy'. When I asked her to explain, she elaborated:

> Briefings are superficial, training is non-existent, debriefing is limited. Even if you write a mission report or lessons learned-type stuff, somebody says 'It's not lessons learned but lessons observed.' We write this stuff and it disappears into the archives and nobody ever reads it again.

Another European woman who had been working for a variety of bilateral and non-governmental organizations stated: 'I don't think that I worked for any organization, including my current job with [NGO], where anyone has explained anything to me.' This included an assignment in the Middle East responsible for protection. She felt that she spent the first six months on the job 'reinventing the wheel'. After ten months, she had the opportunity to discuss her experience with a protection officer and was relieved that they 'were thinking along the same lines'. Nevertheless, she was very frustrated by the waste of time and money caused by the lack of briefing. Her experience documents that lack of briefing and proper handover affects the efficiency of organizations. This was echoed by other respondents who stated that they would appreciate more support concerning the preparation of field trips, for example, being introduced to decision-makers, being told with whom to liaise and talk at the head office, as well as being given information about key documents and publications that would help them to familiarize themselves with the situation. Even if organizations provided such information, respondents felt that it could be done more systematically and more consistently. In the context of professionalization processes within the sector, there are certainly significant efforts to improve the access to training and information which is reflected in the proliferation of short- and long-term courses (Rainhorn et al. 2010; Walker and Russ 2010), and professional networks and research centres which make their reports available through the web (for example, resources provided by ALNAP, HAP, PHAP, ReliefWeb). The question is whether these efforts at the sector level also change the situation within aid organizations and improve the quality of the briefing and debriefing process, given their limited resources and requirements to keep overheads low.

Limited briefing not only affects efficiency; it can have fatal consequences, as the death rate of relief workers is highest in the first three months of the assignment, when they are not yet familiar with the local conditions (Sheik et al. 2000). A European man who had worked for several IGOs and NGOs described briefing, debriefing, training and support from organizations as 'pretty much non-existent'. Recalling his latest debriefing, he felt 'there was actually no one who actually knew what I was doing to debrief me' due to the fact that the responsible desk officer, programme adviser and the staff member dealing with protection had left the organization a few days before his return. However, the debriefing was better than he expected as the newly appointed security adviser was very interested in his views. As discussed in Chapter 1, after the bombing of Baghdad in 2003, the sector increased its attention to security issues. Consequently, assessments of the security situation in debriefings could make an impact on the decision to continue a programme or to pull out, as it would be irresponsible for the organization to put national and international staff at risk. Even though, in this case, it was not possible to talk to the responsible desk officer, there was an opportunity to share experiences with the organization and a belief that the organization took into account the information that was provided. Aside from serving as a mechanism for organizational learning, debriefing can also provide acknowledgement of the stress, anxiety and efforts those working in the field had experienced and coped with, particularly in regions such as the Middle East with a high occurrence of security incidents. The interviews point to the widely shared assessment that the debriefing offered was inconsistent, and varied with the availability and interest of the desk officers. A North American woman in her thirties, who had worked for several non-governmental organizations, explained:

> It's not the organization that's ever really going to listen, it is individuals. And so, there have been times when yes, there has been an individual that works at a particular desk, covering a region who is then really interested and listened a lot. And then there have been times where they did not even have time to meet. And so part of it is the personalities of the individuals and part of it is just the timing of what else is happening within that region and what they have time for.

Respondents varied in their evaluation of organizational support and some praised their organizations for the resources they provided, training programmes and access to reports. My data suggests that overall, preparation for an assignment was considered a personal responsibility and even those who found briefing and debriefing provided by the organization inadequate felt that it was part of their job to prepare for the next assignment and 'hit the ground running'. Although it was stressful to get ready for an assignment at short notice and to figure out what to do with little organizational support, these difficulties contributed to the challenges of the job and respondents took great pride in being able to meet them. Furthermore, a lack of support was contrasted with freedom of supervision and its consequent autonomy. Even though, since the introduction of email, aid personnel tend to be more closely controlled by their head offices than before (Eyben 2011), there is still more freedom than being in a workplace with fixed work hours. Typical for neoliberal work practices, the emphasis lies on self-governance. Work is still regulated, but the emphasis lies not so much in one's presence at the workplace as in completing projects with the desired goals. New information and communication technologies (ICT) make the exchange between field and head office easier and therefore, also, the monitoring of the success (and problems) of programmes. In addition, the internet provides important resources in the form of forums, discussion groups, expert advice and country-based information, and allows expatriates to connect (Glanz 2003; Heron 2005; Bollettino and Bruderlein 2008). Thus even if time constraints, lack of resources and job turnover do not always allow briefing and debriefing in meetings between desk officers and field staff, there are now certainly efforts underway to make reports widely available and to disseminate insights from lessons learned. In March 2014, ReliefWeb announced that it had 'collected and stored more than 545,000 pieces of humanitarian information'.[1] Furthermore, OCHA started to develop a repository, the Humanitarian Data Exchange (HDX), that shall allow easy access to humanitarian data. Research centres such as the Feinstein International Center at Tufts University, Massachusetts, regularly publish field-based research on a range of aspects central to humanitarian assistance. In addition, the ODI-hosted Active Learning Network for Accountability in Humanitarian Action (ALNAP), which was established in 1997 and draws on the expertise of UN agencies, the Red Cross and Red Crescent movements, bilateral and multilateral organizations, international NGOs as well as humanitarian networks, researchers and consultancy groups is surveying the humanitarian system in order to enhance performance and accountability.[2] These are only a few examples in addition to a range of other services hosted by universities and aid agencies.

There are, therefore, multiple efforts to make reports available so that people can learn from others' experience, although it needs to be taken into consideration that reports have significant implications for the future funding of aid agencies and the careers of people working in aid. Pérouse de Montclos (2012) provides a scathing critique of internal evaluations which are driven by the motivation of aid organizations to avoid criticism and by the need of the evaluators to secure further appointments. Thus, as long as reports highlight successes and omit conflicts, problems and failures out of fear that this might jeopardize the future of organizations or the careers of individuals, the insights from such reports may be limited. That one might learn as much from failure as from success has been recognized by some organizations which publish failure reports such as the Canadian development organization Engineers Without Borders, which in 2010 published a Failure Report.³ In addition to the publication of reports, another solution to the problem of high turnover and lack of resources for proper briefing and debriefing which allow individual and organizational learning is the standardization of procedures, for example, through the introduction of 'kits' (Redfield 2008b). A wide range of information is therefore available through websites of research institutions and practitioner networks, which means that the responsibility to obtain the relevant information and prepare oneself for the next assignment lies with the individual aidworker, emphasizing the high degree of self-management required.

Furthermore, regardless of the extent of preparation, people in aid are frequently suddenly confronted with unforeseen circumstances to which they have to respond with limited resources. Although such constraints were frustrating, they were also a source of job satisfaction, as they allowed respondents to prove themselves. They expressed a need for ongoing challenges and learning, typical for professionals who seek self-realization through work (Parment 2011; Ekman 2013). Especially for those on early assignments, each job provided opportunities to get to know different organizations and their operations in different countries. Quickly changing situations, both internally with respect to turnover within an organization, and externally when the political or environmental conditions within the country changed, could also lead to early promotions. For example, a North American woman quickly took on additional responsibilities after starting out on a six-month internship in Sudan. After four months, her contract was changed to a regular work contract. This new administrative role included preparing reports. However, due to the fact that the head of mission failed to maintain contact with donors, she took up this responsibility and handled a multi-million Euro budget. When the head of mission was fired, she became interim head of mission because the organization could not immediately appoint anyone else at a time when violence against aidworkers was increasing in the region. Thus, within a year, she was promoted from an intern to a leadership position, being responsible for the team and a large budget. Just as it was possible to be hired with little prior experience, the urgency of filling posts and the privilege of whiteness meant that people from the Global North in junior positions could quickly take on significant power and responsibility, whereas local staff with more qualifications and experience were not necessarily promoted into a leadership position.

Conflict, cooperation and competition

Another challenge was lack of coordination between organizations in the field or even direct competition, even between national sections of the same NGO. One of the most frustrating aspects of this process were uncoordinated aid responses symbolized by white land cruisers blocking each other in traffic jams. Several respondents remarked on the situation in Haiti in 2010. A European woman found it 'amazing; you had these NGO cars everywhere, you had all the NGOs and maybe some have been created just for the earthquake'. She had a very strong reaction to this experience: 'it was so much that at the end you want to throw up and tell everybody just to go home. Let those people alone and maybe they will get back their dignity, but it is insane.' In particular, badly managed projects that did not take the local situation into consideration and implemented strategies regardless of whether they were appropriate or not were criticized. Again, activities in Haiti six weeks after the earthquake served as an example of such inadequate humanitarian responses. A North American woman recalled:

> We would just show up in one of the most dangerous places in North America, basically, and ripping people's homes apart and installing tents, not having verified, like, how many people were there. Not having checked whether there was enough soil, whether there was enough room in the place, if it was sanitary, if we were respecting *Sphere* standards. It was kind of all over the place. It was really, I had big ethical issues with that programme.

Thus the existence and awareness of standards such as *Sphere* does not necessarily improve the delivery of aid. This badly managed project of a highly respected aid organization did not take the activities of another NGO into consideration which was 'like a street away' and employed several hundred expats. Based on her experience in Haiti, one respondent was very sceptical concerning the contribution of the humanitarian enterprise:

> What should be done? I think that actually it is always the same, there was no coordination, there were big words used from the beginning, 'we rebuild the country' or whatever. A lot of lies; could we stop the lies? I think that everything is about coordination. I am not sure that having all these NGOs around makes sense ... I think that Haiti just is a very good example of the limits of what could be a humanitarian aid.

The introduction of the Cluster approach introduced by the UN Office for the Coordination of Humanitarian Affairs (OCHA) in 2005 and other initiatives sought to improve coordination. Critical assessment of these reforms came to the conclusion that they are problematic by privileging larger organizations and marginalizing those with fewer resources (Dederian *et al.* 2007; Street 2009; Stumpenhorst *et al.* 2011). The efficiency of aid organizations is undermined by the lack of coordination and by conflicting approaches of aid organizations.[4]

The diversity of aid organization that people in aid encounter in the field thus not only provides opportunities for learning, developing networks and for potential job opportunities, but may also be stressful if organizations compete with each other for resources or jeopardize each other's success through uncoordinated and contradictory interventions.

Moreover, conflicts not only occur between but also within organizations. One of the most stressful aspects of work mentioned was difficult work relationships, in particular criticism of incompetent supervisors who did not respect national staff or who misjudged the security situation because of their limited interest and insight into local conditions. A European woman recalled a 'really, really terrible boss' who should not have worked in the field but may have been hired by the organization because

> She came with a lot of money to the organization. And I think that everybody knew that there and to me, I thought, once again for it was not a very good image for the organization, and I think that such a person, honestly should be sacked or should not work there. Like she had a completely disrespectful behaviour towards the national staff, for example. She would shout at them or she had no cultural understanding, she was and she probably did not realize as well that maybe most of the staff she was working with went through war, had a lot of trauma and that I think, working in such type of context you need to factor that in, in what you expect from them.

Due to quick promotions of expatriates to positions with considerable power and responsibility, some observed that one would find 'kings and queens' in the field. Both national and international staff were frustrated when they perceived their supervisors as incompetent and disrespectful of national staff.

Being a supervisor could also be stressful. In fact, being a middle-manager – that is, reporting to head office while managing project staff – is one of the most stressful positions in aid organizations (Antares Foundation 2012). International staff from high-income countries found it stressful to manage other internationals from high-income countries due to their high expectations. A North American woman described her first time managing expatriates from the Global North as 'a pain'. She sensed that she was expected to be 'everybody's shrink and everybody's mommy'. She felt like 'a psychologist all the time', and what she experienced was 'very draining'. Note that her account is quite gendered as she described being responsible for caring for her team members which was at odds with her own understanding of good leadership. She was convinced that good leadership should be characterized by transparency, efficiency and competence. Recall Ekman's (2013) observation that in teams in which high commitment and authenticity play a central role, the relationship between managers and workers, which is characterized by 'fluid, narcissistic mutual recognition' rather than by concrete responsibility, can be highly stressful. The interaction between national and international staff (see Chapter 6) could also be stressful, in particular in cases of accusations of fraud and mutual distrust.

The collaboration with other team members could, however, also be highly satisfying when it was experienced as cooperative and mutually supportive, in particular if a team had to cope with potentially traumatizing events; for example, security incidents. Furthermore, having competent supervisors was highly appreciated and one of the sources of job satisfaction was being able to learn from supervisors and other team members. Working relations could result in strong and long friendships just as much as the desire to never work together again. The work relationships in this regard were highly personalized and individualized. Given that networks play an important role in recruitment, being perceived as 'difficult' and not getting along with other team members could hamper employment opportunities. Addressing problems within teams in a debriefing meeting thus had to be carefully considered. A respondent who had complained about an expat colleague who had abused and fired national staff recalled:

> And [I] went for my debrief to [head office] and had conversations with different people and [had] got to a certain stage with. It was actually with the head of HR and was told that I couldn't take it further, but I should also be aware that he has got friends quite high up within the organization and I would be risking my own career if I would do that within [NGO]. So, I ended up not taking it any further. Because it wasn't to the level of, you know, criminal abuse or anything. And so in a way, there wasn't a lot more that I could say but just very inappropriate behaviour as a manager. But I learned a lot from that [laughs] and I learned that sometimes it is good to walk away from situations that you can't fix and to find yourself in another situation.

She thus experienced the paradoxical situation that, in working for a humanitarian organization whose goal was to support the needy and vulnerable, as a junior staff member she could do nothing about a senior staff member abusing national staff. Of course, such contradictions are not unique to aid organizations; trade unions and other organizations concerned with social justice do not necessarily offer their staff the best working conditions, and the harassment of female staff occurs in all types of organizations.

Edgework

As already noted in Chapter 1, since the 1990s, aidwork is increasingly shaped, in various ways, by security incidents affecting development, relief and human rights work. Aidwork constitutes voluntary risk taking; people working in aid acknowledge that dangerous situations are unavoidable and just need to be dealt with (Roth 2011; 2014). While organizations' security protocols need to be followed, teams also had some leeway to decide whether they should abandon a mission. My data suggest that respondents were critical of security approaches that involved staying in guarded compounds and instead emphasized good relationships with the local community and national staff. They were thus highly aware of the role that perception plays. Respondents emphasized the need to build relationships with the community and took a 'relational approach' (Fast 2014).

Security threats and mitigating measures needed to be considered in the planning of daily activities and could prevent some programmes from being carried out. Security incidents highlight various elements of what is satisfying and frustrating about aidwork, and also shed light on the relationship among team members, often demonstrating the levels of trust among them or the degree of willingness to follow directions of supervisors. The way security was dealt with also reflects the relationship among staff based in the head office and those based in the field who have different access to information and therefore assess the security situation differently. For example, UN security in New York is 'far, far away' and so does not realize how different regions in a country vary as to how dangerous or insecure they are. While head office sets guidelines, it may be difficult to enforce them in the field. In addition, security incidents highlighted the contrast between working and living in Aidland and what respondents described as living in 'the real world'.

Highly restricting security measures which limit movement and interaction with the local population can undermine what attracted people to Aidland and aidwork in the first place. Overall, respondents emphasized that they accepted the risks they were taking and felt that they could decide whether to take an assignment or not (Roth 2011). They were satisfied with the security measures of the organizations they were working for or even found them excessive. They adopted a 'wrong place, wrong time' mentality and pointed out that contemporary societies around the world presented a multitude of risks. Evacuations were accompanied by a whole range of emotions, including relief at leaving a dangerous situation just in time, pleasure to be put up in a comfortable environment, gratitude towards local staff who helped with leaving the country, guilt at leaving national staff and beneficiaries behind, as well as embarrassment at being considered 'heroes' by friends and family back home when all they did was leave the country. Leaving local staff behind was more difficult the longer members had worked together and had got to know each other. Some therefore refused to leave the country or sought to return as early as possible.

Making a difference

One of the most important sources of job satisfaction was the fact that the work was urgent and made a difference in the lives of the beneficiaries. It was experienced as meaningful work and several respondents related the engagement in Aidland to religious and political convictions and thus to self-realization. Those who had made the shift from the private sector to humanitarian aid described leaving their previous career as an irreversible change. This was seen as 'addictive' and thus beyond their control. A European woman explained:

> Respondent: No, I don't feel like increasing the sale of Pampers or whatever [laughs]. I think that the point is [that it is] like drugs – when you get involved in humanitarian aid you become addicted. But I think that it is a very good addiction [laughs]. SR: And what is it that addicts [you] to the humanitarian world? What is the drug? Respondent: The drug is, it is meaningful, and it's about taking care of the others; so altruism, I think that is very important to me, it's about good in a big way. I don't know what it is exactly. And actually it is about goodwill, very much. I would rather say that, because I think that goodwill is much more humble than just good in general.

She was not the only one emphasizing that the work is accompanied by 'emotional highs', 'adrenalin highs' or, as she put it, is addictive. This addiction was not restricted to humanitarian relief, but also shared by 'election junkies' involved in election observation. Respondents appreciated that they had an impact on individuals, organizations or – if they were involved in law- and policy-making – on societies. All these three levels can be connected, as the following statement illustrates. It is by an Asian man who had held a long-term position with a faith-based organization and was active in development cooperation, specializing in education, in East Africa:

> Rewarding is that you are directly contributing to the development of the people ... when you provide education especially. You see the children graduating and then these children going to colleges, after colleges, these guys are getting jobs. So that gives you [the fact] that you have built the human capacity, the workforce of a country. You help [them] to build their own nation ... bringing them back to their own country. So that's very rewarding. Gives you job satisfaction. ... You know most of our guys [staff] were our own beneficiaries.

He thus emphasized that it was satisfying for him to see that those who were recipients of aid were enabled to learn and ultimately to run their own country. The outside help provided by international development organizations like the NGO for which he was working was thus presented as a necessary tool to achieve this aim. Other respondents named the fact that they were able to design and introduce new programmes in collaboration with the stakeholders as one of the most rewarding aspects of their work. Moreover, respondents were not just involved in the design, implementation and improvement of resources; they were also involved in constitutional reform and policy processes. A young European woman described what it was that she found most satisfying in working for a UN agency:

> I think it is being part of policy work. You are part of the policy processes in the countries, the big frameworks which have enormous impact for a large number of people. So I find that very, very interesting.

> Like being part of working groups or comment on new laws ... like youth law and the gender equality law and things like that.

Although she missed the 'small-scale work in the field with the people' which she experienced working for an NGO, she preferred to work for the UN because 'it makes you feel like it has an impact on what you do actually', in contrast to the NGO work.

However, as 'making a difference' was one of the most rewarding aspects of working in aid, both because it contributed to the well-being of others and because it was an expression of efficacy and power, not being able to improve the well-being of those in need of assistance and changing society was experienced as frustrating. Respondents were thus keenly aware of the limits of their work and named a number of aspects that represent obstacles to carrying out aidwork effectively and which include corruption, mismanagement and bureaucratic procedures. A European woman, who held a long-term position in an African NGO providing adult education, explained what she found unsatisfying about her work:

> The circumstances: those political, economic, corrupt stories that turn you into Sisyphus, no matter what one does, which is an awful feeling. Sometimes, I ignore the circumstances and try to focus on my work. Then I don't read the newspaper and don't listen to the radio because that is frustrating me too much, because if I am frustrated myself, I can't get the frustration out of the people, and that is most frustrating. Not to have enough resources in order to do what is necessary to do is very frustrating indeed.

People working in aid must thus confront the fact that despite their best efforts and intentions, the larger context constrains the impact of aid organizations. Not only do external economic and political structures in which aidwork is taking place limit the efficacy of aid organizations, but so also do the bureaucratic structures and inefficiency of the aid organizations themselves. People working in aid are aware of the fact that their work can only bring about limited if any change at all. This awareness was accompanied by questioning the aid industry and could result in career changes. As the quote above demonstrates, this frustration had to be ignored in order to be able to focus on short-term goals.

Although the ability to cope with challenging circumstances was a source of job satisfaction, the perceived lack and waste of resources as well as bureaucratic procedures requiring approval and authorization which slowed down the provision of aid contributed to frustration. Furthermore, aid organizations – UN agencies as well as NGOs – were criticized for resistance to reform and criticism. A European respondent who had held appointments in a range of organizations, both NGOs and IGOs, shared the following:

> There were some parts of IGO work that I didn't like, well, of course, [found] disappointing; it is very bureaucratic, often people are totally unmoved by the populations that they are working to help, and, yeah, so I thought, if I work for an NGO again, it would be a very lean machine, no waste of money, very professional; and I was bitterly disappointed by [NGO].

Respondents not only varied in their assessment of whether UN agencies or NGOs were more efficient, but also in their attitudes towards development and humanitarianism. Some emphasized the urgency of humanitarianism, which in their experience had immediate and visible results, most dramatically if it meant saving lives, but also with respect to alleviating hunger and suffering. Long-term development, however, was seen as less efficient. Such an attitude is typical for French NGOs which make a stronger distinction between humanitarianism and development than do Anglo-Saxon NGOs which are more likely to be multi-mandated (Blanchet and Martin 2011; Stroup 2012). With respect to individual aidworkers, affinity with a particular approach rather than national background was more important. While some found relief work more efficient because it focused on 'getting things done', others were concerned that the effect of humanitarian aid was not sustainable. These respondents emphasized that long-term development was needed in order to accomplish sustainable change. A European man, who had worked for the same project in East Africa for many years, felt that efforts needed to go beyond short-term relief and address the root causes of poverty and suffering.

> Yes, we need to alleviate suffering, do short-term help and long-term help and I think humanitarian aid, development aid are important, but we also need to be advocates and witnesses of what is happening in the South. I think we have all seen the consequences of the policies of international companies. Myself, I have seen enough children die of curable disease, children dying of malnutrition and yet in Geneva, they speculate on food. Or, mothers who are paid like almost nothing for cultivating coffee or such things, [it] really annoys me so much, because I've buried children, I've seen the suffering of a woman who has lost her child and the causes of this are also the policies of our companies here in the Western world.

In this statement, the respondent brought the solution to improving living conditions in the Global South problem 'home' by identifying producers (and consumers) in the Global North as beneficiaries of production processes that result in poverty. He admitted that multiple actors and factors contributed to the current situation, and that he felt more comfortable judging (and blaming) Westerners rather than corrupt and autocratic leaders in the Global South.

Respondents who worked for multi-mandated and development organizations tended to highlight long-term development and those working for humanitarian organizations highlighted emergency relief. Thus the great diversity of aid organizations allowed respondents to find assignments in organizations that resonated with their convictions. However, regardless of their preferred approach, respondents frequently questioned whether their efforts really made a difference in the lives of the communities in which they were active or whether they themselves were indeed the beneficiaries. These doubts motivated respondents to consider acquiring additional knowledge and skills, changing to a different type of organization or leaving the sector altogether (see Chapter 7). Thus, one of the paradoxes of aidwork is that even though the desire to 'make a difference' is one reason to get involved in this kind of work, aidworkers themselves may benefit more than those who are conventionally understood as 'beneficiaries'.

Traumatic experiences and psychosocial support

Aidworkers are exposed to environmental risks such as illnesses and intentional risks such as attacks (Van Brabant 2000). Furthermore, Western expatriates are often confronted with the extreme inequality between themselves, and national staff, and the local or refugee populations. People working in aid are thus exposed to a range of traumatic experiences which include witnessing poverty, inequality or violence. These experiences may be primary (i.e. working in a region marked by poverty, conflict and disaster), or secondary (i.e. working with victims of violence or refugees who have lost everything). Such encounters with individuals who in the most dramatic cases had lost everything but their lives was often presented as one of the most profound experiences of aidwork, which may seem paradoxical. The confrontation with poverty made a significant impression on respondents and was contrasted with (upper)-middle-class lifestyles, which they experienced as shameful. National and international respondents were impressed to observe that people who had lost everything in a conflict or disaster seemed happier and more generous than those living in affluence.

Respondents from the Global North contrasted the strength and dignity of victims and beneficiaries with the egoism, materialism and narrow-mindedness that they experienced in affluent societies and in conflictual relations among expatriates within aid organizations. The beneficiaries were thus admired. It was often mentioned that one 'learned so much from them', although what was learned was rarely spelled out except for showing happiness and dignity in the most adverse contexts. Interviewees also rarely questioned to what extent the behaviour of beneficiaries towards aid personnel may have been shaped by dependency and power relations. It thus came as a surprise when beneficiaries did not conform to the image of grateful recipient and challenged or attacked aidworkers. An Eastern European woman who had lived and volunteered in the Middle East for many years recalled:

> I remember myself being shot by the Palestinians in the camp, because they thought, because somebody said that there was something else that they should get, it was stupid. So for me that was the most difficult thing to overcome. Because I accept to be shot by the Israelis, I accept everything. But if you are shot by the people that you think you are helping, that's terrible. I remember. I just thought I could never go back, to tell you the truth.

Being the target of violence (including homophobic attacks) could be one form of traumatic experience. Furthermore, those who worked as translators with victims of violence underwent vicarious traumatization. The Antares Foundation (2012) estimates that about 30 per cent of returning aidworkers suffer from post-traumatic stress disorder (PTSD). A woman from East Africa, who worked for UNHCR, recalled:

> I met a lot of victims, orphans, minor children, raped women, yeah it was really, for me it wasn't good. I remember the first six, seven months, it wasn't a good memory, I even remember, I had bad dreams, at some point I had to meet some psychiatrist.

She was one of the few respondents who obtained help when the work affected her well-being. Other respondents stated that they had not sought help, even though they had been aware assistance was available for those who had experienced traumatic experiences. They realized in retrospect that they probably needed help. After she felt better, she started to love the work for the aid agency which allowed her to learn about the aid system as well as about her country of origin. She felt 'empowered' through humanitarian work encountering trauma, and stated that helping victims contributed to her personal growth. Thus, like the stressful work environment, lack of resources and stressful working relations, primary and secondary traumatic experiences represented another growth opportunity for respondents. Thus, paradoxically, stressful and traumatic situations can result in burnout and PTSD, but can also contribute to personal growth if they can be overcome.

Aid organizations differ with respect to how much psychological support they offer to staff and volunteers who experience traumatic situations. Although some improvement in the provision of psychosocial support has been noted, overall staff care is not sufficient (Ehrenreich et al. 2006; Porter and Emmens 2009); even if available, respondents did not necessarily make use of such support. A respondent noted in hindsight, 'Looking back now, I realize that I was probably burnt out, pretty much. I had trouble sleeping when I got back, sort of waking, really crazy vivid dreams, that sort of stuff.' She acknowledged that she was 'too proud' to seek support and that she did not realize she really needed it. This was quite typical for respondents who noted that services were available and knew of other aidworkers who had made use of them, but had not done so themselves. For example, some aidworkers will not use services that are not also available to disaster victims (Sharp et al. 1995). Furthermore, there may be strategic reasons for not making use of psychosocial support, as flagging up problems may have an impact on future career opportunities. However, this reluctance to take advantage of available psychosocial support is in various ways problematic: those exposed to traumatic situations do not obtain the necessary help, and the organizations do not learn about these needs and how they can best be addressed. Those responsible for debriefing and psychosocial support need to find ways to flag up problems while assuring confidentiality. One of the paradoxes of aidwork is that being exposed to primary and secondary traumatic experiences can contribute to the well-being of aidworkers because it puts their own privileged position into perspective.

Beyond tourism

The exposure to trauma, suffering and poverty experienced by aidworkers is one side of the coin. Aidwork also offers opportunities to travel to exotic and unusual places, and meet people from different cultures. The opportunity to experience different cultures away from the tourist trail for shorter or longer periods and to interact with a mix of international and national populations was overwhelmingly reported as one of the attractive aspects of aidwork. Professionally, it is rewarding that the work is potentially making a difference to the lives of individuals, communities and societies. Personally, it is very rewarding to experience different cultures and to see places where there are normally no tourists or before they had become tourist attractions. Aidwork offers exoticism as well as the chance of participation in historical events. In contrast, meaningful work that is carried out by nurses, social workers and other care workers in deprived areas in the Global North lacks such exoticism. If such social workers, nurses and other care providers receive media attention then it is for scandals rather than for heroic efforts in a neoliberal context. Thus aidworkers from the Global North emphasize the desire to 'make a difference', but apparently prefer to make a difference in the Global South rather than addressing the needs of vulnerable groups in their countries of origin. Similar to the abolitionists of the nineteenth century, the emphasis is on poverty and need overseas while the discrimination and deprivation in one's own society is not necessarily addressed. Thus, the relationship between Aidland and tourism is complex: people in aid distance themselves from tourists, and yet they appreciate the fact that the weekend or R&R could be used to enjoy tourist attractions such as beaches and safaris (see also Fechter 2012). Africa held a special fascination, though of course there were differences among African countries, for example, French- and English-speaking countries. Some regions were more accessible due to a lack of language barriers and security issues and offered a good work–life balance, which included being able to visit national parks at the weekend. Tourist hotels with their swimming pools, bars and restaurants were part of the infrastructure of Aidland. Furthermore, even if they did not stay at luxury hotels, they were 'tourists' in the sense that they had a choice to stay or to leave (Bauman 1998), in contrast to the local population. However, while respondents noted preferences for certain countries or regions, that did not mean that they would not take on assignments in other parts of the world. As already noted in the context of getting the first job in Aidland, flexibility was required and those who were willing to go to places they were less interested in or had considered avoiding were able to secure employment.

Not only travelling to unusual places, but also the encounters with multicultural teams, was highlighted as a highly satisfactory aspect of aidwork. Respondents believed that aid organizations offered them a unique opportunity to meet people from a range of countries. The international community of aidworkers made possible encounters between groups which are usually separated due to political reasons – for example, engineers from Cuba and from The United States – which enables boundaries to be crossed and ideas and experiences to be exchanged, all of which can help to overcome cultural and political distance. Ideally, aidwork offers opportunities to transcend boundaries and overcome cultural, social and political restrictions. However, visa and work permit requirements hamper the cross-border work. Citizenship mattered significantly with respect to the ability to work in a certain region, both by restricting as well as enabling taking on certain jobs. For example, while a Swiss passport could provide access to a range of countries, other nationalities were more restricted.

As with other aspects of aidwork, the respondents illustrated a number of contradictions about their situation. Aidwork can lead to trauma and deep distress which in the long run can prove life-enhancing if the worker is able to properly recuperate. Aidworkers might distance themselves from tourists, and yet themselves enjoy relaxing in exotic environments. Although aidwork is predicated on border-less or border-transcending work, this itself is strongly restricted and regulated by passports, visas and work permits.

What work–life balance?

Working conditions strongly influence the private lives of people working in aid, to which I will now turn. In particular, I address to what extent it is possible to reconcile work and private life, what – if any – work–life balance can be achieved, and how people working in aid manage 'living apart, together' (LAT). Depending on assignment, status and risk situation, the living and working conditions of people working in aid differ widely. In a stable situation and on a long-term assignment, aid personnel could live on their own or with their families. This guaranteed more privacy and allowed them to maintain some distance from colleagues. Thus some, who worked longer in a country, in particular if they were working in development, for a UN agency, larger NGO or bilateral organization, enjoyed private accommodation and were therefore better able to distinguish between life and work, and in this regard resembled business expatriates. Respondents who held better paid positions were more likely to have a family, and stated that job security – both in terms of the security situation as well as with respect to the length of the contract – played a role when they accepted a position. Aid organizations are facing dilemmas to decide whether to hire experienced aidworkers who cost more due to family commitments or newcomers who have not yet started a family. As one respondent put it, organizations are interested in aidworkers with experience, but 'mature people often come with baggage, baggage life, wife and families'.

> You know, if we want somebody with this profile, that profile often comes with all this other domestic baggage, and so we have to pay for that domestic baggage. And that was a huge dilemma for a lot of people, and still is, because when you look at how much money is involved in supporting that one individual and you look at what you could do with that in terms of the impact on the beneficiaries, it looks disproportionate.

In this account the 'domestic baggage' – i.e. wife and children – of a male aidworker is addressed. In the next chapter, I will address gender differences in combining a career in Aidland with starting and maintaining a family.

Volunteers and those working on short-term assignments, in particular those in high-risk situations, tend to live together in guesthouses or guarded compounds, separated from partners and families. Depending on the circumstances, accommodation in Aidland can be quite basic, and some considered having access to a bed and a clean toilet as good living conditions. While some experienced limited access to water and electricity, others had access to the internet and satellite phones. For expatriate aidworkers from the Global North, a simple lifestyle stood in stark contrast to the affluence they were used to. In this regard, a period in Aidland may be compared to 'slow living' (Osbaldiston 2013).

Living together with expats – and in some cases also 'in-pats', that is, national staff from another region of the country who are also separated from their family – was more typical for NGOs and for high-risk situations in which staff of UN agencies and NGOs lived together in guarded and highly secured compounds (bunkers). Although the opportunity to meet interesting people and socialize in the evening and have time off was highlighted as one of the positive experiences, only a few respondents emphasized that they enjoyed living together with their colleagues. This was experienced as especially stressful if one was living together with sub- or superordinates, regardless of how well one got along with co-workers (Bjerneld et al. 2004, 2006; Antares Foundation 2012). Living together with other expatriates was experienced as 'severe shock' on the first mission. A North American woman in her thirties recalled:

> It was something nobody had warned me about: that it is exhausting to live and work with the same people. Lines are [crossed] I never

experienced that before, even when you are at school, you might be super-close to your colleagues, and you work with them when you are on group assignment when you are in high school, or in university, but you never go home with them at the end of the day. You don't have to see their faces at every meal.

Especially those who described themselves as introverted felt that their need to spend some time alone and remove themselves from the group could be misunderstood as rejection. Living together was even more stressful if problems were encountered, for example, in cases of funding loss, theft, team conflict or work-related stress. Due to the lack of separation between 'work' and 'life', conflicts could spill over from work to life and vice versa. A desire to rest and get sleep could clash with the need to let off steam by partying hard and listening to loud music. However, just as relationships with colleagues and housemates could be highly stressful, they could also be a source of great pleasure and the basis of long-lasting and profound friendships to share challenging situations. In such a context, mutual respect and sharing similar values, for example, a work ethic, can be crucial for smooth cooperation. These accounts show very clearly how living and working in Aidland is intertwined and that conflicts as well as friendships can spill over from the private to the public sphere and vice versa – if it is possible to make this separation at all.

Comparable to closed communities in the military or a monastery, living in Aidland could feel 'institutionalized'. Typical for 'total institutions' (Goffman 1961), work, reproduction and leisure are not separated but integrated. Relationships and life conduct were structured through aid organizations. Aid organizations provided accommodation often including personnel taking care of reproductive activities such as grocery shopping, cooking and cleaning. A European woman in her thirties, who had been on assignments in various sub-Saharan countries, explained:

> And there is this mentality of emergency worker, not a lot of things to do, but people in small communities, and so people will get together a lot and the only common thing is that we have the same work in common, we are expats and so it is a bit like a forced kind of relationship, socially and culturally. With a lot of drinking.

In this quote the aidworker community is described as a bubble which is separate from the local community and apparently does not provide opportunities to interact with people outside this community. Thus, three further paradoxes of aidwork may be noted. First, aidwork can promise an escape from 'normal' life but appears to be highly structured and may be experienced as constraining. Second, private life may be experienced as more stressful than challenging, traumatic and dangerous experiences in the field. Third, despite the interest in foreign cultures with respect to social life in the interviews with international aidworkers, the emphasis lies on the interaction with other expatriates.[5]

Sex, romance, relationships

This characterization of aid organizations as 'total institutions' also shaped sexual and romantic relationships which affected the cooperation of team members. Close personal relationships could result in good communication and trust between these two team members and thus made it easier to accomplish tasks. However, while both team and couple could benefit from such a relationship, other team members could feel excluded and even undermined if the couple were in a leadership position and excluded the others from the decision-making processes. Work itself could also put a strain on the relationship. Respondents gave priority to work and therefore ended relationships if they felt that their work suffered or that it was too stressful. Some aid organizations adopted rules that did not allow romantic or intimate partnerships among team members in order to prevent such relationships from affecting team dynamics.

Given the high turnover of staff and the fact that many people working in aid are either single or separated from their partners, to some extent Aidland is characterized by a 'hook-up culture', a subculture characterized by uncommitted sex which so far has been primarily investigated in the college context (Heldman and Wade 2010; Garcia et al. 2012). Several respondents remarked that it was easy to find romantic and sexual partners, but that relationships usually would not last. That 'everybody was sleeping with everybody' did not mean that they were engaging in orgies; rather 'that you fall in love so quickly and then you fall out of love just as quickly', as one respondent put it. In particular in working and living conditions characterized by intensity and stress as well as boredom, sexual encounters could provide a stress valve and a distraction, whereas long-term relationships suffered. Especially in settings which were characterized by short-term contracts and a high turnover, relationships were seen as superficial, since nobody knew how long they would stay and there was little investment in relationships. Time was considered too short for the compromises necessary for a committed relationship. Given the high mobility of people working in aid, it was also easy to omit information about a partner. An Australian woman explained that she was 'suspicious of relationships in the field' because people on missions would 'reinvent themselves' after failed relationships or would lie about their relationship status.

Although it could be difficult to establish a long-term relationship, respondents noted that it was easy to have sex and that Aidland also provided opportunities for passionate relationships. A number of aspects contribute to these opportunities: the emotional challenges of aidwork, the fact that many aidworkers are single (or apart from their partners) and often young, the close communal lifestyle and isolation from the outside world and local communities. Sexual and romantic opportunities play a central role in aid-worker memoirs (Olson 1999), perhaps most prominently in the title *Emergency Sex and Other Desperate Measures* (Cain et al. 2004). It is also reflected in the scholarly literature, for example, in the term 'sexpatriates' (Verma 2007). Different types of sexual relationships with locals, including temporary marriages and prostitution, are documented (Rajak and Stirrat 2011; de Graaf et al. 1998). This conduct within the expat community was criticized by respondents who observed 'a lot of prostitution' and noted that 'the line between prostitute and not prostitute' could be very thin given the significant inequality between international aid workers and the local population. Intimate relationships could be formed among international aidworkers, with military forces or locals (Charles 2007). In relationships between local men (in particular when they are staff members) and international women, the latter have more power, authority and relationships (Fluri 2011, p. 529). Relationships often ended when one of the partners moved to the next assignment, and it was difficult, though not impossible, for couples to find assignments in the same site, though not necessarily for the same organization.

Although maintaining a relationship while being involved in humanitarian aid was difficult, it was not impossible. Several male as well as female respondents described that they had met their partners or spouses on an assignment. This often involved people from different nationalities which – unless both partners were citizens of EU countries – made it difficult to obtain work permits in the partner's country of origin. Several of the bi-national couples therefore married quickly in order to be able to live together, making it possible for both partners to obtain visas and work permits. Aidland thus speeded up the creation of romantic, sexual and marital relations, but the strain of frequent travelling and the lack of work–life balance and privacy could also undermine relationships and lead to divorce. Based on a qualitative study, Verma (2007) reports a divorce rate of 70 per cent among aidworkers in Madagascar. However, divorce rates are also above average for those working in helping professions, especially in health-related professions, in particular for lower-paid, female-dominated occupations with direct client contact (Balch et al. 2009; McCoy and Aamodt 2010). Thus, while it is easy to find sexual partners, it is difficult to find and maintain families and relationships. A North American woman described the following pattern:

> So usually, what happens is (a) you never get married, I didn't get married until I was 45, 46, 45, and I have no children. I think that was related to my work, lifestyle. And so usually what happens is that you either do it for a period of time and then you go back and take desk office kind of jobs, or it means that the husband will, you know, continue doing this work, but at a cost, I think of the family. I mean I don't know what the divorce and separation rates are among aidworkers, but I would probably say they are pretty high. But yes, it certainly is very hard, I mean you can't just. ... I mean just dealing with this myself.

She described that she had hardly seen her husband during the preceding year due to the fact that whenever she left for an assignment he had just returned, and vice versa. Of course LAT is not restricted to Aidland but is not untypical for dual-career couples and is an increasingly accepted and prevalent type of relationship (Roseneil 2006; Duncan and Phillips 2010) often preferred to family migration (van der Klis 2008).

The interviews also indicate that Aidland is a heteronormative environment. Homosexuality was rarely addressed in the interviews. While Northern aid organizations embrace diversity policies and gays and lesbians may have come to Aidland in order to carry out HIV-related work, they may not be openly gay due to anti-gay legislation and culture around the world (Mizzi 2013). Becoming motivated to be involved in aidwork due to one's sexual orientation, but not being openly gay because one would put oneself and the organization at risk, thus constitutes another paradox of aidwork. A closeted gay respondent was exposed to homophobic remarks by national staff as well as American evangelists. Experiencing a highly traumatic event, this respondent found it impossible to reach out for help, as this may have involved disclosing his sexual orientation. Given the dense networks within the aid community, even if he was in his home country he carefully guarded himself in order to avoid jeopardizing his future work opportunities.

In addition, several respondents commented on the fact that the expat community was characterized by a culture of partying and drinking. In this sense, the expat community might be compared to Mafessoli's (1996) notion of a 'neo-tribe'. Some respondents resented this subculture. A European woman in her thirties remarked:

> What I don't like about being abroad is, I am sick of, it is all one generation, even if people are married, it is like one big singles party and everybody is drinking all the time, you don't see grandparents, of course hundreds, but not international, and you don't see children, it's all one big Friday night in the pub kind of session. Every single day, and I find that tedious. And you are all doing the same kinds of work. There is no one who is going to talk about fashion or in banking or anything, they are all there for the same reason. So I find that all rather boring.

This quote illustrates the strong division between the expatriate scene and the local population which results in the invisibility of nationals ('you don't see grandparents', 'you don't see children'). Working overseas also meant missing significant family events such as weddings or funerals of friends and relatives. The lack of separation between work and life in Aidland may thus be contrasted with a separation from friends and family, including from those in the home country as well as from those whom one has met during a previous mission. How is this experienced and how can the experience of living in Aidland be communicated to their friends and family at home?

Separate spheres?

While living and working in Aidland is very attractive, frequent and unavoidable separations can be painful. There is a tension between the attraction to foreign countries and a desire to spend time with friends and family at home. Especially when someone has been assigned to a mission at short notice, the days of getting ready to take up the assignment are filled with obtaining necessary permits and equipment, and there is little time to reflect and anticipate the consequences of accepting the job offer. A European woman recalled:

> On my way to [country in Middle East], you are rushing, you are getting everything organized, you are sitting on a plane, you are watching a film, as the film was finishing and you get the end credits afterwards, I suddenly realized where I was going and what I was doing and it was only in that aeroplane that I thought 'Oh, my goodness, what I am going that way towards the sun when all the people I care about are this way, my family, my friends, my new little flat, that I need to decorate. Why on earth am I again having to upheave myself, take myself away, I am going to have to make new friends, I have to earn the respect of everyone, I am going to have to battle with all the problems there.' It just seemed particularly hard on me. I did not know why I had done it.

Respondents found it to be a major challenge to maintain contact and hold relationships together. However, although maintaining friendships and other relationships is difficult, it is not impossible, and some respondents even reported that their relationships with friends and family had intensified since they had entered Aidland. Distance can strengthen as well as undermine relationships which are based on common interests and may be weakened if there are fewer opportunities for mutually beneficial exchange (Willmott 1987). However, distancing may also be employed as a strategy of boundary-setting which contributes to maintaining relationships (Hess 2002). Some respondents spoke of difficult relationships with their parents and found it helpful to create some distance and to reconnect. 'Relationships with the family might get easier through the international work because one is going away', in particular when the relationship with parents is 'difficult', which some thought was typical for many aidworkers because it provided an opportunity to avoid difficult relationships. Overall, respondents felt that their relationship with friends and family became stronger since they had entered Aidland. Several respondents emphasized that they were rooted in close-knit families and some came from families with extensive experience of travelling and living overseas and distance hardly mattered, although here there were some class and regional differences. While middle-class respondents from the Global North either emphasized their close or their problematic relationships to parents and other family members, working-class and immigrant respondents from the Global North and respondents from the Global South noted that their parents had been initially disappointed by their children's occupational choice.

Spatial distance plays a significant role with respect to family members and also in friendships. Long-distance friends and longer-term friends may be even emotionally closer than the ones who live close by and whom one sees more frequently (Adams 1998). However, while they are able to reminisce as well as update each other, they don't necessarily have the opportunity to create new memories. Such emotionally important but somewhat stagnant friendships may be considered 'latent friendships' (Shea et al. 1988). One of the European respondents who found it easy to reconnect with old friends at home described her circle of friends as a 'frozen thing'.

> Actually, I nearly see them more often than they see each other, it is like without me, they don't meet anymore. So I guess it is more like a frozen thing, for me it is frozen. My time in [home country] is still with my old friends, and I am the link. While for them, they went in different directions, but I have a place. And it is very funny because if I am calling, when I am on a mission, and I call 'Hey, how is it going?' 'Well, I just came back. And I went to my mom and like straight away, they reintegrate me in their day-to-day activities. Last time I called was last week. So that's very easy.'

Respondents not only described the deliberate efforts and emotional commitments to maintain friendships with close friends from their country of origin, but also maintained relationships with friends they had met on missions. Thus friends lived all around the world. This is of course not unique to people working in aid, but it is a characteristic of today's mobile societies which are shaped by global networks maintained through web-based communication and frequent travelling.

Sharing experiences

Furthermore, respondents found it difficult to share their experiences with friends and family members who were not familiar with or exposed to poverty, conflict and suffering. This also highlighted the contrast between Aidland and 'normal life' for the respondents from the Global North. People working in aid are thus confronted with the paradoxical situation that there is a lack of opportunity for exchange and everyday interaction which represents the basis for friendships (Willmott 1987; Fehr 1996), whereas friendships are particularly important in challenging situations (Rebughini 2011). Respondents felt that it was easier for them to share challenging and traumatic experiences with other people working in aid, rather than with friends and family at home. As one respondent explained:

> You find yourself cut off from people and it is quite difficult that you have a different type of life. It is not just a different country, everything about your day-to-day experience and anxieties and concerns are so different to normal people.

Although a few respondents felt that family and friends were interested to hear about their experiences, overall there was a lot of frustration about prejudice and lack of interest in development, human rights and humanitarian issues. This experience was not unique to respondents from the Global North, but was shared by those from the Global South. Respondents noted that no one wanted to listen for more than 'five minutes' and that, as a Latin American man put it,

> People are more interested in the anecdotes, of how do we live, and what about the animals or this. It is difficult to understand or to find someone who wants to go deep and wants to know about the humanitarian issue itself.

They found it difficult to share the complexity of their experiences and emotions associated with their lives in Aidland. A European woman explained:

> I guess, people have a lot of clichés about relief. And I guess, I think I need to talk about things, like all the things that I described, about the system, but if you don't work there, you can't see them. And people have this idea that ... you are doing such a good job, and you are so good, those are irritating to be honest. ... I never really know how I should answer ... I think it is good to be proud of what we are doing, but it's wrong to think that we are needed, that's what I wanted to say. And this for me is very difficult to explain to the people and yes, I never really know how I want to answer this question.

This account highlights tensions and contradictions that are encountered in the attempt to share insights from working in aid. People working in aid frequently encounter a lack of interest and understanding, and feel uncomfortable being perceived as heroes when they have doubts about the contribution that the aid system makes to the lives of the so-called beneficiaries. The desire to talk about one's insights and practices is juxtaposed with doubts about whether critical assessments of the aid system can be conveyed to outsiders who are not familiar with Aidland. Respondents felt that outside Aidland people were bored or did not want to listen to accounts of poverty and traumatic experiences; interest was restricted to adventures and 'sexy stories'. For some, this lack of interest was hard to bear and a Latin American woman separated from her husband because he did not want to listen to what she had gone through. She explained:

> One of the most difficult things for us as humanitarian workers is that nobody wants to hear about our job. I mean they want know the sexy

stories: 'Did you see the guerrilla? How do they look like? Do you know the paramilitaries?' But it is like more of a, how do you say that? I don't know the word in English. But it is curiosity. They want to know the sexy aspects of it, but nobody wants to hear about the massacre or the corpses or the tough thing that you have to go through.

However, lack of interest in the aid world may be related to a lack of interest of life outside the aid world, as one European woman who left the aid business experienced. She recalled a situation in which she came together with representatives of various humanitarian organizations and realized that the Aidworld 'is a small microcosm, which actually turns around itself and not a lot of outside perspective'. Not surprisingly a number of respondents felt that they were living two separate lives – one overseas and one at home. One European woman perceived her work for the UN and her life at home in Western Europe as 'two different lives which do not have anything in common'. Another European woman explained that when she was at home, she only spoke about her work overseas with close friends and family members, especially those who also had experience with overseas work. Overall, she felt that people could neither understand nor relate to her experiences and had the impression that 'people are oblivious about living conditions in Africa'. She gave the following example:

> But even the positive letters that I wrote home from [African country] seemed to be negative when they got here. Like I said, 'Oh we are very happy today, because the water dispenser has come and has filled up our tank with water. And we are so happy we really can have a good wash.' Because that was the only water to wash with. And the electricity has come back on, and we hadn't had electricity for a week. And people took that as a negative thing, but it was a positive thing. So anything that seemed to me good news when I was out there, was bad news when it got here. 'Oh, poor thing hasn't had electricity for a week!' 'Oh, poor thing hasn't had enough water to even shower.' But if you are living in different conditions among people who haven't got as much as you, that is wonderful when the water came.

In particular, Western expatriates felt that their values differed a great deal from those of their friends and family in their home countries, who pursued their careers and started or raised families. With respect to the exchange with their old friends, respondents not only spoke about their overseas experiences, but also about the fact that their friends had started families, while many of the respondents were single and childless at the time of the interview. They felt it was difficult to explain to friends at home what they enjoyed about this work/life. Furthermore, they felt it was difficult to reconcile the poverty they had witnessed in the field with the materialism they experienced at home. Some aidworkers thus have difficulties fitting in back home (Bronner 2003; Stirrat 2008).

Conclusions

On the one hand, work in Aidland is stressful, demanding and challenging. On the other hand, Aidland can take place in regions with beautiful landscapes and pleasant climates, and workplaces could be close to wonderful places, or in particular for those from the Global North, it is possible to go to the beach or visit national parks over the weekend. Living and working in Aidland thus combined stressful living and working conditions, the exposure to poverty and trauma with a tourist dimension. People working in aid strongly distanced themselves from tourists and emphasized that they did this work because they wanted to 'make a difference' and sought the close contact with culture and community that tourism and other travel experiences do not offer. However, the desire to gain new skills and work in regions in which one had not previously worked shaped the decision to accept an assignment. Nevertheless, respondents distanced themselves from those whom they considered 'humanitarian tourists', referring to aidworkers who were interested in seeing different parts of the world through this kind of work, rather than putting the needs of those affected by disasters, conflict and poverty first. I interpret this criticism as an ambivalence, as many respondents from the Global North pointed out that travelling and learning about other cultures was one aspect that attracted them to this kind of work while at the same time emphasizing that they were motivated by the impact they had on other people's lives and proud of their accomplishments dealing with challenges.

Aid organizations tend to be 'greedy organizations' (Coser 1967) which are characterized by long work-days and work-weeks. This was especially the case in emergency situations but could also apply to desk officers or consultants who carried out field trips and assessments in development cooperation. Access to email, skype and satellite phones which allowed communicating across time zones lengthens the working day, starting in the early morning or ending late at night and including weekends and holidays. 'Work', which is characterized by mobility, flexibility and intensity, clearly dominated and shaped 'life'. Especially in situations in which staff and volunteers share accommodation, a separation of 'work' and 'life' or a 'work–life balance' is hardly achievable. But even outside of shared accommodation, the expat community tended to be close knit and somewhat insular. Working and living conditions shaped private relationships in the field, enabling sexual encounters to take place, while making it difficult to establish and maintain committed relationships. In the next chapter, I will address how Aidland is gendered; that is, to what extent the experiences of men and women working in aid differ.

Notes

1 See http://reliefweb.int/blogpost/what-have-humanitarians-been-reporting-over-past-decade (accessed 8 December 2014).
2 See www.alnap.org (accessed 8 December 2014).
3 See http://www.ewb.ca/ventures/admitting-failure-af-fail-forward-ff (accessed 8 December 2014).
4 For example, respondents working for secular organizations were highly critical of proselytizing, faith-based organizations.
5 The relationship between expatriate and national staff and their interaction with the local population is discussed in Chapter 6.

5 Doing gender in Aidland

> Where gender comes into [play] is career planning, career management. And that is something I was talking to a friend about who has this old ICRC guy as a mentor and he basically told her 'Well, either you are going to be a delegate, or you are going to have a life and a family.' And he was basically telling her 'How silly, how stupid you are, if you want to have a life, you should not be a delegate.' And he did not see the injustice behind having to make this choice, while he did not have to make it, because he had a wife and children and she took care of them.
>
> North American woman, thirties, married
without children, February 2013

> But if I am a woman I am not working in Iraq or wherever else, I would take care of my kids. … As a man if I had the choice and I am given the choice, I would rather prefer to work in a war context and to be able to provide for the family than to stay at home with the kids and having my wife in Iraq or wherever else. I don't know if I am a macho if I think like this, but in this case, I would not have been able and I do not think that I would have had the same kids, if I would have taken care of my kids. I think that children need much more the mother than the father to say this in a different way.
>
> European man, sixties, divorced with
grown-up children, February 2013

These quotes highlight gender and generational differences: whereas the female respondent highlights the injustice of women being asked to choose between career and family, the male respondent defends conventional gender roles of the male breadwinner and the female carer. However, both respondents highlight that aidwork leaves little space for raising a family. As the previous chapter demonstrated, aid organizations are 'greedy organizations' that have a significant impact upon aidworkers' private lives. Work and relationships, the private and the public sphere are characterized by gendered divisions of labour. Gender is an integral part of organizational processes and is expressed in expectations concerning men's and women's position and performance in organizations (Acker 1990, p. 321; Halford and Leonard 2001; Martin 2003). Development and humanitarian organizations have rarely been analysed from a gender perspective (Hyndman 1998; Dema 2008), even though gender analyses are long established in development (Porter and Sweetman 2005; Campbell and Teghtsoonian 2010) and there is a rich literature on gender and development (Jackson and Pearson 1998; Fraser and Tinker 2004; Porter and Sweetman 2005; Boserup 2007; Momsen 2008; Rai 2008), but this body of scholarship focuses primarily on those who are the recipients of aid. More recently, gender issues have been addressed in humanitarian assistance (DARA 2012; Hoare et al. 2012).

I suggest that a number of factors play a role that makes Aidland open to gender renegotiation and allows women and men working in aid to ignore and play with conventional gender expectations and to reconcile 'femininity' and 'masculinity'. Gender constitutes an important frame for organizing interaction (Ridgeway 2009). The concept of 'doing gender' (West and Zimmerman 1987), that is, accomplishing gender in interaction, has been further extended to 'doing difference', acknowledging the intersection of race, class and gender (West and Fenstermaker 1995) as well as 'undoing gender' (Deutsch 2007). Whereas *doing gender* stresses, invokes and perpetuates gender differences, *undoing gender* challenges differences between men and women, masculinities and femininities. The concepts of doing and undoing gender are useful in analysing forms and behaviour and constructions of femininities and masculinities that conform to or challenge contemporary gender ideologies (Risman 2009). Feminist movements have emphasized gender differences as well as gender equality (Ferree and McClurg Mueller 2007). I suggest that emphasizing gender differences, for example, highlighting women's nurturing role or experience as mothers, while integrating women into leadership positions, represents a form of 'redoing' gender. Factors making Aidland open to gender renegotiation include the fact that it is very heterogeneous with respect to ethnicity and nationality; it is also diverse with respect to organizations and professions, and it is characterized by a high degree of turnover and fluctuation as contracts tend to be short term. This diversity and fluidity as well as the power differences between expatriates from the Global North and nationals and internationals from the Global South contribute to an opening up of negotiations as to how gender is done and undone. This chapter addresses how gender differences are perpetuated as well as challenged in Aidland and how they intersect with other forms of inequality.

Familiar patterns

Working long hours, frequent travel and work-related entertainment or meetings which put pressure on family life are of course not unique to Aidland and characterize the experiences of other expatriates (Shortland and Cummins 2007) as well as many careers in domestic labour markets. However, a high degree of flexibility, mobility and the prevalence of short-term assignments make balancing a career with a family particularly difficult for those involved in humanitarian aid or human rights work. As the previous chapter demonstrated, working conditions in Aidland shape living conditions and relationships. Phases of high intensity alternate with times of waiting around for visa or work permits, a change in the security situation or for the availability of resources. Of course, depending on position and type of intervention, working conditions vary with respect to mobility. Development cooperation allows some expatriate staff to stay for several years in the same assignment and place and to bring their family members to the field. Staff in aid organizations working in emergency relief as well as long-term development tend to adopt an emergency work style; meaning long working hours that, due to peer pressure or tight deadlines, take over leisure time such as evenings or weekends undo the separation between 'work' and 'life' even in non-emergency situations (Hilhorst and Schmiemann 2002; Gilbert 2005). These circumstances make it difficult to start and maintain long-term committed relationships when partners have to accept being separated for shorter or longer time periods. Long work hours and high-risk situations are more compatible with a lack of family commitments. Many international aidworkers enter the field in their twenties and early thirties when they are still single or before they have children. Many of my respondents were 'expat girls' (Fechter 2007) and 'expat boys', who moved independently without a partner and children, although they had intermittent relationships. However, some of the respondents said that they were able to find missions together with their partner or that they met couples in the field. As already noted, some of the respondents had found a partner on an assignment, but did not yet have children. Some anticipated leaving Aidland in order to start a family (see Chapter 7). Depending on the security situation, national staff also lived separately from family members who resided in a different region of the country, whereas local staff could return home after the working day. Middle-aged and older respondents, who had been in the field for a longer time or who started working in aid after they had raised their children, felt that aidwork tended to be an 'adventure' for young people, who come to Aidland for a few years after finishing school and before settling down. Some respondents stated that they would like to see more aidworkers who are older and have more experience in the field.

Keeping in mind that my sample was small and therefore potentially unrepresentative, overall, the vast majority of respondents were single, although there were some noticeable regional and gender differences. Men from the Global South were more likely to be married and to have young children than women from the Global South, and men and women from the Global North were more likely to be single, divorced and without children. Some women from the Global North had become involved in aidwork after their children were already adults. In contrast, an African woman with young children who was working as a national staff member for an international aid organization and earned more than her husband was supported by her mother and her husband who looked after her children when she was working in another region of the country. Two fathers from the Global North had both married Latin American women whom they had met when they were on an assignment. Their wives followed them from assignment to assignment and looked after the children. One of these marriages ended in divorce. Apart from the fact that it might be too dangerous for the family members or too expensive for the aid organizations, a further obstacle for bringing a partner or family to a post is the unwillingness of the partner to come along. Overall – and perhaps not surprisingly – my data suggest that it is easier for men to find support from their wives and partners than for female aidworkers to find support from their male partners.

Studies of expatriates working for a range of industries indicate that female expatriates tend to be younger, single and childless, while men tend to be older, married with children and hold more senior positions (Forster 1999; Selmer and Leung 2003). In contrast to male expatriates, it would seem that women have to choose between expatriate careers and raising a family (Linehan 2001). This is echoed in the interviews with people working in aid. A European woman in her early fifties, who had met her partner during an assignment, was married and did not have children put it like this:

> Somebody once said to me, 'A woman can have three things, the three things being job, partner, children. They can't have all three.' Or rather than job I should say career, very difficult to have all three, as a woman. Men take it for granted. You can have a partner and children and still have a career, but something suffers. You may not be able to be as far with your career as you want. Certainly in this sort of life, you can't have all three. So much for equality.

Female respondents also felt that within aid organizations as well as in other labour markets gendered expectations existed which made it easier for men to interrupt a career. A North American woman in her thirties felt that men could take time off to 'backpack around the world' or go 'kite surfing in South Africa for six months' without jeopardizing their careers. In contrast, she felt that women put their career at risk if they interrupted it in order to start a family. Not surprisingly, she found this double standard unfair. She was planning and looking forward to having children, but was very worried that motherhood would have a negative impact upon her career in the humanitarian sector. Her concerns were confirmed by a European man in his sixties who expressed his conviction that it was the woman's role to raise children, quoted at the beginning of the chapter.

These two respondents quoted at the beginning of the chapter represent two different generations – a woman in her thirties and a man in his sixties – and there are certainly generational differences with respect to the gender division of labour. However, my sample did not include female breadwinners and male trailing spouses or partners who take on childcare and reproductive labour. Younger female aidworkers were confronted with a lack of support and felt that they had to choose between a career and a family. Those who chose aidwork explained that although from time to time they missed companionship they appreciated the fact that they did not have to make compromises. A European woman in her forties who was single and did not have children explained:

> And I am always afraid that I might fall in love and that I am not longer free to do what I want to do. So every now and then I miss having a partner, but I am more afraid that [a relationship] would keep me from what I really want to do.

It is very clear from her statement that she did not expect to find a partner who would support her career. Her expectation is reflected in the experience of an Australian woman in her thirties who described the reaction of her former boyfriend when she was interviewed for an overseas position which she was very keen to get.

> And I got short-listed, and I got a call at twelve a clock at night. And they said, 'Would you like to do the job interview?' And I said, 'Yes!' ... And I was really ecstatic. And I was with my then boyfriend at the time. And I said, 'This is fantastic, this is great, this is exactly what I wanted.' And he said, 'Oh, well, that's the end of us then, isn't it?' And immediately, I was going into a job interview, in which my mind was split right down the middle. ... And now I feel, that was the main reason why I didn't get the job.

She attributes the fact that she did not get the position because she felt that she had to choose between the job and her relationship, and thus felt ambivalence when she participated in the job interview. It should be noted that she took it for granted that she was asked to do the job interview in the middle of the night, the demands of the aid organization thus clearly overruling any form of work–life balance.

Male and female respondents remarked that they felt it was easier for men than for women to find a supportive partner who would follow them on an assignment. However, men also found that reconciling aidwork with starting or maintaining a family was problematic. Furthermore, my data suggest that there are not only gender differences with respect to the difficulties of beginning and maintaining relationships but also similarities. In particular, women and men from the Global North were equally likely not to have children. Men who were single and divorced found it as difficult to sustain a relationship as women. One of the men from the Global South noted that his parents were disappointed that he had not yet started a family. However, most men from the Global South were married and half of them had young children. These respondents lived separately from their wives and children because it was not possible to bring their families into crisis situations. Even when they lived together, frequent travelling meant that respondents saw their spouses and children rarely. One of the respondents recalled that his son called him 'Uncle' when he returned from a trip, which made him consider quitting aidwork. However, his wife convinced him that he should continue in his position.

Both female and male respondents felt that working in Aidland posed challenges to their relationships and families. Many of the respondents were single and did not have children, but those who had a partner spoke about the difficulties of finding assignments in the same place or being separated from partners and children. In some cases this led to separation and divorce. Despite these commonalities, there are also gender- and region-specific differences. Overall, it seemed easier for men from the Global South and men married to women from the Global South to reconcile a career in Aidland with having a family. In contrast, women felt that they were being forced to make a choice between a relationship and their career because the partner did not support them or because the organizations penalized the interruption of a career for family reasons. While some of the women stated that they were not interested in a relationship, especially if it would force them to give up aidwork, other women were anticipating ending aidwork once they found a partner or in order to find a partner and start a family (see also Fechter 2007). Many of the female respondents did not have children or had started their involvement in Aidland after their children were adults. However, the ability to reconcile having a family and a career in Aidland is not only shaped by gender and nationality, but also by the type of work (development cooperation vs. emergency relief; work in headquarters vs. work in the field) and the organization (UN organization vs. NGO; big NGO vs. small NGO) and the benefits it can offer (for example, maternity leave), which all play important roles. Moreover, the easy entry, flexibility as well as the fact that expatriate aidworkers can afford household help may contribute to gender equality (Fechter 2013). Furthermore, female national staff members of international aid organizations enjoy the support of partners and other family members due to their comparatively high incomes.

Recruitment and promotion

In some respects Aidland is similar to the other labour markets: overall, more men than women will be found in leadership positions, with some professions being dominated by one or other gender. Of course, in Aidland (as elsewhere) one may also find men in female-dominated professions (for example, male nurses), and women in male-dominated sectors (for example, security or logistics). Furthermore, Aidland may be compared to the public sector as well as to the third sector, in which one finds a higher proportion of women among volunteers, staff and in leadership positions than in the private sector. Knox Clarke (2014) found women in 40 per cent of staff and leadership positions in aid organizations, and once the proportion of women reaches 40 per cent, gender starts to matter less (Allmendinger and Hackman 1995). Paradoxically, the high proportion of women as staff and as leaders of development organizations as well as the fact that men and women take on roles which are 'inconsistent traditional gender norms' can contribute to an invisibility of gender inequalities in development organizations (Dema 2008, p. 442).

Male as well as female respondents noted efforts to recruit and promote women in aid organizations. Overall, gender was downplayed, in particular with respect to holding women back from leadership positions. Female respondents were keen to emphasize that they did not feel discriminated against on the basis of gender, and highlighted the role of nationality, job qualifications and experience, age and marital status, which in their experience mattered more. Moreover, and most importantly, region mattered. Women from the Global North benefited from (neo)colonial continuities and the 'whiteness of power' (Goudge 2003), and their daily practices and identities were shaped by multiple and contingent discourses of power (White 2006; Cook 2007; Heron 2007). Development projects, in particular those focusing on gender, represent career opportunities for feminists from the Global North (Syed and Ali 2011), who represent 'masculine patriarchs' (Dogra 2011) compared to women from the Global South who are the intended beneficiaries of empowerment projects. The similarity between men and women from highly developed countries who participate in the same activities and are taking on masculine roles emphasizes the distance between international and national women working in development. Although asymmetrical gender relations play a role in Aidland as in other contexts, 'it would be ethnocentric, if not racist, to assume that gender is always and everywhere the primary basis of oppression, persecution or exclusion' (Hyndman 2004, p. 309). Not surprisingly, women from the Global South felt that they were not disadvantaged as women but as national or non-white staff.

Male respondents – both from the Global North and from the Global South – stressed their good working relationships with women and, in contrast to the female respondents, tended to emphasize gender differences. They gave various examples of why hiring women was important to guarantee the success of a programme. For example, the presence of female staff members made access to the female population easier, and in some cases impossible without them, for example, in the context of health provision. This was particularly so in communities that were characterized by a separation between the sexes. A male national staff member who worked for an international NGO in Asia described the advantage of integrating female staff into the programme:

> It was very difficult in the early days ... male members were not able to deal properly with ... issues related to health and hygiene, water and sanitation as women's issues. So this is where the lead role was taken by female staff. But then gradually we also moved into that role. I mean

> going with them and learning from them ... having a female colleague at your side, how she talks and tries to understand the issues which are related to women. It helped me a lot basically to understand from that perspective and engage with the conflict.

In this case, highlighting gender differences and the acknowledgement of the need to understand women's perspectives and experiences contributes to integrating men into women's fields of access and expertise. The cooperation between male and female staff described in this account thus contributes to overcoming a gendered division of labour. This is an account of an undoing of gender insofar as the acknowledgement of gender differences leads to more gender equality by integrating men into a women's sector. Furthermore, expatriate men gave examples of hiring national women in positions overseeing national men because they were best qualified for the job. One European man in his sixties who had worked for various organizations in a variety of post-conflict situations for several decades explained that he had hired a woman for a senior security position because she could access information through her male relatives and thus was able to provide crucial information.

> I had to compromise on a lot of things, including my own [male] guards, accusing me, I don't know what, pushing them to have a woman on top of them or whatever. I said, 'No, this is not the point, do you have the information that she has? I am going for the information, and this information has to come from wherever.'

He thus emphasized that he was keen to hire the best person for the job. Gender played a central role in his decision-making process. It seems ironic that she was hired due to having the requisite male relative and assuming that as a mother she was more interested in peace for her children than a man. Furthermore, he was convinced that if she was able to take care of her children she could also take care of the project staff. This respondent was keenly aware of gender differences and contributed to challenging and undoing gender norms by putting a woman into a senior position over male national staff in a typically male-dominated field: security and society (Afghanistan).[1] He was thus un- and redoing gender. At the same time, he also asserted his power over the male national staff and disregarded the cultural context.

Throughout the interviews, male respondents emphasized that women were well integrated into aid organizations. However, men were more likely to address gender differences than were female respondents, highlighting that these differences had advantages for the work of the team. Overall, female respondents tended to downplay gender differences between expatriates. A woman who was working for the UN expressed her ambivalence about being young, female and 'looking innocent'. However, it could be useful:

> because one is not seen as a threat, at the same time I found it difficult because it was always the boys that were taken more seriously. And you

are labelled as a secretary rather than as a political affairs officer or a media affairs officer.

She thus describes ambivalence at feeling stereotyped. Furthermore, although she had a supportive line manager, she believed that it took her longer to establish herself than 'the average person', i.e. a male colleague. Eyben (2007) recalls that in the early 1970s due to her status as wife she had no chance to find work as a development professional despite the fact that she was a trained anthropologist. This changed in the late 1970s when she started to work for various UN agencies and became a women-in-development specialist. Those who first entered male-dominated fields had to prove themselves in a macho development culture and often sacrificed partnerships and plans for a family for their career. The under-representation of women in leadership positions may lead to competitive behaviour traditionally associated with a male leadership style. Thus, they may not support female colleagues but compete with or distance themselves from other women in a way comparable to other male-dominated sectors (Rhoton 2011).

Women from the Global South were aware of the fact that aid organizations sought to employ or offer scholarships to women from low(er) income countries. My data suggest that there was a widespread perception among male and female respondents that women were not disadvantaged, were perhaps even advantaged, as aid organizations sought to increase the proportion of women among staff. However, they also felt that gender was not the only aspect that played a role in hiring decisions. When I asked an African woman in her twenties what role gender played in her work, she answered:

> Okay, now you speak like a UN [agency], because that is what they say, when you apply for a job. 'Woman are encouraged', and everyone is assuming that women are weak and maybe sometimes, you know, they might be different in how they would contribute to humanitarian assistance sphere than men. But I would say, in a way, me, like, me I am not only a woman, I am a [African] who is from the Diaspora.

Her reaction demonstrates very clearly that gender in Aidland needs to be approached from an intersectional perspective. This means that how gender intersects with other systems of privilege and disadvantage needs to be taken into consideration. Not only nationality, but age, marital status, religion and education matter. Women from the Global South did not feel disadvantaged compared to men from the Global South, but compared to international aidworkers from the Global North. An African woman in her thirties felt that she had to work more and harder than 'European women to prove that I am as capable and competitive as you guys, you know'. Another African woman who had worked for several years on short-term contracts as a translator for a UN agency in the Middle East said that she felt disadvantaged. In addition to gender, nationality and ethnicity were central for hiring decisions.

Overall, with respect to discrimination experiences gender was downplayed by women, whereas men highlighted gender as a reason to hire or promote women by men. Women from the Global South felt ignored, overlooked and disadvantaged, not due to gender but due to their nationality, race and ethnicity. Furthermore, age and marital status mattered. This also informed work and leadership experiences, to which I now turn.

Gender-specific leadership and work styles

Respondents characterized Aidland to some extent as 'macho' but distinguished between different types of organizations and forms of intervention. Perhaps not surprisingly, the military was characterized as macho. Although peacekeeping troops and other military forces are not usually considered as aid organizations, troops and people working in aid had various encounters: in briefing meetings, but also in the context of troops providing security or in the context of transport and logistics. Furthermore, military staff and people working in aid socialized in expatriate spaces. In addition, some respondents contrasted UN agencies which were considered 'macho' with non-governmental organizations.

'Macho' had a number of meanings and usually referred to taking on a dominant position, and was contrasted with a more team-oriented, communicative style of interaction. Development was considered 'less macho', as more emphasis was put on communicating and collaborating with so-called beneficiaries, whereas relief was described as 'more macho', since expatriates were in charge of projects with less consultation of national staff and local communities. Human rights was also characterized as 'macho-dominated culture' regardless of being a female-dominated field (see also Hopgood 2006). In post-conflict situations 'hard' masculinized interventions such as policy and advocacy work and humanitarian relief which are more visible, valued and rewarded may be contrasted with 'soft' feminized interventions (social and cultural rather than technical, longer-term development rather than short-term relief) which are less visible, attract less money and are not valued as highly (Williams 2004, p. 321). Respondents distinguished two different types of Western expatriate aidworkers: the 'cowboys' and 'ex-military types', and the 'liberal development workers'. Despite the ongoing professionalization processes, 'humanitarian cowboys' were still there, 'throwing bags of rice around and jumping into this and jumping into that'. Such 'cowboys' could be very useful in the early phases of a crisis. They were charismatic figures who had a track record of 'getting things done' and were thus able to raise funds based on this reputation, but were not necessarily good team members, and their ability to contribute to the transition from emergency to recovery and capacity building was seen as more limited.

Men as well as women spoke about performing 'macho' or 'masculine' behaviour as needed and appreciating 'feminine' behaviour such as mentoring, good communication and team-building skills. Such 'feminine' skills – performed both by men and women – put emphasis on listening and understanding colleagues, and being respectful and attentive to local culture and good at negotiating. In contrast, engaging in reckless behaviour which put oneself and others at risk was another meaning of 'macho' behaviour. An Australian woman recalled the event of an international aidworker who had provoked a local guard by violating the curfew when he was on a date with a local woman. Rather than threatening the international aidworker, the guard shot and killed the national woman. However, women also jeopardized themselves, their colleagues or their hosts through careless behaviour. For example, a European woman admitted that she had put herself and her team at risk when she insisted on driving a car herself rather than letting a national staff member drive. On the other hand, a male respondent emphasized that keeping his team secure was based on communication with multiple stakeholders. However, even if men and women were consciously undoing and redoing gender, they were nevertheless confronted with gender stereotypes and were evaluated differently for the same behaviour. A North American woman in her thirties said:

> But I think women are judged much more. And women as soon as you scream, you are 'hysterical', but the guys would scream and they are 'manly'. And I think a lot of the women, also who I know would be much better managers than the men and therefore have less security incidents, less highs and lows and whatever and less emergencies and just can manage things just better in general. But that actually works against us because this very macho environment where you have, I suppose, bragging rights. Like if you have been in ten security incidents you are a better humanitarian than if you have been in none.

Thus, the experience and avoidance of security incidents appears to be gendered insofar as an emphasis on information gathering, communication and good respectful relations with the local population is seen as typical for female leaders. Male and female respondents felt that women had a different leadership style to men which was described as nurturing, mentoring and non-confrontational. They highlighted that women were more attentive than men to the needs of national and international staff, and invested more time in team building. Several male respondents emphasized how much they had learned from the communicative skills of female colleagues and bosses, and said that they had spent a considerable amount of time listening and learning. They admired and had learned from women who were perceptive about the views and expectations of various stakeholders and were able to negotiate with different groups. A young Latin American man, who did an internship with a UN agency, described one of his female bosses as 'one of the best bosses I ever had'.

> She was very, very intelligent and also sensitive with people and maybe, I think it was, so I think maybe she thought, the qualifications, they are

> there, he has the degrees he needs for that. But maybe she felt that I was sensitive for humanitarian things and we had a good chemistry, when we had like a talk like this. And she was also very close to like, she had this capacity of being very close to the people. ... I think this is it, I don't know, but I think, she felt she could teach me, what I needed, what I did not have could be learned. But what was needed were the things that cannot be learned, that you cannot teach. But that was there, and she could hold my hand and work very closely and I could learn what I had to learn.

It is clear from his account that he was full of awe and admiration for his manager, using metaphors that described the relationship as intimate, affectionate and emotional. He explained that his boss gave him a chance although he had little experience in the field. What he brought were academic credentials, good recommendations and a 'sensitivity' which was compatible with his boss who taught and nurtured him. He admired her intelligence and empathy and was eager to learn and be taught by her. Several respondents commented that the nurturing leadership style and ability to build relationships was particularly effective in conflict situations and appropriate in the collaboration with national staff. Both men and women emphasized that good leadership qualities involved integrating masculine as well as feminine behaviour. Femininity was associated with listening, taking care of others and negotiating, whereas masculinity was associated with confident and assertive behaviour, being in power and being able to make decisions.[2]

Thus, different work styles were identified, even though they could potentially be performed by both men and women. Overall, however, women were described as working harder and being more dedicated than men, who were more likely to be 'distracted' (a euphemism for having sexual relationships while on assignment) or to focus on their job without consideration of the team. A European woman who had worked for different NGOs and international organizations in different post-conflict situations described men's and women's attitudes to team work as different:

> I think, largely speaking, women are failing when they can't make the team work, whereas I feel that men, if the team is not working, it does not matter because as long as they can do their piece of work, it's okay. ... I definitely got the feeling in meetings that it was always the women trying to make things work.

While women were described as perceptive, communicative and team building, men were described as task oriented and more focused on individual achievements than on the success of the team.

Similar to hiring and recruitment discussed above, male respondents tended to emphasize gender differences, whereas women in general tended to downplay the role of gender with respect to carrying out the work. However, due to the different positions which expatriate and national women held, there were some differences in the way they discussed inequality. White, expatriate women from the Global North described situations in which they were in leadership positions of national as well as international staff. As described in the previous chapter, it was relatively easy to be quickly promoted to leadership positions. Young female respondents said that being the boss of expatriate as well as of national staff was stressful. However, the sources of stress varied with respect to supervising national or international staff. In the case of being in a supervisory role over national staff, the stress could result from the fact that a young expatriate woman felt that she was less qualified than (older) national staff (see Chapter 6). Internal team dynamics and expectations from the team leaders could be more stressful than a potentially dangerous situation, as a North American woman, who was quickly promoted to a leadership position, explained:

> You are like a psychologist all the time and that's draining. And that's the point when the technical work gets to be super-easy. 'Yeah, I can deal with rebels' we are woken up in the middle of the night because the rebel leader comes with nine armed guys, and I am in my pyjamas and he asks me to use my phone and I have to tell him 'No, because I can't give rebels access to my communication.' And that was super-easy and I would get everything I needed and access on the ground and negotiate anything.

Gender dynamics are clearly at work in this account with respect to her management of expatriate staff who – she felt – simultaneously expected and resented a nurturing leadership style, and she felt that her colleagues expected her to play a mothering role or serve as a psychologist. She found such expectations from other expatriates much more stressful than encountering rebels. She described how her nurturing leadership style within the organization was complemented with assertive behaviour towards rebel leaders. Thus, in contrast to the 'Rambo-litigators' in a male-dominated job and 'mothering paralegals' in a feminized organization discussed by Pierce (1995), she reconciled assertive and nurturing emotion work in her role. As noted above, humanitarian culture has been described as macho and this macho behaviour was performed by men as well as women. This is also addressed by a European woman who worked as a logistics coordinator for an international NGO in Africa. She felt respected by drivers, mechanics and other male national staff because of her understanding and respect for the local culture and her supportive leadership style with national staff. However, she described that when she felt that her authority was not respected she switched to what she called 'male ex-pat behaviour' which she described as a change to masculine body language and projecting toughness rather than empathy and caring.

> If I see that the balance is being changed then straight away I would take a cigarette [indicating changes in body language], and then, and then it is completely changing and it's like, 'Okay, if you don't know the limit, it is like now we are playing it different, and I just become an ex-pat.' And even kind of a male ex-pat.

In addition to drawing on her competence as a logistician and her empathy for national staff, this respondent employed a masculine style in order to assert her position. This is a good example of how gender, nationality and power interact. In this case, nationality (as Western expatriate) trumps gender and allows this female international respondent to maintain authority over the male national staff. She and her team know that she holds the leadership position and thus can make decisions affecting national team members. If needed, she mimicked masculinity, but felt that she gained the respect of her team through her respect for the local culture and concern for the wellbeing of her team. In her experience, local staff and beneficiaries see female expatriates not as women, but, as one of the respondents put it, expatriate women 'they are just seen as third sex'. Women from the Global North thus found themselves in positions of power and authority over national male staff (Fluri 2009; 2011). It was not just Western expatriates but also national female aidworkers who were working for international aid organizations who mimicked masculinity in order to gain respect from male colleagues. An African woman in her thirties explained:

> I tend to have very different characters. I adapt myself according to the situation, so sometimes I need to be a man, you see ... for example, the way I walk ... so I walk like a soldier ... sometimes when you are leading a programme, okay, you have to be playing your role, so now, this is when you have to be playing the man's role.

Gender is thus fluid and redone depending on the demands of the situation. Overall, women from the Global North as well as from the Global South emphasized that they were respected by male team members and, if they felt that their leadership roles were challenged, they mimicked masculinity. They also gained respect for looking after their teams, which entailed displaying more conventionally feminine roles.

Gender and culture

It was remarkable that international aidworkers when asked what role gender played in Aidland usually gave examples that concerned 'locals', male or female national staff, beneficiaries, local counterparts or the general population. Although gender differences with respect to career planning and leadership styles were noted, overall gender differences among expatriates were rarely addressed. An emphasis on gender equality is therefore presented as a characteristic of advanced Westerners, whereas 'local traditions' result in gender differences, privileging men and disadvantaging women. The 'local woman' is constructed as a victim who needs to be empowered and rescued (cf. Dogra 2011). International women from the Global North pointed out that they were respected by male national staff and that they could assert themselves when working with local men who were subordinate to them.

In these accounts a number of things were going on. On the one hand, international men and women presented themselves as more sophisticated and more attuned to gender equality than local men and women who were constructed as more backward and constrained by local traditions and religion which confined women to the private sphere and excluded them from education, the public sphere and decision-making. While women were seen as the victims of backwardness, men were the perpetrators or beneficiaries of outdated beliefs in gender differences. International men could then demonstrate their openness to gender equality by promoting local women and putting them into a leadership position above a male local staff member.

On the other hand, international men and women pointed out that it was important to respect local culture and the local gender order. Again, this was focused primarily on women. The emphasis was on the behaviour of Western women to respect the local mores, for example, with respect to clothing, in general not wearing revealing clothing which is either tight or low-cut, and covering their arms, legs and perhaps also their heads (cf. Cook 2005). In contrast, it was rarely addressed that men should respect the local culture, although a few male respondents spoke about showing respect to older men. Several female respondents also pointed out that when they were in leadership positions they deferred to local men who were subordinate to them, in order to demonstrate respect to a culture in which women defer to men. Thus the respect for local culture is inextricably intertwined with gender.

An intersectional perspective enables us to see that gender can present the foreground or background to the relations between national and international staff. When women defer to men's authority citing cultural reasons, gender is at the forefront. Ethnic and national differences can also replace a conventional division of labour and help national and international women assert leadership. This can mean that gender becomes less salient, even to the extent of disappearing in a 'third sex', whereas country of origin and the privilege associated with whiteness, European, Northern or Western origin matter more.

Conclusions

Scholars of gender generally assume that in interactions and power relations gender is most salient, but this does not seem to be the case in Aidland. Respondents were highly reflexive about how they employed gender in order to signify power. Thus gender is separate from biological sex when a female international aidworker describes how she assumes male expat behaviour in order to gain respect from male national staff. A number of factors come into play to make Aidland open to gender renegotiation: power differences between international and national staff, heterogeneity with respect to organizations and professions, a high degree of turnover and fluctuation. These factors allow men and women working in aid to ignore and play with conventional gender expectations, and to reconcile 'femininity' and 'masculinity'. Gender relations in Aidland shed light on power as lived experience and how gender gets 'done' under exceptional circumstances.

Aidwork seems to challenge as well as perpetuate the gendered division of labour. Aidland and aid organizations are gendered organizations in which men still hold the majority of leadership positions, and male- and female-dominated fields can be distinguished. However, the proportion of women in leadership positions appears to be higher than in the private sector. Thus, Aidland offers opportunities to negotiate gender relations, stretching and bending gender. For women this can mean taking on leadership roles at the field, regional and head office level, overseeing budgets and operations. Several UN agencies and non-governmental organizations are now led by women (see Chapter 1). It also means that women are working in conflict zones and other areas of high risk. Aidland also offers men opportunities to engage in caring and skills-building activities with vulnerable populations, and thus in activities that are often labelled feminine, although given the context of a high-risk environment, engaging in such activities does not undermine masculinities. It is thus a space in which gender can be un- and redone, allowing men and women more scope to reconcile 'masculine' (assertive, risk-taking) and 'feminine' (caring, communicative) behaviour. Aidwork thus offers opportunities to men and women to engage in a wide range of activities and escape narrow understandings of masculinity and femininity challenging stereotypical notions of 'men's' and 'women's' work.

Aidland and aid organizations thus provide an interesting context for studying un/doing gender for a number of reasons. First, aidwork appears to be quite open to newcomers of both sexes who enter the field as volunteers, on secondments or as consultants. Volunteer positions can turn into staff positions once field experience has been gained. While aidwork comprises a wide range of occupations, field experience plays a crucial role in hiring practices although aidworkers are highly educated and use time in between assignments for further education and training (Roth 2012). Second, due to unforeseeable circumstances and the distance to head and regional offices, work in field offices requires flexibility and independence. Due to frequent and unplanned staff turnover, this also means that it is easier to move into positions of responsibility than in other labour markets, although international staff have significantly better chances of assuming a leadership position than national staff. Women as well as men benefit from such opportunities of quick promotion. It may be easier for women to assert leadership positions in aid organizations than in other labour markets. Third, and closely related to the last point, with respect to recruitment, class and nationality appear to be far more important than gender, though staying in aidwork appears to affect male and female life-courses differently. While women may have more opportunities to gain leadership positions in aid organizations, the consequences of pursuing a career in aidwork are still gendered, making it more difficult for women than for men to sustain an aidworker career with raising a family and maintaining a relationship. Not only gender, however, but region of origin mattered with respect to marital and parental status. An analysis of the gendered division of labour within aid organizations requires an intersectional perspective and needs to take the relationship between expatriate and national staff into consideration, which is the focus of the next chapter.

Notes

1 Nevertheless, he also appropriated her knowledge when he presented it at interorganizational meetings without identifying his source because this would have compromised her security.
2 Hyndman (1998), who characterizes the UN discourse as 'implicitly and explicitly gendered', points out that UNHCR's gender policy is contradictory because on the one hand it essentializes and prioritizes gender differences by casting women as 'vulnerable', while on the other hand it pursues 'mainstreaming and integration', and considers women as equal partners (Hyndman 1998, p. 248).

6 Othering and otherness

> Frankly speaking, for the organization I am working for, [faith-based NGO], we are doing our best to make sure that there are good working relationships between the two groups. But I can tell you, the relationships are not that good.
>
> African man, expatriate, large INGO, June 2005

> The UN – sometimes you feel that it is not a fair community, you know. In terms of the way they treat the national versus the international. So we do the work, we know the country, we have the networks, we have the communication, we do everything and we get paid less.
>
> African woman, national staff, UN agency, June 2006

> I'm below the executive secretary, I don't want that, I would prefer to be further down [the organizational hierarchy], but it does not matter what I want. ... This means that I have very, very much power. ... Sometimes it is good to have power and say 'This is how we are going to do this' and by now I do this sometimes, but I don't think that it is good for the sustainability of the organizations if an outsider has so much power.
>
> European woman, expatriate staff, African NGO/European donor, 2006

International aidworkers who represent about 10 per cent of the aidworker population constitute an interface (Long 2001) between the rich(er) countries of the Global North and the poor(er) countries of the Global South. This chapter addresses how aid encounters reflect and perpetuate North–South relationships at the micro level, how national and international staff experienced working together and how they perceived each other. Although national staff and expatriate staff come from all regions of the world, leadership positions are still predominantly held by Europeans and North Americans (Knox Clarke 2014). The terms 'expatriates', 'local staff' and 'beneficiaries' are racialized terms which are rarely questioned and which signify the unequal relationships between international and national staff members, beneficiaries and local population (Crewe and Fernando 2006). Different forms of knowledge and how they are evaluated play a central role in these encounters. This chapter addresses how otherness and sameness, insiders and outsiders are constructed with respect to race, ethnicity and nationality. What role do ethnic background and skin colour play? What does it mean to be a Bangladeshi woman in East Africa? A North–South dichotomy on aid relations would be simplistic, naïve and problematic. In order to capture privilege and power within aid relationships, not just region of origin, but ethnicity, class, gender and age, also need to be taken into consideration. Relationships in aid organizations need to be analysed from an intersectional perspective.

Of course, intercultural communication is central to living and working in Aidland.[1] How long one stays on an assignment shapes relationships with other internationals, nationals and locals. It also influences how much time there is to learn about local conditions or to apply knowledge acquired in other contexts. International aid involves crossing borders to provide short-term relief or to engage in long-term processes. The desire to travel and to experience different cultures is one aspect that attracts people from the Global North to Aidland. A whole range of different encounters may be distinguished – between internationals from different countries and regions, between international and national staff in programme and in support positions. Furthermore, volunteers and staff of aid organizations interact with beneficiaries, household aids[2] and the local population. These interactions are central to aidwork and its previously discussed characteristics which include the desire to pursue meaningful work that 'makes a difference', opportunities for personal growth, the perceived exceptionality of aidwork and stressful encounters within teams.

Hierarchies, respect and capacity building

The opening quotes to this chapter reflect that national and international staff are acutely aware of inequalities within aid organizations. The complexity of social interactions and unequal aid relationships has been addressed in development literature (Crewe and Harrison 1998; Grammig 2002; Lewis and Mosse 2006) but have so far found less attention in humanitarian studies. Of course, distinctions between 'nationals' and 'internationals', 'Global North' and 'Global South' are overly simplistic. Slim (1995, p. 168) distinguishes between three categories of humanitarian practitioners: first, the 'international relief elite' which comprise 'the civil servants and employees of the government, UN and NGO organizations who dominate the relief and development business and form the humanitarian establishment' and come from the Global North and to a lesser extent from the Global South. Second, local staff of international aid organizations who are involved in running the programmes and are 'intermediaries between the host population and the foreign development workers who control communication and usually produce what is expected of them'. Presumably, this 'compradore class'[3] shares the worldview of the donors, but not the experience of the poorer members of the population (Rajak and Stirrat 2011; Eyben 2011). Third, there are the 'founders of members of national NGOs or community-based organizations' or 'local NGOs', who may eventually assume government positions (Slim 1995; Yarrow 2008). Of course, aidworkers from the Global North who work as volunteers or staff in national NGOs or community organizations are subordinates and report to local staff. It is thus important to consider the origin of the aidworker, her class background, the type of organization she is working for as well as her contract or position within that organization. A respondent from a less developed country working for a UN agency may earn a higher income and have more power than a respondent from a post-industrial society working as a volunteer for a local NGO (Shutt 2012). Nevertheless, as long as development policies and decisions about donations are made in the richer post-industrial countries of the Global North and those from less developed countries are underrepresented in leadership positions of international aid organizations, the crude distinction between 'North' and 'South' may serve as a signpost of differences. However, the emergence of 'new' or non-DAC donors (Grimm and Harmer 2005; Grimm et al. 2009; Six 2009; Binder et al. 2010) may change the relationship between international and local staff, donors and beneficiaries. In order to address power differentials within humanitarian communities, the de-Westernizing of humanitarian aid through an increased and more visible involvement by non-Western aid agencies is needed (Hilhorst 2005, p. 362). Some international agencies have taken steps to internationalize; for example, Action Aid International moved its Head Office from London to Johannesburg in 2003 in order to express its commitment to overcoming the North–South divide. In 2014, Oxfam International decided to move its headquarters and split them between Nairobi and Bangkok. Furthermore, at the assembly marking MSFs fortieth birthday, four new sections – MSF-Brazil, MSF-East Africa, MSF-Latin America, MSF-South Africa – were approved. Although the MSF movement is still dominated by sections based in Europe and other high-income countries, this development marked an awareness of a need to become truly international and global (Fox 2014). Some NGOs employ expatriates only as volunteers or only if qualified nationals cannot be found (International Health Exchange and People in Aid 1997; Crewe and Harrison 1998; Owen 2010). International agencies have also started to replace expatriate staff with local staff, thus giving positions to local staff which had previously been reserved for expatriates (Crewe and Harrison 1998; Owen 2010).

Currently, international staff are still overrepresented in leadership positions and are likely to be higher paid. Expatriates tend to earn on average four times as much as local workers, despite equal levels of education and job experience (Carr et al. 2010, p. 330).[4] Such pay differences have significant consequences, as higher salaries indicate ability and worth, while receiving a lower salary can result in a sense of injustice which leads to demotivation, mobility and, therefore, higher staff turnover (Carr 2000; Carr et al. 2010), and may result in 'disappointment and resentment' (Arvidson 2009, p. 228). In order to achieve commitment and motivation, donors and NGOs have to invest in national staff in order to ensure that fieldworkers do not feel 'underpaid, undervalued, overworked and underappreciated' (Ahmad 2007, p. 349). A further problem is that the high turnover of international staff may require national staff to get to know or even train new international team members on a regular basis without having the opportunity of being promoted into leadership positions themselves (cf. Shevchenko and Fox 2008). However, national staff appreciated the fact that international aid organizations paid better than local employers and, even though they resented pay and power differentials, they made use of the opportunities the aid system provided. Furthermore, respondents realized that Western expatriates provided crucial links for the mobilization of resources that benefited both national and international staff. Overall, respondents were keen to assert that relations were good, but a whole range of tensions and problems were mentioned. In particular, it was noted as problematic when international staff managed higher-skilled but lower-paid national staff.

National staff criticized international staff who did not pass on knowledge and instead sought to increase their experience through moving from one post to the next in order to further their own careers rather than contribute to capacity building (cf. Owen 2010). Whereas the relationships between international staff in leadership positions and national staff in programme positions could be tense, the relationships between international staff and national staff in supporting positions (for example, as drivers or as translators) were described more positively from both sides. For example, Western international staff mentioned that they taught their drivers English or showed office staff how to use email and computer programs. They also acknowledged the capacities of interpreters and, rather than asking them to translate an interview, gave them the opportunity to conduct interviews themselves, aware that the local translators might be in a better position to show awareness of cultural norms and gain trust. While work as an interpreter represents one route to Aidland, interpreters could also be frustrated if they were not adequately compensated for the additional responsibilities they were taking on. It depends on the disposition of line managers whether national staff in supporting or programme positions were supported and promoted. Several respondents who had started out as national staff members, some of them in support positions as drivers or interpreters, appreciated the fact that they had been mentored, supported and promoted by Western international staff which allowed them to study at Western universities or to enrol in training programmes which led them into leadership positions at the regional level or head office.

While this inequality was primarily frustrating for national staff, international staff also felt uneasy about these arrangements and found it stressful managing national staff. For example, international staff were aware that national staff had more local knowledge and in some cases were better qualified, but earned less and were managed by international staff who frequently changed.[5] Age, gender and language also mattered when young female staff from the Global North managed national staff. Western expatriates expressed unease about their privileged position and some mentioned that language barriers, in particular not understanding their colleagues, could contribute to their insecurity. A European woman recalled the difficulty of 'trying to manage people in another culture':

> Sometimes it was difficult to know if you offended someone if you upset somebody because you couldn't necessarily tell from their behaviour. And you might hear them talking to their colleague in their own language. You wouldn't know whether they had a moan about their work or something entirely different. You miss out on all the nuances you can use when you are working in your own culture.

Some Western expatriates, therefore, were not only aware of the inequality between national and international staff, but also questioned their own knowledge and actions (cf. White 2002; Crewe and Fernando 2006; Schondelmayer 2010). Paradoxically, even though working in a different culture is one of the main motivations for Western aidworkers to get involved in aidwork, it is also a source of stress. Furthermore, the desire to 'make a difference' was firmly embedded in unequal power relations which were perpetuated within and through the work of aid organizations. The ideals of expatriate aidworkers were thus confronted with the reality of unequal aid relationships and affected the interaction between both groups. For example, a European woman recalled 'a lot of banter' between national and international staff, and added:

> Ostensibly the local staff really respected the expats. In reality, I think they probably looked down on them, and thought they were stupid, because they were cheating, they just did not realize. And so we came out with our ideals and they were there I think pretty jaded with the turnover of staff and saw all these people come and go, 'they have great ideals but real life continues, whether they are there or not', that was the impression I got.

Western expatriates were aware of their privileged position and criticized the preference of aid agencies to hire expatriates from Western countries for leadership positions (Carr *et al.* 2001), even if they benefited from this practice.

While inequality is part of the structures of the aid industry, some expatriates try to overcome these inequalities on the personal level by supporting local friends and their families financially. This included paying for education or medical bills, or inviting colleagues for drinks after work. Some Western expatriates returned from assignments without any money or savings because they had spent it all in the country, aware of the income difference.

These income differences also shaped expatriates' attitudes towards alleged cheating and stealing by national staff. Several respondents described that they overlooked and excused such betrayals due to the significant inequality between nationals and internationals. One respondent explained that she had 'a good relationship' with her colleagues, even though she thought that 'they would steal stuff from me, but I have a lot more than they do so it is not surprising if the temptation is too much'. Her seemingly tolerant attitude, however, may also be seen as disrespectful insofar as the accusation of theft was apparently not openly addressed and the presumed perpetrators did not even have the chance to demonstrate their innocence. This generous attitude therefore includes a paternalistic element, although not following up on (alleged) theft may also contribute to the security of international staff, because disgruntled national staff is one source of insecurity for international aid personnel (Fast 2014).[6] The relationship between national and international staff is clearly multi-layered and includes (alleged) betrayal as well as friendship, trust and loyalty. International staff provided numerous examples of situations in which national staff had protected them and saved their lives, for example, by warning them to leave or by standing between attackers or police and defending the international aidworker who was the target of an attack or had got into difficulties with the police. Some expatriates acknowledged that they had got themselves into difficulty, sometimes while also putting their co-workers and hosts at risk. Thus expatriate aidworkers were very keenly aware that having a good relationship with national staff and the local population was central for their security in the field (Roth 2011).

Respecting local culture

National staff were critical of Western international staff who did not respect local culture, for example, through the way they dressed, partied and engaged in sexual relations or by not respecting local holidays. In contrast to Western expatriates, who frequently gave examples of Western women showing respect through covering their bodies or showing deference to local men, national staff did not make such gender differences with respect to the behaviour of expatriates. They expressed frustration about the lack of respect their international colleagues demonstrated by pursuing a Western lifestyle. Nonetheless, they were protective by warning their colleagues about the potential consequences of their behaviour, as an African woman explained:

> I noticed what international staff are doing which is also taken as negative is that they also try to live their kind of life there. You know what I mean, it is like free lives, you know, like practising sex and you know all of these Westernized activities, this has actually a very big negative implication culturally. You see it is not a free world, you can do this in the States, but you cannot do it in Darfur, because if you do it in Darfur, the next day you can get your neck chopped.

National staff noted whether or not their international colleagues made an effort to gain the respect of the local population as well as their national colleagues by paying attention to local customs (for example, covering their hair), and pointed out that they were disrespectful and pursued a Western lifestyle at their own peril. They recommended that organizations should brief international aidworkers more concerning local culture and customs before sending them on assignments; at the same time they remained sceptical about whether providing expatriates with information would actually make a difference. An African woman explained:

> It would be very good if they would have been briefed, because they will brief you about the situation when they send you somewhere, okay, it is blablabla. But they won't brief you about the people, the nature of the people, the culture, the values. And even if they give it to you on paper, you don't read it, people they don't read it, who cares, you know.

In the context of the debate about the professionalization of aid, the relationship between international and national staff, staff and beneficiaries has obtained significant attention and is addressed in the various codes and standards. Aid organizations provide different types of immersion exercises and seek to hire staff who demonstrate familiarity with the region of operation and good cross-cultural skills. Fechter (2011, p. 145) reports that an 'inverse relation between job responsibility and country-specific training' may be observed: development fieldworkers and volunteers obtain the most extensive training, while the 'development elite', the technical experts in high-profile positions, receive very little training (ibid.). Furthermore, an interest in national culture and traditions does not necessarily imply contact with beneficiaries and clients of aid interventions (Nowicka 2006; Eyben 2011). MSF has carried out a 'perception study' (Abu-Sada 2012), which is used in humanitarian studies programmes. Although many aid organizations have policies which stress cooperation with indigenous actors and the strengthening of local capacity, Minear (2002, ch. 5) characterizes these commitments as rhetorical and instrumental. Furthermore, an emphasis on 'local knowledge' may restrict the added value and job opportunities of Western expatriates, as it raises the question of why qualified national staff should not be hired. The familiarity of the political, social and cultural context in which aid organizations are operating also challenges standardized approaches which are more easily implemented if aid staff have little knowledge about any particular place (Eyben 2011). Aid organizations still tend to ignore local conditions and instead apply universal, neoliberal policies and practices in order to secure funding (Rajak and Stirrat 2011). Rather than relying on idealized images of partnerships between donors and local NGOs, it is important to recognize that these relationships are 'highly fluid and change with circumstances' and thus need to be analysed on the ground (Fernando and Hilhorst 2006, p. 298).

Not surprisingly, some Western expatriates felt that Western aid organizations and Western aidworkers could be quite 'alien' to local communities. A European woman greatly enjoyed working with national staff because it gave her the feeling 'that you are part of the country', but acknowledged that 'we are Sputnik, we are from another world'. Like other respondents she believed that it was very difficult to establish good working relationships and respect. Although she felt that it was easier to bond with women, she was fully aware that insurmountable differences remained. She was one of the few respondents who explicitly addressed race.

> So to me, meeting the local staff we had a laugh, especially with women, because then you create a complicity very easily. But you have to be very cautious with this cultural gap that will stay forever. Because when I think about [Africa], because I am not black, I am white, because my experience is different. But just to realize how important it is to have local staff who know the place much better than you. For a lot of them, they have been through experiences that you will never know ... without those people we will never be able to work.

Referring to race as well as gender, she experienced closeness as well as distance. She appreciated that she would never know the local area as well as the national staff and had not experienced loss, trauma or poverty.

The success of international organizations thus depended on the support from national staff. As noted above, organizations and networks that seek to support the professionalization of aidwork increasingly highlight the good relationships between national and international staff, with accountability not only towards donors but also towards beneficiaries, and the importance of capacity building and resilience for sustainable development and disaster risk reduction (see e.g. Harvey *et al.* 2010; *Humanitarian Exchange Magazine* 2011). These demands may be to some extent rhetorical and, if one takes debates within development studies into consideration, not particularly original. Moreover, the emphasis on 'internationalization', that is, bringing more non-Western nationals and expatriates into programme and leadership positions, intersects with increased concerns about staff security and the effects of the financial crisis which affected aid budgets in 2008 and the following years. Due to the unequal pay of national and international staff, shifting responsibility to national staff is saving staff costs. Furthermore, security measures of aid organizations have so far primarily focused on international staff and have included removing expatriates from conflict regions, with the result that national staff are now facing higher risks (Stoddard *et al.* 2006). More leadership opportunities for national and non-Western staff may, therefore, be a side effect of cost-saving and litigation-preventing activities of international aid organizations rather than affirmative action and equal opportunities.

Retreating into the expat bubble

The expatriate community of aidworkers has been described as a 'fish bowl' (Verma 2007) and an 'expatriate bubble' (Fechter 2011), and represents a 'very parochial form of cosmopolitanism' and 'imperial nostalgia' (Rajak and Stirrat 2011). The interviews suggested that there were marked contradictions between seeking authentic 'non-tourist' experiences and the fact that like tourists, international staff can retreat into white spaces (Leonard 2010) in which they are served by nationals, but hardly interact with them on the same level, i.e. like peers or similarly positioned colleagues. Hotels or villas of expatriates become 'Club Med under bombs' (Yala 2005; Muenz 2007; Pandolfini 2011). Even though respondents from the Global North described living together with other Western expatriates as one of the most stressful aspects of living and working in Aidland (see Chapter 4, this volume), some of them also pointed out that at the end of the day, they preferred to socialize with other expats rather than with their national colleagues (cf. Rajak and Stirrat 2011). Some felt guilty for retreating into an expat bubble, but, especially if the encounters with national staff at work were experienced as stressful, there was less desire to spend time and cultivate friendships with national colleagues outside of work. A European woman stated:

> I think I could have made more of an effort to build up friendships with local people, staff, then I am sure I could have visited them weekends or gone to see their place up country on the weekend but I think, I did not make as much effort as I might have done. I found the job quite stressful and quite draining and I didn't always find it easy to manage [African] staff ... I guess because of that I did not necessarily want to see them over the weekend [laughs] as well.

This respondent felt that she needed to explain and justify why she did not spend time with her African colleagues outside of work hours. Of course, she could have insisted that it is her right not to socialize with work colleagues in her free time, but she was embarrassed not to spend time with her African colleagues or other Africans who were not her colleagues and instead to spend her leisure time with other international workers.[7] Respondents presented a number of explanations for the preference to spend leisure time with other international aidworkers. Native speakers of English gave linguistic reasons. After a long day working with an interpreter or speaking in the local language, they preferred to communicate in English. An Australian woman explained:

> I was living with a Bosnian family, so it was a lot of pressure on them, a lot of pressure on me. And after a full day of working and constantly working not in your language, at the end of the day, it was really a big relief to sit around with people who understood you, understood what you were saying.

For those who used English as a lingua franca, language was less relevant as a reason to socialize with other expats. Instead, culture, education and lifestyle – that is, sharing a Western lifestyle (Cook 2007) – mattered. Some mentioned that they wanted to spend time with people who were familiar with their lifestyle and values. They were aware and respected local norms, for example, following the local dress code or refraining from sunbathing, but did not want to have to comply with these norms all the time. A North American woman admitted:

> My personal view, and it is very politically incorrect, but I don't think they want to be stuck with us at the end of the day and I don't think we want to be stuck with them. We already have basically no, work–personal barrier, but at the end of the day you also need to just be able to relax and not worry if I am taking my shower and I am coming in with my towel, I don't, how will that guy perceive me … I just need to go and take a shower.

She thus made a very clear distinction between international ('us') and national staff ('them') and was unapologetic about the desire to follow the Western (un)dress code (Cook 2005). Again, it should be a matter of fact that one can relax in leisure time and not feel constraint in the privacy of one's own home. But as in the previously discussed example, 'internationals' and 'locals' are juxtaposed. Interacting with national staff and being observant of local norms was thus experienced as straining and exhausting. This also demonstrates that women felt under more pressure to comply with local norms and therefore may have had a more ambivalent relationship with national staff than men. My data thus suggest a tension between the desire to have authentic and profound experiences in another culture and at the same time retreating into expat bubbles which allowed maintaining a Western lifestyle. Paradoxically, international aidworkers from the Global North were eager to pursue experiences that were not available to tourists while, like tourists, they withdrew from the exotic environment if the constraints on their Western habits and lifestyles were experienced as stifling.

Some respondents were defensive about this tendency, however, and mentioned self-critically that they spend 'too much time' with other expats. They were aware that their desire to become immersed in other cultures stood in contrast to socializing with other Western expatriates. A European woman explained why she was ashamed 'to admit' that she primarily spent her leisure time with other expats:

> I don't really like the idea to go to another country and then you stick with your own. It doesn't sit entirely comfortably with me and, if you are going to a different country I feel you should make more of an effort to get to know local people and experience what is life like for them. It feels like the easier option, selfish.

Her desire to spend time with other Western aidworkers clashed with an ideal 'to get to know local people' and developing an understanding of their everyday lives. Thus, she highlighted the gap between local and international staff. Other Western expatriates explained the distance between international staff by the fact that local staff had families and wanted to spend time with them, in contrast to the single and largely child-free group of expatriates. Thus rather than the difference between a Western lifestyle and the local norms, differences in marital and parental status were emphasized.

Whereas language and lifestyle might suggest that a preference for socializing with other Western expatriates is a matter of convenience, there are also more strategic reasons for a separation. The security situation was presented as one reason for refraining from contact with locals and socializing with them in their leisure time. For example, in a politically charged situation, socializing with other expatriates rather than locals was presented as a conscious decision to avoid the perception that one would favour one group over another. Humanitarian workers and the organizations for which they work need to know who is benefiting and who is losing out from the aid provided by aid agencies (Slim 1995). Furthermore, some internationals felt that they would put local friends at risk by spending time with them. The segregation between international aidworkers and local populations could also be enforced through guarded compounds and curfews which limit the interaction between expatriates and locals. In the most extreme case, this meant 'bunkerization' (Duffield 2010); that is, the seclusion of expatriate staff in guarded compounds and their use of fortified vehicles that protected against attacks. However, rather than contributing to the security of international staff, the retreat into expat bubbles could increase the risk of attacks (Fast 2014) and an alternative approach to security is building relationships (Van Brabant 2000). Thus, Western expatriates presented a number of reasons for socializing with other international aidworkers from the Global North rather than with local staff or locals more general. This retreat into the expat bubble could be a preference as it allowed pursuing a Western lifestyle, or it could be enforced through the security policies of aid organizations.

Of course, the expat bubble includes locals who supplied services in the public and the private sphere – or provided transport between these spheres – but they are rarely mentioned and thus remain mostly invisible. Expatriate staff did have drivers for security reasons as well as due to poor roads and transportation infrastructure. In addition, Western expatriates whether living in joint or private accommodation often employed household help. This could include gardening, cleaning, cooking, doing the laundry and buying groceries. Given long working hours and cheap labour, employing local staff helped to create jobs and enabled international staff to pursue long working days. In addition, employing locals to run errands also allowed international staff to avoid public space (for example, going to the market or to shops) and being addressed by locals (for example, being asked for money or to buy something). The practice of hiring locals as household aides has a neo-colonial aspect and is a lifestyle which is different from home, at least for those who could not afford to hire cleaners or nannies. Some Western expatriates subsequently found it difficult to get back to their old lifestyle where they had to do everything themselves. However, international aid-workers also expressed unease about employing staff, being aware of the income inequalities that made it possible for them to afford having personnel (Mangold 2012). Furthermore, some missed privacy due to the fact that they had gardeners or other household help (cf. Eyben 2011), but considered this apparently unavoidable.

Encounters with the local population

Just as international staff presented different reasons for retreating into the expat bubble, there were various reasons given for interacting with the local population. Overall, this was motivated by a genuine desire to become immersed in the local culture, although it could also have had more instrumental reasons, as one of the respondents recalled. This North American woman had been instructed to leave the confines of the aid organization and step outside in order to gain the respect and acceptance of the local community.

> The first time you go on a walk in the village like on a Saturday, it is a bit daunting as everyone is staring at you and everything, but then I had a very good PC [Project Coordinator] in [Muslim country in Africa], who said 'No, this is part of the job, we need to in our time off go to the village, spend some money there, be seen, hang out with the kids, whatever. We need to be seen not just as these guys in their bunkers.' And that was a big part of it, and that made our project more accepted, because we were also more, quite respectful, I mean it is in [African country] there are Muslims so I would never go with a miniskirt. So I was not veiling myself but my arms would be covered and you know very respectful and something, respecting that you don't shake men's hands, because there is an issue with that. You don't go, a woman would not go to town to buy a case of beer, [laughs], you know, it is fairly simple.

This approach implements insights from MSF's perception study (Abu-Sada 2012), and various codes and standards that highlight the importance of getting to know and gaining the respect of the local population and national staff. Several factors shaped the experience and practice of interacting with locals. Language played a central role. International aidworkers who spoke the local language were usually more interested in socializing with locals who became acquaintances and friends than within the expat community. Speaking the local language or even sharing the same cultural or political background can make it easier to gain the trust of the local community (De Cordier 2009).

Third culture individuals (TCIs) who grew up in different cultures found it easier to relate to the local population, indicating 'heightened perceptual ability' and 'interpersonal sensitivity' (Lyttle et al. 2011).

Some distanced themselves from the expat community. A European woman explained that she was known as 'the white woman who walks' because 'I used to walk to church, I used to walk to the supermarket, they saw me around, I was not scared to go to the community, I just talked to people, made friends with them'. She represents those who were comfortable interacting with local people. It is noteworthy that she explains that she was not scared, which implies that there might be reasons for being so. The sources of such fear could lie in the economic inequality and cultural distance between aidworkers from the Global North and the local population. She distanced herself from international aidworkers from the Global North who 'stayed inside watching DVDs' in the aidworkers' residence and attending the international church together with other expats. She thus noted that international aidworkers from the Global North preferred to stay in white spaces (Leonard 2010) in their leisure time. In contrast, she preferred to attend the local church.

> I love African culture, so why wouldn't I go locally? So I just went locally. Yeah, I don't know. So I had loads of friends among the local staff, I went to their houses, I saw their children. I just enjoyed relating to people, to understand them a little bit more.

Thus, while some Western expatriates found it necessary to retreat into the expat bubble in their leisure time, others clearly preferred spending their free time with local friends and acquaintances. This group had less interest spending time with other Westerners for a variety of reasons. For example, those who stayed for a longer period of time in a particular site were not so interested in meeting those who only stayed for a short period of time. Another reason was that they found that they did not always share the interests of other expatriates, whether they were Christian missionaries or young people interested in partying. Expatriates who were interested in getting to know locals usually knew or made an effort to learn the local language. They enjoyed playing with children and teaching them English, or socializing with colleagues and their families after work. Language skills of international aidworkers as well as of the local population mattered. International staff who did not speak the local language appreciated it if the local population spoke their language (for example, English), which made it easier to interact. Not just for linguistic reasons it was easier to interact with nationals who were (highly) educated.

Furthermore, living with a local family rather than with other expatriates provided opportunities for getting to know locals and to feel more integrated. In some cases, the relationships went beyond banter in the marketplace or friendships and led to romantic relationships or marriage. Several men from Europe and North America had married 'local' women whom they had met on assignments. The wives would follow their husbands to the next assignment and accepted that they would be temporarily separated from their partner if it was not possible for the family to be together at a family post. While mobility and separation can lead to the dissolution of a relationship, the relationship can also lead to leaving Aidland and staying permanently in a country which initially was just a 'post' or 'mission'. A European man recalled, 'there are quite a few colleagues who got married there and stayed there', referring to the Balkans. Some women mentioned that they had started relationships with local men. However, sexual and romantic relationships with locals were rarely addressed in the interviews. Power imbalances in aidwork are reflected in sexual relationships, most notably with respect to child sexual abuse by aidworkers and peace-keepers (Fechter 2015), but also with respect to prostitution and other (more or less) consensual sexual relationships (Charles 2007; Verma 2007; Fluri 2009). Given the economic inequality between aidworkers and locals, the line between different types of relationships may be quite subtle.

Respondents were sad to leave local friends because despite skype and email they found it difficult, if not impossible, to maintain these friendships. They very rarely mentioned that they returned to countries in which they had worked before, mostly due to security issues but also because they found it hard to be faced with poverty and need without being able to do something about it. It was much easier to maintain relations with other international staff who one might meet again on another assignment. Respondents contrasted their experience with those of tourists. They emphasized that they grew closer to the local population and local culture than tourists. However, those who were working in head offices or who worked as consultants and thus spent shorter time periods in the field felt that they lacked the credentials of those who stayed in a country for months instead of weeks, or a year or more rather than several months.

Respondents thus differed with respect to their desire to get close to the local population and to distance themselves from the expatriate community. Some had a genuine desire to make local friends and to immerse themselves in local communities, some by learning the local language, others by relying on the language skills of their hosts. Others understood that building trust was part of their work and would contribute to the success of their work. Thus the type of assignment and the time spent on a mission also had a significant impact upon the relationships that developed – or not.

Race, ethnicity and expatriates

Apart from a distinction between the 'expat bubble' and the local population, the expat community is highly multinational and provides opportunities to meet people from different nationalities and cultures. Thus, even if the expat bubble represented a retreat from the unequal relationships between national and international staff, it provided an opportunity to engage with expatriates from different countries and cultures. The expat bubble itself includes a range of subcultures. Military, UN, NGO and faith-based organizations have different organizational cultures and attract different constituencies. The military and the UN are perceived as 'macho' by those working for NGOs, whereas the military perceived NGO workers as 'tree-hugging hippies'. Relief and development NGOs differ in their approaches, as do secular and faith-based organizations. Thus the expat community encompasses a range of organizational and national cultures and cross-cultural exchange as well as the opportunity to form more homogeneous sub-communities. This includes linguistic communities – in addition to using English as a lingua franca, French, German, Spanish, Swedish, etc. speakers are attracted to one another. Larger cities allow expats to re-create 'little Italy' or 'little America' (Verma 2007). Furthermore, the celebration of holidays such as St Patrick's, St Andrew's and St George's day enables national identities to be sustained (Rajak and Stirrat 2011). A shared cultural and linguistic background alone did not explain an acceptance into the expat community, however. A European woman in her thirties, who was born to Asian parents and adopted by a European couple, recalled that when she attended an expat party in an Asian country, based on her appearance she was considered a 'local' rather than an 'international' and no one talked to her until she was introduced as being from Europe and working for a UN agency.

> Then, oh, suddenly I was interesting to talk to. But your face and your appearance is so important. And that's a bit scary I think. And it's nothing, it's nothing mean, it's nothing deliberate. It's just the human being, I think. Because I think I do the same thing. I think that when I go to a party, maybe I speak, I prefer to speak to somebody from Europe than I prefer to speak, it's not actually that I prefer, prefer is not the right word, but automatically you, you go, you move towards the group that you think you have most in common with.

In order to rationalize this painful experience of racism in a Western expat-only zone, she explained the behaviour of her peers who had a preference to interact with those who are similar. Similarly, an African expatriate felt that Western expatriates kept their distance from non-Western expatriates. Her account shows very clearly that the term 'expatriate' is a racialized term which tends to be reserved for white Northern aidworkers.

> Yes, but always to be an African expatriate, it's different because, yeah sometimes I find that some of the expatriates, some they don't consider you as an expatriate. So, they are just, I would say there is a little bit of racism. Because they don't talk to you, but they talk with the white people.

This African respondent was a trained medical doctor with research experience, and had worked for various international NGOs as a member of both national and international staff. She had experienced being invisible to her Western colleagues until they acknowledged that she did excellent work after she had submitted an 'amazing report' which was circulated among her Western colleagues. Marginalized by Western expats, non-Western expatriates she appreciated the opportunity to socialize with well-educated African expatriates. This is a good example of how race matters in the aid community (White 2002; Crewe and Fernando 2006; Syed and Ali 2011). White Western expatriates were aware of and uncomfortable with their racial privilege and expressed dismay about the dominance of white leaders in aid organizations operating in African countries.

Non-Western expatriates who had started out as national staff played an important role in connecting national and Western staff. They had started their careers as national staff members and thus could relate to the experiences of national staff, or they had the language skills to communicate with national staff. They thus enjoyed more respect from national staff than Western expatriate staff, in particular if they lacked language skills or did not seem to deserve their privileged position. Thus national staff turned to non-Western expatriates. An African expatriate observed different work styles of national and international staff and felt that she could provide a connection between the two groups, and she described herself as 'a bridge between the national staff and the expatriate staff'. She thus held a crucial position in the organization, mediating between two separate groups who relied on her for communication.

Encounters with 'beneficiaries' and 'locals'

National and international staff described the encounters with beneficiaries and the local population as one of the most rewarding aspects of their work. Some Western expatriates preferred to work in local NGOs rather than joining international aid organizations in order to learn from locals. They admired the resilience of people who had experienced disasters and conflicts and were humbled by the ways in which refugees or internally displaced people coped, despite their poverty and loss. International aidworkers frequently contrasted the generosity and gratitude of the recipients of aid with the conflicts and competition they perceived among the expat community, and the egoism and consumerism in Western societies.

Sometimes this representation of beneficiaries appeared idealized. On the one hand, potential conflicts between different groups of aid recipients (for example, within refugee camps) were not addressed in the interviews. On the other hand, the power differentials and inequality between aid providers and aid recipients were overlooked. In Chapter 4, I discussed a respondent who found that one of the hardest experiences was 'to be shot at by the people you think you are helping', clearly indicating the mismatch between the intentions of aidworkers and the perception of the so-called beneficiaries.

Her experience was an exception, however, as overall respondents described the encounters with recipients of aid as highly satisfying because it was an expression of efficacy, and allowed them to 'make a difference', 'have an impact' or 'give something back'. To provide someone who is starving with food or provide medical services to those in need could save lives. Moreover, in conflict zones, the presence of international staff could also increase the safety of the local population while putting the lives of aidworkers at risk. The impact on the individual level thus justified the presence of the international aid community. The experience of helping others in humanitarian settings therefore combines this whole range of aspects – providing someone with much-needed resources, experiencing power and efficacy in challenging circumstances and engaging in voluntary risk taking. The encounter with beneficiaries could be 'a marvellous experience', for example, if refugees stayed in well-run camps, became gradually independent of aid and expressed joy. In contrast, it was hard to accept that international aid organizations were not necessarily able 'to provide the right answers to the needs' of victims of conflicts and natural disasters.

Although the accounts of aid encounters differ considerably, what they share is that the contribution of the international aid community is described as limited. On the one hand, the resilience and ability of those living in the camps able to look after themselves is stressed. On the other hand, providing only material contributions is sometimes seen as insufficient. Furthermore, respondents realized that they reacted differently to various groups of beneficiaries, in particular to Europeans and Africans. A European woman who had worked for several decades in a wide range of countries compared the needs assessment in the former Yugoslavia to that in African countries. Even if the situation was much worse in many African countries, the situation in Europe was considered to be more critical. She explained:

> But as a European doctor you were used to Africans being in a bad stage, so actually you consider it as normal. And then, when exactly the same doctors started to work in Bosnia with the prisoners who were quickly compared to prisoners of the Second World War and things like that, when you were sending people there, what is the status of the prisoners' population, they were usually overestimating that, they would say 'We have never seen it that bad'. And it was not that they were in a good shape, absolutely not, but they were not in as catastrophic a shape as they were reporting about, [while] the Africans were in a worse shape than they were reporting about.

She realized that she found it more difficult to 'protect yourself because they are cousins, they are not brothers yet, because it is a different culture. But still it is more difficult to work with people who are so close to you.'

Not only nationality and religion, but race, in particular, played a central role in these experiences of closeness and distance among people working in aid and beneficiaries.

Conclusions

Overall, nationality rather than qualifications mattered in who occupied what position in the organization, and Aidland may still be characterized as a 'racialized project'. Western expatriates are overrepresented in leadership positions and engage to a greater or lesser extent in capacity building and mentoring of national staff. Some national staff who held supporting positions such as drivers or interpreters had university degrees or language skills which helped them to move from support to programme and later on to international positions. I argue that some types of knowledge and expertise become essentialized and thus invisible, whereas others have high currency. The value of different forms of knowledge is both related to where it has been acquired as well as who holds it, which in turn affects the standing within aid organizations. For example, certificates and degrees from elite universities in the Global North are valued more highly than those from less prestigious institutions, including those located in the Global South. Language skills hold a particular significance in multinational teams. English as a lingua franca is privileged in Aidland; thus native speakers of English do not necessarily have to learn another language and instead rely on multilingual national and international colleagues. In contrast, international aid organizations consider multilingual national staff with local knowledge as being in need of 'capacity building'; that is, learning to conform to the meeting and report culture of Western-led aid organizations. Whereas relations among Western expatriate staff and national staff in support positions were described positively both by national and international staff, the relationships among Western expatriate staff, non-Western expatriate staff and national staff in programme positions appeared more difficult. This may be due to the fact that inequality between international and national staff in status, pay and career opportunities is most pronounced when it comes to programme positions which should be based on qualifications and merit, but appears to be based on region of origin. Thus, some national staff were confronted with Western international managers who were less qualified than themselves. Pay differences between international staff in programme and management positions and national staff in support positions (drivers, interpreters, guards) can be more easily justified than between international and local counterparts, especially if national staff have more context-specific knowledge and greater language skills, and so serve as intermediaries. While internationals noted that well-qualified nationals leave the country or pursue more lucrative careers than those in the aid sector, national staff experienced that they had little chance of being promoted if they stayed in their own country and therefore pursued international careers. If the positions and salaries of international and national staff were more comparable, this might encourage qualified nationals to stay and enable them to pursue careers while remaining in their own country or region, which at the same time may make overseas assignments less attractive to Western expatriates.

The analysis of interactions and relationships among international and national staff and their encounters with local populations and beneficiaries thus reveals further paradoxes of aidwork which are related to differences in power and privilege. It is not unusual that Western international staff are in positions of responsibility including capacity building while being briefed by national staff who are in possession of 'local' knowledge, networks and language skills that are crucial for the success of aid projects. Regardless of their skills and knowledge, national staff are confronted with limited career options which cause some to pursue expatriate careers. The often cited 'brain drain' of qualified national staff may thus be a consequence of the hiring and promotion practices of international aid organizations. A further paradox of aidwork is that although working in a foreign culture represents one of the attractive aspects for Western international aidworkers, the interaction with national staff and the adherence to local norms may be experienced as quite stressful. Furthermore, violating local norms and engaging in a Western lifestyle can put international aidworkers at risk. The separation of Western expatriate aidworkers and local population and staff seemingly contradicts the desire to immerse oneself in the local culture. Thus, even though aidwork addresses the symptoms of global inequality, these are re-enacted in the interactions between national and international staff. In the final chapter, I will address how the respondents coped with the paradoxes of aidwork and its inherent inequality and paternalism (MacLachlan *et al.* 2010; Barnett 2011).

Notes

1 It should not even be necessary to point this out, as it seems so self-evident. However, the discussions around World Humanitarian Day (19 August 2014) that highlighted the necessity to establish good relationships with national staff and local populations suggest that this still needs to be emphasized.
2 Household aids include cooks, cleaners, gardeners and other household staff who contribute to the safety and reproduction of international aidworkers. Drivers and guards might support international staff both at the workplace as well as outside work.
3 The term 'compradore' refers to an intermediary or go-between the country and international agencies (see e.g. Kamurazzaman 2013).
4 In this study, 202 organizations, including aid organizations, government agencies, educational organizations and business organizations in developing countries, were surveyed. Unfortunately, the authors of the study do not reveal whether the wage gap differed among different types of organizations; that is, whether aid organizations had a smaller wage gap between national and international staff. However, MSF's financial report for 2010 indicates that although international staff represent only 10 per cent of the field staff, 43 per cent of the expenses for field staff are allocated to international staff (MSF International Movement 2011).

5 Respondents gave not only examples of well-qualified national staff. Some expatriates criticized lack of punctuality and understanding of Western forms of management.
6 Respondents also gave examples of keeping staff even if they were not satisfied by the quality of service they provided, for example, not preparing food so that it would meet Western standards. Again, this was presented as a generous attitude while the question could be raised whether such an expectation is appropriate or realistic.
7 She does not refer to the international aidworkers as white or European.

7 Should I stay or should I go?

[*How long are you planning to do this kind of work?*] Until I get forced to stop. Now I have no intention of stopping. But I, you see, I'm also in a different position to most people. I was 39, nearly 40 when I started this sort of life. I know what I gave up in order to do this. And for me, that's fine. You give things up to live this life. You don't give up the middle-class lifestyle, because of course I have a middle-class lifestyle here. But you give up a lot, you give up security, you give up the nice car, the nice TV, the nice all the rest of it. You give up permanence. You give up a family in many ways.
European woman in her fifties, married, no children, July 2004

The ideal would be to find a good, likeable job in a good, likeable place where you could stay indefinitely. I tend to think that it is really like a lucky, lucky shot. It is one of the things that as compared to other jobs hands you another dimension of choice, but also uncertainty, which is not just the kind of job, but where? Of course nowadays all jobs are more flexible, but I think that it is one thing to move from Rome to Milan or Milan to Paris, as compared, as say, London to Jerewan.
European man, forties, single, no children, February 2013

[*Can you imagine going back to [country of origin] to do work there?*] Not now, because we still have the crisis and I have the plan to build a school there. So with my [domestic] salary I could not do this, I need money to realize my project. Maybe after I am going back, but I am sharing everything with my friends there. [Country of origin] is really one of my main problems, but I think I have to start to build a school first and I will see what I can do.
African woman, early forties, single, no children, February 2013

Just like the reasons for entering Aidland, the decisions to leave aid organizations are also related to values, career and family planning as well as to structural conditions. There are a whole range of different personal and professional motives for leaving specific aid organizations or Aidland. As with any other career, careers of people working in aid are shaped by social, organizational and personal change. For some aidworkers changing the workplace within Aidland proved to be a solution for criticism and discontent, but others came to the conclusion that there was no hope of reform or of finding more efficient aid organizations and decided to leave the aid system altogether. Another group were forced to leave the aid sector, for example, due to health issues, an attack or discrimination. Finally, consultancies, studying, teaching and research enabled some to alternate between being more and less immersed in Aidland and to engage in critical reflection while still being committed to the aid sector and seeking to improve it.

Changing organizations or assignments

Given the prevalence of fixed-term contracts, moving between organizations and assignments is as much a structural requirement as it is a personal preference. Only larger organizations (for example, UN agencies, bilateral organizations and some large NGOs) offer certain career opportunities within organizations, including more permanent positions and opportunities to take on different assignments. Smaller NGOs offer fewer opportunities for permanent jobs and mobility within the organization, so a career change often means moving to another organization (including secondment opportunities). Multiple changes among different sectors, positions and organizations and enrolling in further education are necessary because they enable aidworkers to gain additional skills and widen their networks which makes it possible to remain in Aidland. I was frequently told in interviews that 'one has to change after five years' otherwise one would run out of ideas and the work would become routine. The sector itself is also constantly changing, including a shift from development to humanitarian relief, the inclusion of rights-based approaches and peace-keeping, to name but a few (see Chapter 1). Aid personnel thus need to be familiar with the transformations (and justifications) of aid interventions and position themselves on the spectrum between relief, development and human rights-based approaches. Critical self-evaluations and professionalization efforts seek to enhance the effectiveness of aid. Aid professionals have increasingly become a 'learning elite' (Wilson 2006).

It is therefore not surprising that respondents emphasized that they were interested in challenges and acquiring new knowledge. This could be achieved by finding an assignment in another country, working for a different organization or taking on a new responsibility. For example, this could involve changing from a desk job in the head office to a position in a regional office or a field position, or it could be a change from emergency relief to development or vice versa. Learning and gaining new experiences played a central role in the choice of assignments and was crucial for job satisfaction. Job changes were also shaped by respondents' doubts and discontent with the impact of aid. Changing organizations and aid sectors (for example, moving from development to humanitarian aid or vice versa) was a strategy to address disappointment with the perceived lack of impact of aid or the efficacy of specific aid organizations. Respondents were looking for assignments which had more effect, gave them the opportunity to learn and experience new challenges and, depending on life-stage and partnership status, would enable them to start a family or spend more time with their partner and children. My data suggest that career considerations of Western expatriates tended to focus on the content of the job rather than income, prestige or job position. However, while some were financially independent, others had to consider how to make a living. National staff had similar motivations for changing organizations. In addition, this group left organizations out of frustration when they felt that their contributions were not acknowledged, and that they were barred from permanent positions and promotion as long as they were national staff members.

Different forms of impact

Respondents were aware of the tension between the idea(l)s of humanitarianism and development and the 'real existing aid industry'.[1] They observed competition between individuals and organizations, bureaucratic procedures or a waste of resources and were frustrated about inefficient and dysfunctional organizations. There is a wealth of studies which critically evaluate the contributions that development, human rights and humanitarian work can make (De Waal 1997; Terry 2002; Kennedy 2004; Riddell 2007; Ramalingam 2013). While some emphasize that the aid project is self-serving (Hancock 1989; Maren 1997; Polman 2010), others are more optimistic and come up with suggestions for reform (Minear 2002; Barnett 2011; Slim 2012c; Weiss 2012; Donini 2013). People working in aid experience ambivalence concerning the impact of the aid sector as a whole which is often seen as quite limited, and a desire to be involved in a specific project that has a positive impact on the individuals and communities that are involved in it.

Western and non-Western expatriates as well as national staff expressed criticism and discontent concerning the impact of aid while at the same time believing that aid could make a difference and thus constituted meaningful work. In order to reconcile discontent with the aid system with the desire to pursue a career in aid, different approaches (development and humanitarianism), and organizational cultures (NGOs and UN agencies) were distinguished. Thus, rather than criticizing the sector as a whole, aidworkers focused on specific organizations, projects or interventions which they perceived as ineffective; for example, badly managed projects or projects serving other purposes than helping the victims of poverty, conflict and disaster. Consequently, it was a matter of looking for work in another organization; for example, moving to/from one NGO to another NGO, to/from an NGO to the UN or a bilateral organization, to/from short-term relief to long-term development. A critical perspective on specific organizations or forms of intervention allowed criticizing the aid system without abandoning it – and a career in aid – in total. The solution to nagging doubts about whether the aid actually can 'make a difference' was therefore to look for the 'good project' (Krause 2014).

Changing from an NGO to a UN agency or vice versa usually had something to do with the mandate of organizations, the resources to which they had access and their organizational culture. For example, some respondents appreciated that working for a UN agency allowed them to effect broader social change, for example, through the introduction of regulations or by influencing the political process. Others appreciated that working for an NGO gave them more opportunities to interact directly with beneficiaries. Furthermore, criticism was directed at specific organizations. Internships and other forms of work experience gave insight into the work cultures and practices of aid agencies and resulted in enthusiasm as well as disillusionment. Such disappointment could be caused by all types of organizations, small unprofessional and large professional NGOs as well as UN agencies. The type of criticism varied. NGOs tended to be criticized for being not professional enough while UN agencies were scorned for being too bureaucratic. Larger organizations, NGOs as well as UN agencies, faced disapproval for wasting resources and for decisions driven by personalities and internal politics. Thus, different types of organizations, including well-known and highly respected development and humanitarian NGOs and UN agencies, failed to live up to the high expectations of respondents. Of course, every sector of the labour market is facing criticism, and education, health and welfare may serve as a few examples. Thus, the criticism of the aid sector is by no means exceptional, but Western expatriate aidworkers stated that they chose the aid sector expressly because it promised an opportunity for more meaningful work which they apparently did not expect to find in jobs in their countries of origin.

If aid interventions may have little positive or sustainable and perhaps even negative impact, what then justifies a career in aid? Some felt that aid interventions were 'too much about the development worker, too much about the donor'. Nevertheless, even those who believed that fundamental change was needed to achieve global justice expressed the conviction that short-term relief was better than not intervening at all. Looking for another assignment – despite doubts and criticisms of the aid system – was also for many an economic necessity (Fechter 2012; Shutt 2012). However, the incomes of aidworkers differ widely and, due to the prevalence of insecure and fixed-term contracts, employment in the sector can be precarious. Furthermore, other helping professions – for example, law, medicine or education – also offer career opportunities and can be extremely well paid.

Learning and new challenges

As we have seen, self-realization, personal growth and development have played a central role in the decision to engage in aidwork. The interviews suggest that the desire to learn and be challenged is at least as important as the wish to make a difference. Thus not only doubts about the efficiency of particular aid projects or organizations motivated respondents to look for new assignments, but also the search for new experiences and the acquisition of additional skills. This 'learning elite' (Wilson 2006) sought new trials through working in different regions or countries, different organizations or on different types of assignments. Similar to the dissatisfaction with their previous work which had led them to aidwork in the first place, once aidwork felt routine or was no longer challenging, it was time to look for a new job. Respondents emphasized that acquiring additional skills through changing jobs contributed to their ability to make a valuable contribution to the aid sector. They emphasized that learning and being challenged contributed to their job satisfaction, whereas the desire to gain more money, prestige or power was hardly mentioned. This was recognized by the sector which could provide limited financial incentives and career opportunities, but sought to keep staff motivated by providing training opportunities and secondments (Loquercio et al. 2006). However, while some respondents, in particular respondents from the Global South, were very satisfied with the training and career opportunities that their organizations offered, respondents from the Global North tended to look for such opportunities themselves. Despite the heterogeneity of the respondents, it was remarkable that throughout the interviews the desire to gain additional skills and work experience was highlighted. This could be explained by the fact that I carried out the majority of the interviews in the context of university-based training courses, but this applied also to respondents recruited from outside these courses. Respondents in the early stages of their careers expressed the desire to be exposed to different organizations, positions and stakeholders in order to understand the system better. This did not mean that they were dissatisfied with the organizations with which they had worked before; on the contrary, some were proud of them, but they believed that they needed to gain an insight into different sectors of the aid system. In some cases, changing to a different type of organization or assignment made respondents realize what they really liked about their work, for example, that a powerful position was not necessarily the most satisfying. A European man in his thirties who had taken on a position as country coordinator recognized that he did not like the work in the capital and much preferred working directly with beneficiaries.

> And it was such a political mess between all the stakeholders, including the UN, the European community, the [Middle Eastern country] government, that I spent all my time speaking English and French in the offices of the capital. And I had such a limited touch with my beneficiaries and also with my local staff.

Although he appreciated that he learned a lot during this assignment, he became aware of the fact that he much preferred assignments in the field, learning the local language, getting to know the local culture and interacting directly with the local population. Those who could look back on a longer career in aid organizations noted that over time they grew bored and did not pursue their work with the same curiosity and enthusiasm as before. A European woman felt that she was 'slipping slowly into a kind of busy expert'. She had carried out assessments over a long period which involved returning to countries and sites where she had worked before. Due to this extensive experience, she was able to carry out the work much more efficiently than at the beginning of her career, but over time felt less fulfilled through the work. Another respondent asked her organization 'to give me something different, I need to see more, otherwise I can't develop'. Several respondents gave examples of turning down assignments because they did not offer opportunities to learn something and gain new experiences. Respondents mentioned that it could become boring to be 'pigeonholed' because one had acquired expertise in a particular field and therefore would not find different assignments. Some respondents therefore turned down job offers in order to gain additional skills to avoid being 'put into a box'. This could mean that rather than taking a job in a country office doing administrative, HR and finance work they might hold out for a logistician position in a refugee camp. Such a desire to find new appointments seems to be at odds with the professionalization ambitions of the aid sector. After all, aid organizations should be interested in hiring staff with a track record of HR, election observation or nutrition rather than hiring someone with no previous experience in logistics. However, as long as aid organizations are under pressure to hire at short notice and give higher priority to field experience than job training, such 'boundary-crossing' will be possible and contributes to the training of the aid workforce.

Boundary-crossing not only included changing between NGOs and UN agencies, but also working in government organizations. For Western aid workers, this meant working for bilateral organizations. For national staff from the Global South, this included a broader range of public sector organizations. A Latin American man in his twenties described the reason for his decision to leave the UN agency he was working for:

> So I resigned from the UN and I worked with the government, I wanted this experience, because I thought that it was very interesting. And this [government agency] had a lot of money, I think it was the biggest project from the EU, European Union in [Latin America]. And it also had funds from the World Bank and the [national] government. So, then I started working with the government. I remember, my boss at the [UN agency] said, 'how can you resign from a job here at [UN agency], to work for the government?' He was kind of upset. I said, 'I don't care, I just want to learn. This is the period of my life when I want to learn.'

He was aware of the fact that national governments have much higher budgets for development and humanitarian relief than international aid organizations.

He thus put into perspective that the contributions of the international aid system are actually quite small when compared to the efforts of national, regional and local government. Moreover, this example illustrates that within Aidland, it was expected that someone would move from a smaller NGO to a larger NGO and from there to a UN agency, while there it was less understood if someone left an aid organization in order to join the private or public sector, emphasizing the notion of separate spheres and the distinctive character of Aidland.

Family planning

Another reason to look for a different assignment was related to family planning. Respondents who wished to have more time for romantic partners or to start a family hoped that changing to a different assignment would make this easier. Those active in emergency relief considered looking for positions in regional or country offices or in headquarters, or to move to development cooperation, where the postings are longer lasting and more secure, and therefore make it easier to bring the family to the post. Thus an important aspect concerning decisions about staying in Aidland was respondents' age and life-stage. Respondents in their twenties and early thirties who were working in emergency relief and on assignments which were short term, characterized by high risk and which did not allow a partner to come along, stated that they were planning to move to more long-term and stable conditions when they were older and wanted to start a family. Some of them had partners who were also working in aid and who they usually did not see very often as the partners were on similar assignments. As already discussed, although the intensity of emergency relief encouraged a hook-up culture and led to breakups, it also speeded up marriages between partners with different citizenship. Aidworker couples, especially those of different nationalities, who were ready to start a family thus carefully considered their options. A North American woman in her thirties who was ready to start a family explained that she had said to her European partner:

> 'Well let's push for this. Let's get you to the [head] office and then I will just follow you.' At this point, we just need to make a move and need to be based somewhere where we have the same rights.

However, both head or regional office positions and consultancies demand travelling to some extent; they thus require having a support structure, for example, a partner, relatives or paid help who can cover care obligations during trips overseas. Both male and female respondents stated that starting a family would be a reason for a change in career while noting that for women 'the clock is ticking', which is still less the case for men. Although younger respondents (in their twenties or early thirties) remarked that starting a family might be a reason for them to leave aidwork, quite a number in their late thirties and forties were single and without children. Thus the plan of leaving Aidland was not necessarily realized. Some left Aidland and returned to their home country because they felt that staying longer at one place might make it easier for them to meet someone, although some who do not then start a relationship return to Aidland.

Leaving Aidland

Some respondents left the aid sector altogether, either voluntarily or involuntarily and also for a variety of reasons. Some respondents developed fundamental doubts about the aid system which they felt could not be resolved by changing to a different organization. They believed that neither long-term development nor short-term relief was sustainable and that neither addressed the underlying causes of poverty, conflicts and disasters. They believed that instead of addressing the symptoms, it was necessary to engage in political and economic reforms that contribute to changing living standards in low(er)-income and less developed regions in the long run. This did not necessarily mean that they felt that they personally could bring such change about. For example, a European woman who had worked in a development project in an African country for several years stated:

> I think the whole development cooperation is just a drop on a hot stone. I think we can do what we will, we can initiate as many wonderful programmes but as long as the political framework does not work, not just in this country, it will go on like this forever which is a shame, but even if this is so, I won't go into politics, I am not diplomatic enough.

Another respondent considered getting involved in advocacy organizations promoting fair trade and challenging pharmaceutical industries. Like other respondents he saw aid as treating the symptoms of global inequality and felt that it was important to address the root causes, for example, through a reform of trade regulations or through sustainable political solutions to conflicts. Thus, some felt that advocacy and political engagement was needed to bring about social change and address the underlying causes of poverty and disease.

Other Western expatriates concluded after working in aid organizations for several years that business rather than aid would make a better contribution to development. These respondents had immersed themselves in local communities, spoke the local language and had made friends with locals. Based on their observations of the aid system, they felt that supporting the start-up of small businesses (for example, an internet café or taxi) might contribute more to the development of the local economy than interventions of aid organizations. A European woman who had worked in various African countries became convinced that aid recipients were 'spoon-fed' and, rather than developing their own initiatives, 'waited for someone to come along and tell them'. She decided to help an African acquaintance by supporting his university studies and providing him with a small loan which allowed him to contribute to a micro-credit scheme, aware that she was taking a risk with her investment, but potentially also profiting from it.

> So I gave him some money to invest, with the view that I get the money double back within a year. That was the terms, and he explained how it worked and it was fascinating to see how they managed to live without banks, and they did their own things. And of course there was a risk and I knew that.

In addition to this investment, she returned to Europe to train as an accountant, believing that 'the way forward was business and not aid'. Another respondent with long-time involvement in an African community after a while doubted that an orphanage offered the best solution to help children. He came to the conclusion that it was important to provide adults in the village with income opportunities which would make it possible for children to stay with relatives rather than in the orphanage. He recommended that the orphanage be transformed into a centre that the children could visit from time to time. Initiatives such as these were developed in collaboration with local partners in Africa and with sponsorships from individuals and organizations in Europe. Thus, rather than implementing standardized programmes, partnerships with local communities enabled projects to be developed that were based on knowledge of local conditions and needs.

Some respondents questioned the presence of Western expatriates rather than the goals of aid organizations, given that there were equally or even better qualified national staff. They felt that the high turnover and privileged position of international staff was problematic. A European woman who had enjoyed working in humanitarian relief left the sector because she did not want to stay in Africa unless she was 'contributing something worthwhile'; she explained:

> Well I guess when you are in a country with a high unemployment rate, yeah, I guess I would feel very guilty fulfilling a role that [was] taking a job away from a local person. So, I think you do feel, you do feel privileged if you get a job in this kind of environment. I was always very conscious while I was there, we employed a gardener and a cook and we had local staff in our office and there was no way that they could afford that. And that does not sit very comfortably with me. I think it would feel very selfish to apply for a job wherever just because it would be an enriching experience for me. If that would mean that a [African] then would not have a job.

In particular, she was uneasy about the involvement of expatriates like herself who did not have the specific skills needed to support national staff (e.g.

specific medical or engineering skills). Thus, although she shared the widespread desire to learn and embrace challenges as an opportunity for personal growth, she rejected this wish as selfish and one that would cause difficulties for national staff who have to deal with the turnover of a succession of expatriates who had to be briefed by national staff and counterparts.

In contrast to Western expatriates who left the aid system due to their doubts about what contributions they could make personally or to the aid system overall, some of the respondents of the Global South saw their involvement in aid organizations from the outset as temporary. They perceived their careers in Aidland as an important stepping stone towards future goals. A young man from Latin America explained:

> I think the humanitarian work and the relief is very important, but it does not solve things, problems, just alleviate them, which is important, because it makes a difference in the lives of people between life and death. It is not nothing but it does not change the conditions and I think that this is important. So I would bet now, that maybe after five or ten years, I would move to the development field and probably after some years of international experience go back to [Latin America], because there are many things to do also, but with some international experience it could be also very enriching and maybe my contribution could be more valuable. Yeah, and then we will see.

Similarly, an African man in his twenties had a clear vision that this work in the aid system would provide him with resources, skills and prestige which would enable him to pursue a career in the private sector which would help him to run for a high political office in his country. This young man was reading for a Ph.D. at a European university and was keen to contribute to African development. Other respondents from Africa also wished to return to their home country but rather than plan careers in the private sector and politics, they saved money in order to open a school or an orphanage. In these cases, pursuing an expatriate career for a number of years was a means to learn and gain material resources which could be used to contribute to development and humanitarianism in their home countries. This means that the much-cited 'brain drain' may be only temporary. Instead, non-Western expatriates accumulated transnational capital in order to 'make a difference' in their country of origin, while also supporting development and engaging in relief efforts in other countries in the Global South. Some African respondents expressed a Pan-African identity.

Aidworkers from the Global North faced the risk that skills and experiences they gained in Aidland were not valued in 'the real world', i.e. in the public and private sector of high(er)-income countries. Professionalization processes notwithstanding, people working in aid, in particular volunteers, may be seen as mavericks. While it is possible to transfer experience from commercial logistics to humanitarian logistics, this seems to be less possible the other way around. Furthermore, spending longer periods outside the private sector or not having access to the latest technologies and tools can result in de-skilling as well as a loss of networks. One strategy to avoid de-skilling processes and the disintegration of networks is to alternate international assignments with employment in the private, public and third sectors in the Global North. An Australian human rights worker who had worked for various aid organizations in Eastern Europe and Asia explained that she had carefully considered which postings to take in order to avoid de-skilling as a lawyer.

> I had made the decision after the second posting in [Asia] that I wouldn't take up anything, any other international postings that didn't involve hard law basically. This was soft law, refugee law, working with one specific convention … because at the end of two postings, that's for me two years out of the legal profession and already you start to [think], 'Am I going to be able to go back into court, have I lost my skills?'

Given the difficulty of transferring skills and experiences out of Aidland, just what resources aid organizations can offer those who want to change positions is crucial. Some organizations offer those who had been in security incidents a position in the head office. However, NGOs were also criticized for exploiting their workforce and not providing support for returning aid-workers. A respondent who had been involved in a faith-based organization was concerned that

> The NGOs as institutions are so much into business that they forgot their identity, forgetting their identity means they have no time to think about how to take care of their people, and they become cruel. They use the people in the field, in very difficult environments, and they use them, they take advantage of them and they leave people alone. And people go back to [their] countries, sitting without support, broken, lost, depressed, frustrated, and some of them become alcoholics or drug addicts or kill themselves! This is the reality.

The organization People in Aid was established after the Humanitarian Practice Network found significant weaknesses of staff management in aid organizations and recommended an agreed HR standard for the aid sector. In 1997, the People in Aid *Code of Best Practice* was first published. A revised code, called the *Code of Good Practice*, was published six years later. In 2012, the organization had over 200 members. People in Aid regularly surveys sector practices and provides training and resources for HR management, emphasizing that the investment in staff and volunteers results in an improved performance of aid organizations. Better staff care thus benefits both people working in aid as well as donors and service users. However, budget cuts after the

2007/2008 recession affected aid organizations and the hiring, promotion, benefits and training opportunities that are offered.

Larger aid organizations may offer support for additional training that can enable a career change. It therefore matters greatly whether organizations are able to provide resources that allow those leaving Aidland to acquire new or updated skills and develop new networks, for example, through enrolling in training and university courses or through attending conferences. However, given their tight budgets, aid organizations must minimize their overheads and demonstrate that resources benefit the target populations rather than (former) staff. Thus, given the difficulties of leaving Aidland, people may look for another overseas assignment even if they would prefer to change sector or accept an appointment in a head office. Although theoretically opening a business, for example, in tourism, may provide an employment opportunity for those who wished to stay in Africa, Latin America or Asia rather than returning to Europe or North America, this would not necessarily be reconciled with a humanitarian identity. For example, a European respondent who would have liked to stay in Africa after his assignment with an aid organization ended said:

> I did not have a chance to stay in [African country], because I am not yet a good businessman in tourism or importing European tools or something else. And although there were many NGOs, there weren't any in the capital. Therefore I left [African country] and my girlfriend stayed there.

Aside from the professional and material aspects that make the transition out of Aidland more or less difficult, there are also emotional and relational aspects of this transition. This included 'falling into old habits' rather than engaging with global issues. Thus, respondents not only experienced that their horizon widened when they got involved in aidwork, but also that their world had shrunk when they returned to their home country and resumed their old lifestyle. For example, even though Western societies offer many opportunities to engage with people of different nationalities and ethnicities, this is not necessarily perceived as a chance to engage in multicultural communities and develop and sustain cosmopolitan solidarity.

While some experienced that they very quickly returned to old patterns, others found it harder to adjust. Some respondents who had worked in emergency relief felt that they no longer fitted into highly developed post-industrial societies which had been for some of them the reason they worked in the aid sector. They felt that they had changed through leaving their country of origin and through their experience of being confronted with different cultures. Furthermore, some found that their skills and experiences were not valued in the private sector. Resources provided to those seeking to exit Aidland appear to be crucial; without such resources people might return to Aidland despite their intentions. In addition, for those who had been involved in aid missions for long periods it was no longer clear where 'home' was and where they belonged. Furthermore, it could be difficult to adjust to losing the privileges connected to a well-paid position and the practice of having assistants and household staff running errands. A European woman who had worked for over 20 years in the sector observed that some of their colleagues found it quite difficult to become reacquainted with life in Europe or other high-income countries.

> I think is sometimes the problem that people are not knowing what they do afterwards. If you [are] in the humanitarian field for too long, it is actually kind of difficult to resettle in the world here. ... But you actually lose the reality on how it is to actually live in Europe. So if you are [a] highly considered person in the field and then you have to find a job and then have this tiny little apartment which is overly expensive. You are kind of going for a regular job somewhere it is sometimes a huge difficulty to go through. And I think people are kind of sometimes just afraid of doing so.

How easy or difficult it is to leave Aidland depends on one's life-stage and available resources. Furthermore, the exit from a particular organization or the sector more generally may not be a choice but enforced. Such an involuntary exit may be related to health issues, severe illnesses, attacks and burnouts, including primary and secondary traumatization. The interruption or end of an aidworker's career due to health reasons could result in a re-evaluation of one's life and career, and lead to a reorientation including leaving Aidland – just as health reasons could also be the cause of starting an aidworker career. In addition, gay and lesbian aidworkers may be forced to leave due to the threat of homophobic attacks and anti-gay legislation in some countries. Aid organizations may not hire or renew the contracts of openly gay and lesbian aidworkers if they fear that they would jeopardize the success of a project in a homophobic environment (Mizzi 2013).

Younger respondents went to university or took on job training in order to pursue a career in the private or public sector after leaving the aid sector. For those who were close to retirement, the exit from Aidland also appeared unproblematic if they were financially secure. Regardless of age, financial security and expertise made the transition easier. Some organizations provided leavers with resources which could be used for university studies, job training or to fund the start of a consultancy. However, such support was rare. Only two respondents mentioned that they were offered financial support when their assignments ended. Some organizations offer career counselling. Thus, perhaps leaving Aidland may be even more difficult than entering it, and for Western expatriates it may be easier to transfer skills gained in the private, public and third sectors into Aidland than the other way round. Some of the older respondents stated that they had to stay in the aid system despite their doubts because they felt that they had lost the necessary networks and skills to find a job outside Aidland. One would think that, given the importance and emphasis on internationalization and globalization, employers would be very interested in hiring people who are able to work in stressful working conditions with limited resources in different cultures. However, given the experience of 'separate spheres' (i.e. the fact that those who live and work in Aidland find it difficult to share their experiences with those who live in the 'real world') this is not necessarily the case. Of course, the experience of leaving Aidland varies with skills and resources as well as with respect to the length of time spent in Aidland. For those who had been involved in Aidland for a short period of time, either after school or university and before starting a 'real job', the experience of leaving Aidland is different from that of those who have worked in Aidland for an extended period of time.

On the boundaries of Aidland

Additional strategies to reconcile conflicting motivations and the paradoxes of aidwork that have been addressed throughout this book encompass consultancies and the participation in training programmes, and are to some extent intertwined. Consultancies appear to take on a particular significance in Aidland which is characterized by liminality, a constant transition between different positions, sectors and countries. Consultancies play a role in gaining access to Aidland, maintaining contact with Aidland while one is holding another position (for example, at a research institution), make a living in between appointments as well as providing an exit strategy. Consultants have contracts of varying lengths lasting from a week to several months, and usually work in teams (Stirrat 2000). Consultancies provide interesting job opportunities tailored to skills, expertise and experience. A European woman in her thirties who had worked for several NGOs and had left the aid sector because she had become disillusioned with aid explained why she had returned to working for a NGO as a consultant.

> I did not go back because I believed in aidwork particularly. I went back because it was a project that interested me. And I thought I've got the skills and with my background I would be the perfect person to do the job, I could make a difference. So that is where I still find myself. Although I have now been back there as a consultant for about a year and a half. And I could go on for at least another year. So we will see.

Her statement sounds contradictory – on the one hand she did not believe in aidwork, on the other hand she thought she could 'make a difference'. She explained that one important reason to support the project was that she did not want to let the team members down. Thus even though she was sceptical about the aid system as a whole, she felt that she could make a contribution on a small scale.

Above, I addressed the fact that respondents resented being pigeonholed and felt that carrying out the same type of assignment – although in different countries and regions – did not offer new insights and challenges. In contrast, consultancies require specialization as well as networks in order to secure contracts, for example, to carry out needs assessments, project evaluations or training. Thus consultancies were experienced as less constraining and offering more flexibility. A North American woman who had worked in several field positions which required a lot of travelling and separation from her partner described how she envisioned the future:

> What my life will be in the next couple of years? I think the consulting/research will take up, I think I would like to get a job where I can. I mean right now, if it goes on like right now, I can make a living out of that, so I hope that continues. Eventually, let's say in the next five years, I would like to have a more stable position, more you know, based with an NGO or university, I need more stability because, yeah, I would like to have a family, have some kids ... maintain the humanitarian connection absolutely. I don't know, I never thought I would do consulting, maybe something else will happen, maintain the humanitarian connection for sure.

Although consultancies require even more flexibility and mobility than other fixed-term jobs in the aid sector, they also offer more control over assignments than being employed by aid agencies. Furthermore, the boundaries between (long) consultancies and (short) fixed-term positions are not that clear. The status as consultant can camouflage un- or underemployment and is a strategy for creating one's own workplace. Furthermore, even more than the fixed-term, project-related employment in Aidland, consultancies fit into the neoliberal framework which emphasizes self-governance.

Training programmes, university based or otherwise, can both represent job opportunities as well as competition for consultants. Respondents participated in training courses for a whole range of interrelated reasons. Participation was motivated by the need to acquire additional knowledge and skills, but also by the desire to find a space to reflect on the effects of aidwork. Participating in a training course thus was as much about building networks and gaining certificates as about learning and reflection.

As noted in Chapter 1, some development studies programmes have their roots in programmes for colonial administrators, while others were founded when development aid took off in the second half of the twentieth century. Human rights and humanitarian studies programmes emerged in the 1990s (Gonzalez et al. 1999; Rainhorn et al. 2010). In addition to degree programmes, a broad range of online and offline courses are offered by aid organizations and university-affiliated institutes (Walker and Russ 2010). Respondents were aware of these training opportunities and made use of them. They participated in online courses, short-time courses or enrolled in Master's degree courses between assignments. Some organizations paid for the participation of their staff in short-term or regular university courses. However, such support was not offered in all organizations or to all staff members. Some of the respondents from the Global South had obtained scholarships or bursaries, and some organizations paid for the training of their staff. Other respondents, from the Global South as well as from the Global North, paid for the courses themselves. Courses were taken during paid or unpaid leave or in between assignments.

For some respondents it was important to obtain a university degree in order to improve their career opportunities, either working for aid organizations or becoming consultants. For example, despite many years of practical experience, respondents felt that it was necessary to have a certificate that demonstrated academic accreditation. For example, a European man in his sixties who had worked for many years in development and humanitarian assistance and had contributed to innovations in the aid system summarized his motivation succinctly:

> Let's complete the transition from development into humanitarian assistance and put academic credit on this process.

Thus, even if he had developed and implemented programmes in a variety of organizations, he felt it necessary to gain a formal recognition of his abilities. His experience indicates that professionalization processes highlight the increasing importance of certificates, even though field experience remains crucial. Some of the respondents from the Global South countries appreciated that scholarships offered them a unique opportunity to obtain a degree from a university in the Global North. They were convinced that they needed such degrees in order to pursue a career as an expatriate aidworker and felt that the degrees they had obtained in their country of origin were not acknowledged. An African respondent explained:

> Why? Because, I think it was one of my dreams to attend a school in a developed country, and it felt like continuing as an expatriate also, I need to have a degree. Because with my, because some of the countries they do not accept my degree from [African country].

Respondents from the Global South believed that degrees from a prestigious university in the Global North would help them to secure employment in Aidworld. My data suggest that non-Western expatriates who held leadership positions (for example, at the regional level) had benefited from studying for postgraduate degrees at European and North American universities. Similarly, respondents from the Global North who had studied at universities in Africa or Asia because they felt that they could learn more about development studies if they were taught by activists and studied together with beneficiaries felt that in order to pursue careers in international NGOs they also needed degrees from Western universities.

Several respondents were pursuing or planning to pursue doctoral research with the intention to work in academia, aid organizations, as consultants or setting up organizations drawing on their field experience and academic training. The desire to gain postgraduate degrees was not just instrumental; respondents also appreciated that enrolling in a university programme gave them space to reflect and learn about alternative approaches. An African woman explained, 'the objective is that you leave the field and you think about what is wrong, what is good. So I think that this time I'll really get many skills about analysing humanitarian work.' Similarly, a Latin American woman who had worked as a national staff member in a number of NGOs had several reasons for enrolling in a humanitarian studies programme in the Global North.

> So I wanted to come here just to breathe and to think about the humanitarian action, to challenge it a lot, not to criticize, because I know there are many critics, very critical, but not to criticize it also, but also to have some answers to understand better. So this is a second thing: to learn to challenge, I think it is the other reason why I came here. And the third one I thought it was a very good transition to my plans to getting a job at an international organization, maybe a humanitarian one, maybe development.

In addition, several respondents explained that they took a year out to study in order to regenerate from exhausting working conditions. One respondent explained the decision to enrol in a year-long university programme with being physically exhausted from the missions she had been on.

> It was a one-year programme, so it was perfect, I would just take one year off, do my thing ... you think you can make a lot of connections, things like that, sort of push my thing, and I needed a year to be back. That was really the thing, I sort of needed a year-long debrief about everything that I had seen to make sense of it. Because I knew that the work I had done was great, but I had a lot of questions, I needed, just ethical questions, management and efficiency questions, I needed to think about it.

Thus, in addition to enrolling in a postgraduate degree or participating in a training course combined three aspects: getting a break, finding a space to reflect on humanitarianism and finally finding jobs. In particular, those who were trying to enter the field or who were looking for a new assignment, making contacts and networking was also of high importance. This included the practitioners among the teaching staff and guest lecturers as well as fellow students who were or had been employed in various organizations.

These courses therefore offered learning additional skills and acquiring credentials while simultaneously providing opportunities to leave Aidland temporarily and still keeping a foothold in the sector. This was important for professional and personal reasons. Given that many respondents felt that their friends and family had little interest in and understanding of their work, on the courses they met people who were familiar with aidwork and it was possible to reflect on these shared experiences while being outside the field. Postgraduate degrees also promised an academic career which included temporary stays in Aidland – for teaching, research and/or consultancies. It appears that so far the majority of teaching and research staff in humanitarian and development studies have a background as practitioners and have spent considerable time working for aid organizations prior to joining academic programmes and continuing the involvement, not only through research and teaching, but also through consultancies and participation in evaluation panels. Academics can be critical friends who provide critical assessments about the sector and produce additional knowledge.

Moreover, academic staff of development and humanitarian studies programmes are also 'producing' the next cohorts of aidworkers. Thus, paradoxically, the partial withdrawal from aidwork into academia relies on the 'production' of new aidworkers in order to sustain academic programmes. The question is to what extent these new cohorts of aidworkers can be absorbed by aid organizations, in particular those without prior field experience who may find it challenging to enter aidwork. Humanitarian studies programmes were initially offered to practitioners who had already got field experience in order to provide them with a space to reflect and learn more about the sector. However, programmes are increasingly open to those with no prior experience in development or humanitarian relief who find it difficult to find the first field position. EU Volunteers, a programme of the European Union, seeks to address this problem by offering university students volunteer opportunities and thus supplement academic training with practical experience. Thus academic programmes have a variety of functions: they can serve to recruit those without practical experience to aidwork, provide a temporary break for those involved in aid organizations and offer a career opportunity to those who no longer wish to work for aid organizations but who want to conduct research or train future aidworkers. Academic programmes are therefore both a path into and out of Aidland. Of course, academia is not the only career that builds on practical experience in aidwork. Experiences in aidwork have also been published in journalistic and autobiographic accounts, and have, for example, led to careers in the media as well as in the private, public and third sectors. This is well documented for former VSO volunteers (Bird 1998). In contrast to training and recruitment, retirement and pensions of aid personnel have so far barely attracted attention in the debate around professionalization.

Conclusions

Decisions about leaving particular aid organizations or the aid system in general, either on a temporary or a more permanent basis, are intertwined with the characteristics and paradoxes of aidwork that have been explored throughout this book. First, to a certain extent, changing assignments and organizations is a strategy to stay within Aidland given the small number of permanent positions and career opportunities in aid organizations. My data suggest, however, that even more important than this structural requirement to change is the desire of those working in aid to be exposed to new and challenging experiences which provide opportunities for learning and personal growth. This means that a job in an aid organization is not in itself meaningful and exciting and there is a need for constant change. Second, this need for change and the desire to gain additional skills and experience, either through work experience or through participation in training workshops or university programmes, is tied to self-doubt and criticism of the aid system. My data suggest that respondents were very keenly aware of the limited (long-term) effect of aid in general and their personal contribution in particular. For many, the solution to dealing with these doubts was to look for better, more efficient organizations and interventions, and to become better trained and experienced as well as taking some time out to reflect about the contradictions of Aidland. Thus, although they were aware of their limits and contradictions, they did not give up on the 'good project' (Krause 2014). Third, the interviews suggest that there is a tension between 'job satisfaction' and 'making a difference' which may not always be the same. In particular, if respondents felt that they were being 'pigeonholed' due to their specialization and expertise, the emphasis lies more on variation and new challenges than on applying experience in order to help beneficiaries. Gaining additional experiences in different aid organizations and sectors certainly contributes to the qualifications and capabilities of aidworkers which is beneficial to the aid sector. However, the opposition to being pigeonholed is remarkable, since it suggests that individual job satisfaction may be more important for aidworkers than how they could make the best use of their accumulated experiences to 'make a difference'. Fourth, consultancies play an important role in various stages of entering, maintaining and leaving careers in Aidland. While consultancies promise more control over assignments, they also require a high and perhaps even higher degree of mobility and flexibility than short-term positions in aid organizations. Thus they also highlight the high degree of self-governance needed in the aid system. Fifth, obviously career considerations are intertwined with decisions about personal lives shaped by health issues, including burnout. Both men and women spoke about plans to have children which would affect their career decisions. Sixth, just as it seemed easier for national staff from the Global South to enter aid organizations, it also seemed easier for this group to leave the aid sector again and find jobs in the public or private sector in their country of origin. Thus, for respondents in the Global South, the boundaries between aid organizations and other sectors of the labour market seemed more fluid than for respondents in the Global North. They also felt that they could contribute to the development of their country by working in government organizations, volunteering or by working in the private sector. Seventh, even though some respondents from the Global North had serious doubts that aid projects could 'make a difference' as they had initially hoped, they continued to pursue their careers, raising the question about who actually benefits from aidwork: those who are the intended 'beneficiaries' or those working in aid organizations.

Note

1 See e.g. Slim (2005) for the tension between idealism and realism.

Conclusions

This book is an attempt to make sense of aidwork and to understand what attracts people to work under challenging, dangerous and stressful conditions which confront them with physical and social violence and why the most difficult and possibly traumatic experiences are viewed as 'the best time of my life'. It also speaks to a potential turning point in humanitarianism, an increased awareness of the colonial and postcolonial legacies that shape aid encounters, something that until now has found more attention in development studies. Furthermore, I propose that a dialogue – if not integration – of humanitarian and development studies is needed to better understand how the work opportunities in Aidland structure the life-courses and work histories of people working in aid. I also believe that a dialogue between 'aid' studies and studies of social work, social movements and the third sector would be fruitful in order to develop a more integrated global perspective on social action and social change. This may help us to move beyond some of the paradoxes of aidwork and Aidland.

So what are the paradoxes of aidwork and how do they shape the lives of passionate professionals working in Aidland? Both development and humanitarianism are rooted in modernization, colonialization and decolonization processes. They are at the same time addressing the consequences of these developments as well as perpetuating them as long as power relations between rich(er) and poor(er) countries are not changed. Inequality not only persists between countries, but also within them. Gaining access to aid organizations, whether as an international or national staff member or volunteer, requires a significant amount of economic, cultural and transnational capital. Furthermore, inequality also exists within aid organizations. Citizenship, race and class differences matter with respect to access to as well as position and promotion within aid organizations. This means, for example, being able to afford doing unpaid internships or to volunteer for extended periods of time. Paradoxically, volunteering has become part of the professionalization processes in Aidland, so those who cannot afford to work without pay or to pay for overseas experience find it more difficult if not impossible to join Aidland. However, there may also be less of a need to 'make a difference' in the lives of distant strangers, but more of a desire to improve the living and working conditions in one's own country. Thus I argue for more integration in thinking about development and humanitarianism in rich(er) and poor(er) countries, to consider continuities of thinking about social work in poor communities in the Global North with development in the Global South. Of course, there are huge differences between the situation of refugees and victims of violent conflicts in the Middle East, sub-Saharan Africa and other crisis zones around the world and deprived areas and communities in the Global North, but it is important to keep in mind that within the highest income countries zones of exclusion and violence exist as well. For non-Western international staff who started out as national staff, this continuity of social problems at home and overseas is more obvious than for many Western expatriates.

Skills and prior job experience play a different role for national and international staff. This is particularly noticeable when international staff from the Global North are trained by their local counterparts or act as line managers of national staff despite having fewer skills, in particular language skills and local knowledge. This indicates that the aid enterprise is still a 'racialized project'. While qualifications of national staff are not always acknowledged and remunerated, Western international staff have the opportunity to gain qualifications by learning through trial and error. Aid organizations thus perpetuate the inequalities they seek to address. Furthermore, although Western expatriate staff perceive a difference between aidwork and 'normal life', it is important to keep in mind that the global inequalities that shape Aidland inform the segregated domestic and global labour markets. In contrast, for national aidworkers there is much less of such a distinction between Aidland and 'real life'.

The establishment of university programmes, research institutes and academic journals is part of the professionalization processes that are going on in the aid sector. In addition, organizations such as People in Aid and Antares focus on human resources and psychological issues in the sector. While it is important to establish that people working in aid have the necessary skills and resources that ensure high-quality work and work satisfaction, it is also important to consider the career opportunities and exit opportunities for people working in aid. In addition, given that 90 per cent of the aidworker population are national staff and a further decrease of Western expatriates in leadership positions (currently about 40 per cent) may be expected, there seem to be few career opportunities for European and North American aidworkers. This means on the one hand that it is important that professionalization processes should target and benefit national staff. On the other hand, it may be frustrating for graduates of the recently emerging Humanitarian Studies programmes from the Global North who may find it even more difficult or even impossible to pursue a career in Aidland. It is therefore important to consider not only what skills may be transferred into Aidland, but also what skills that are gained in intercultural encounters with limited resources in challenging environments may be applied to other contexts (cf. Burrell Storms et al. 2014). Such a knowledge transfer would bring the separate spheres closer together and contribute to learning processes and exchanges between social workers and people in aid who are working with ethnic minorities, refugees and asylum seekers in different contexts. Such an exchange should be beneficial both for the beneficiaries of aid organizations as well as the workforce.

An intersectional perspective is required in order to understand the role gender, citizenship, race and class play in Aidland. Gender interacts with other systems of privilege and disadvantage. This means that in the interaction between national and international staff, citizenship can be more important than gender. Gender can be an advantage for promotion into certain jobs, especially if aid organizations seek to enhance the participation of women. However, aid careers affect the life-courses of men and women differently. Some organizations have started to monitor the diversity of their workforce. Such data will enable strategies to be developed which will promote a more diverse workforce. Internationalization efforts include moving head offices from Europe and North America to Asia and Africa as well as seeking to appoint staff from less developed countries in management positions. Aidland is characterized by multiple forms of inequality which inform the access to and promotion within aid organizations. Furthermore, the aid system as a whole stabilizes and perpetuates global inequalities rather than challenging them, unless it addresses underlining structures.

Does this mean that aid is bad and should be abolished? By no means. Rather, 'aid' needs to go a step further and needs to be transformed. A first step would be to openly acknowledge power differences and inequalities which shape the interactions within aid organizations and that create the relationships between donors and recipients. This requires more attention to the hiring and promotion practices within aid organizations. For example, this could mean that Western expatriates get involved on secondments and as volunteers, obtaining salaries that are comparable or even lower than those of national staff. It could also mean giving national staff more say in the hiring of expatriate staff. This would put national staff in decision-making positions, recognizing that skills are needed and who can best train national staff – on a temporary basis. Turnover would thus be minimized as national staff would have an opportunity to move up and pursue a career within the organization, while international staff would temporarily volunteer to help fill skills gaps. In order to make it possible for those on lower incomes to participate in volunteering and secondments, enterprises and governments in high-income countries could offer income replacement or tax incentives for those providing expertise that has been requested by Southern aid organizations. Furthermore, governments, universities and other enterprises could invite representatives of Southern aid agencies not just to learn at Northern institutions but also to teach about the needs, perspectives and demands of those living in low(er) income countries. This would involve a shift from a unilateral knowledge transfer to a dialogue which can inspire new sustainable and fair production and working conditions. A rethinking of economic growth which, rather than financialization, involves 'use value' would inspire and underpin the development of technologies that stop rather than foster climate change, that promote economic democracy in terms of sharing resources as well as decisions of how to invest in them. Thus, there are plenty of opportunities to 'make a difference' and 'bring about change' which affect individuals around the globe, no matter where one is engaged.

So is there an alternative – and perhaps more efficient – way of engaging with these global inequalities, and what implications would this have? For some of the people working in aid whom I interviewed, in particular those from high-income countries, quitting their previous careers and entering Aidland was an attempt to leave late modern societies behind and address the consequences of global inequality, whether these are underdevelopment, political conflict or natural disasters. This career change was grounded as much in the desire to help as in the frustrations of a meaningless and materialistic lifestyle or the lack of impact in social and helping professions due to increased regulations and public sector cuts. However, this raises the question of whether 'meaningful work' only exists in Aidland. What makes Aidland so attractive? Moreover, an involvement in Aidland in the quest for self-realization appears rather selfish. Perhaps a high-earning professional could have more impact if he or she would support a local project financially and at the same time lobby or campaign for fair trade agreements, policies addressing climate change, and boycotting firms benefiting from military production. Direct contact with 'beneficiaries' is not only possible overseas but also in the interaction with patients and clients in care homes, hospitals and homeless shelters. Asylum seekers and refugees are in need of legal, financial, political and social support. In the context of a care deficit, many of the carers come from low(er)-income countries to provide care work in the high(er)-income countries. Thus, while English nurses join NGOs to make a difference in the Global South, women and men from the Global South leave their families behind in order to work in hospitals in the UK. This highlights a further aspect of aid: remittances (that is, money sent home by various diasporas) far outnumber aid provided by 'donor' countries, many of which do not meet the millennium goal of 0.7 per cent GDP. 'Donor' countries however profit from segregated labour markets in which migrants and ethnic minorities are usually positioned in the lower skilled, less prestigious jobs. More fairness and observing workers' rights in the global division of labour may increase the remittances further, perhaps even making 'aid' obsolete.

Thus, bringing Aidland home does not mean a disengagement from global relations, but rather it means acknowledging the advantages and disadvantages that characterize contemporary global societies. The protest movements associated with the global financial crisis and inspired by the Arab Spring resulting in the widespread Occupy movement in 2011 suggest a resurgence and revitalization of social critique and may also result in an alternative politicization of aid. Such a politicization would result in solidarity movements and acknowledge that the vast majority of people working in aid are national staff whose career opportunities are thus far restricted. Such an approach would represent a critique of – rather than an attempt to escape from – neoliberal societies, and would be a protest against exploitation of various forms. Such a broad social justice movement would address climate change, trade regulations, labour law, racism and other forms of discrimination. This could result in support of diaspora networks or activism to provide free access to education rather than charging national students high and international students even higher student fees. Thus, rather than addressing the symptoms of global inequality, such activism would address the root causes. One of the attractions of Aidland for people from the Global North seems to be that it promises enchantment and exoticism in a disenchanted late modern society: solidarity movements may result in true partnerships and 'pleasures of participation'.

Nevertheless, does a starving child or adult, a family that is under threat or an individual without shelter have time for such political solutions? Humanitarians rightly point to the necessity of addressing immediate needs and thus provide invaluable assistance. I am not advocating against development and humanitarian work, but for paying attention to what extent aidwork perpetuates what it seeks to undo and to complement short-term interventions with long-term strategies to really make a difference. As long as humanitarian interventions are needs based and do not address underlying structural inequalities, aid interventions fit into and stabilize a neoliberal framework.

Methods appendix

Between 2004 and 2013, I conducted biographical interviews with over 60 people working in aid. The interviews were conducted in two waves (2004 to 2006 and 2011 to 2013) and I got in touch with the respondents through a variety of means. The first interviews were conducted with a snowball sample of people whom I contacted through friends and other networks. The majority of interviews were conducted in 2005 and 2006 during a humanitarian studies course at a North American university. The course offered an excellent opportunity to obtain a purposive sample including men and women who had work experience in a range of organizations (including UN agencies, smaller and larger NGOs, Red Cross organizations, faith-based organizations, the military and government) working in relief, development and human rights work. In 2011 and 2012, I carried out additional interviews with former aid personnel in the South of England and via Skype with former aid people. In 2013, I conducted 12 additional interviews with participants of a humanitarian studies course at a European university which attracted French speakers, even though the language of instruction was English.

The 33 women and 24 men who were included in the analysis[1] originated from Australia, Barbados, Belgium, Canada, Colombia, France, Georgia, Germany, Ghana, Hungary, India, Iraq, Italy, Japan, Macedonia, Madagascar, Nepal, Pakistan, Philippines, Rwanda, Somalia, Sri Lanka, Sudan, Sweden, Switzerland, the United Kingdom, the United States and Venezuela. The organizations they had worked for included NGOs (Aga Khan Rural Support, Amnesty International, Help Age International, International Rescue Committee, Jesuit Refugee Services, Médecins Sans Frontières, Medair, Mercy Ships, Mines Advisory Group, Oxfam, Plan International, Save the Children, Tearfund, World Vision as well as smaller NGOs), UN agencies (IOM, UNFPA, UNHCR, WFP, WHO), the International Committee of the Red Cross, the International Federation of the Red Cross and OSCE. Respondents had been on assignments in Asia (Bangladesh, Burma, Cambodia, East Timor, Hong Kong, India, Indonesia, Nepal, Philippines, Sri Lanka, Vietnam), Africa (Angola, Burundi, Darfur, Democratic Republic of Congo, Ethiopia, Ghana, Guinea, Kenya, Liberia, Madagascar, Mali, Mozambique, Nigeria, Rwanda, Senegal, Sierra Leone, Somalia, South Africa, Swaziland, Tanzania, Uganda), the Middle East (Afghanistan, Gaza, Iraq, Kurdistan, Lebanon, Pakistan, Syria), Central and Eastern Europe (Albania, Bosnia, Croatia, Georgia, Kosovo, Kyrgyzstan, Serbia, Tajikistan, Ukraine) and Latin America (Bolivia, Brazil, Colombia, Ecuador, Nicaragua, Peru) and the Caribbean (Barbados, Haiti), and some had worked in head offices in Geneva, London, New York or Paris.

I first asked respondents to describe how their life developed up until they became involved in the aid world. The second part of the interview focused on the aidwork itself, how the lives of the interviewees changed and developed since they started in this field, how long they planned to do this kind of work, and under what circumstances they would leave (or had left) the aid world. Issues which had not been addressed in the narrative or have been unclear were addressed through follow-up questions. I had an extensive interview schedule which I handled flexibly. Some of the interviews were carried out in public, including in cafés or bars as well as university cafeterias. Interviews that were conducted during lunch breaks were usually shorter (30 to 60 minutes) than interviews conducted in the evenings or at weekends which lasted up to three hours. In several cases, the interviews were carried out over two sessions, as the interview could not be completed in the first session.

Interviewing people working in aid

Interviewees gave the impression that they enjoyed talking to me. They found themselves and their work interesting and the interview provided a neutral space for reflection – I was neither a (potential) co-worker, nor a friend or family member. Several respondents told me that they appreciated the fact that the interviews gave them an opportunity to reflect on their lives and careers. This was particularly important if they were at a point where they were considering a career change. Given that the interviews took place in Europe and North America rather than during an assignment, they were in a liminal position: both intellectually and emotionally engaged with, but temporarily removed from, Aidland while they were considering their next career step. Some found that through talking about their experiences in the interview they had gained a new perspective on past decisions. The respondents were very reflective and frequently considered what attracted them to aidwork and discussed the reasons for their career choice with friends and colleagues. As previously mentioned, virtually all respondents had graduate degrees and most had postgraduate degrees. Some were working on their Ph.D.s, several had used qualitative methods in their studies and some had even conducted life history interviews. Some had published reports and peer-reviewed journal articles. They were thus familiar with research methods and some were skilled interviewers themselves, including one respondent who was trained as a military debriefer. They were therefore familiar with the interview process and made conscious decisions about what they wanted to disclose.

All but two interviews were carried out in English, the remaining two in German. Some of the respondents were native speakers of English (from the UK, US, Canada, New Zealand or Australia) but for many, English was the second, third or more language. Thus, in the majority of interviews English served as lingua franca. Some respondents apologized for their lack of English-language skills. If that was the case, I apologized that due to my limited language skills I was only able to carry out interviews in English and German. I emphasized that if anyone should be embarrassed it should be me, not them, given that many of them spoke more languages (French, Spanish, Arabic, etc.) than I did and that my English was not perfect either. If they were not native speakers of English, they usually had more language skills than I had. Several respondents from African, Asian and Eastern European countries thanked me for being interviewed; they mentioned to me that they were happy that I was taking their perspectives into consideration, indicating that they felt marginalized and overlooked by Western expatriates, something which they discussed in the interviews. As a white, Western, highly educated woman, I shared characteristics of some of their expatriate colleagues, but I was also an outsider, not being a (former) aidworker myself. My outsider position was also relevant with respect to Western expatriates with whom I shared whiteness and cultural capital. Respondents wanted to know how I had become interested in the subject and whether I had been an aidworker myself. I explained that my interest in learning about aidworkers' careers was rooted in conversations with a friend working in aid and visiting her in Rwanda where I met some of her friends and colleagues in 2001, and again 12 years later when I visited her in Tanzania. I had never worked in aid myself, however. Thus, it was very clear that I was an outsider, which meant that respondents could not take for granted that we shared experiences and therefore had to explain to me how they experienced living and working in Aidland.

Both insider and outsider positions have clear advantages. Much research on people working in aid has been conducted by insiders (Harrison 2013) who have generated rich data and insightful analyses of processes in the field. However, I believe that conducting research as an outsider brings an additional perspective that allows for capturing the heterogeneity of the field, which also raises the question: who 'really' is an aidworker? Does it depend on the length of time spent in the field (contrast between consultants and fieldworkers), the type of organization (staff at the UN, for example, are more removed from 'beneficiaries' than NGO personnel), the sector (where relief is more urgent and risky than development) and the skills (generalists vs. trained medics or engineers)? Interviewees hardly referred to themselves as 'aidworkers' and instead referred to more specific and shifting positions.

Conducting research as an outsider also highlighted the distinction between 'Aidland' and the 'real world' or 'real life'. As I explain in this book, Aidland was often described as separate and distinct from 'normal life', more so for international than for national staff. However, international as well as national staff mentioned that it was difficult for them to find interest about their work from outsiders. While they could relate their experiences to other aidworkers, they sometimes missed understanding and validation from those living in the 'real world'. As an outsider and as a scholar taking an interest in their lives, I provided validation.

Following conventions for ethical research, I informed interviewees about my research interests and encouraged them to ask me further questions about the project and assured anonymity and confidentiality. All participants signed an informed consent form. I also emphasized at the beginning of each interview that respondents should only answer questions they were comfortable answering. In a few instances, interviewees did not provide information about their age, relationship status or sexual orientation, either because they felt that it was not relevant for the interview or because they did not want to share this information. However, overall, respondents were very open, even disclosing personal information they had not shared with friends or co-workers, fearing consequences for their careers. In this regard, being an outsider and being removed from the field had a clear advantage for conducting the interview. Interviewees were also interested to learn to what extent their experiences were comparable or what I had found out so far. I answered such questions by providing some preliminary observations which elicited further comments from the interviewees. Furthermore, when I noticed contradictions or inconsistencies during the interview, I pointed them out to the respondents in order to give them an opportunity to comment and elaborate on them.

The biographical interviews were supplemented with interviews with human resources (HR) officers and staff members of an organization supporting HR management of humanitarian organizations, several lecturers of humanitarian studies courses, including a trainer who works with NGOs and UN agencies. Furthermore, I spoke with former refugees and with individuals who considered becoming aidworkers but had not yet joined an aid organization. Furthermore, participation in humanitarian studies conferences and workshops and other occasions at which I presented my research led to informal conversations with (former) people in aid.

Analysing life-history interviews

I greatly enjoyed listening to the respondents which I did not only during the interviews but also while transcribing the recordings. I summarized the biographical interviews immediately after the interview and later on transcribed and coded in NVivo. My coding scheme encompassed the dimensions of biographical continuity, identity, interaction; resources, values, and empowerment. Furthermore, the analysis included gender and intersectionality as well as risk and danger. *Biographical continuity* focuses on the biographical trajectory as well as turning points; for example, if working in the field of humanitarian aid is constructed as a gradual development in the life-course or if there was a turning point which led to this activity. *Identity* addresses if and how the identity changed through working overseas and what influence the location (being at home, being in the field) has on identity. This dimension includes political attitudes and religious values as well as national and cosmopolitan identities. These two dimensions – biographical continuity and identity – in particular inform Chapter 3, which addresses how the respondents became involved in aidwork. The dimension *Interaction* gives attention to the relations in the field with local staff and beneficiaries; within the organization, within the expat community, and with friends and family in the field as well as during a visit at home or after returning to the home country. The dimension *Resources* encompasses education, travel, volunteering and work practice as well as networks in development cooperation, human rights work and relief aid. The dimension *Values* captures the motivation to become active in development and relief work, for example, political, social and religious motives. *Empowerment* addresses how aidworkers deal with challenges, danger and feelings of helplessness and what role these issues play in the satisfaction or dissatisfaction with their living and working situation. Furthermore, this dimension captures what importance capacity building and empowering of local staff has for aidworkers, as well as how expatriate aidworkers deal with their privileged position compared to the local population and to their comparatively disadvantaged position with other expats (diplomats, businesspeople). The dimensions are not mutually exclusive but overlapping, and include subjective and objective aspects (Bertaux and Kohli 1984). This means that they capture the trajectory as well as encompassing how the interviewees perceive and construct these trajectories. The analysis of these trajectories revealed three patterns: an early interest in development and relief that started in childhood or youth, a gradual involvement which was the result of social or political engagement or grew out of overseas experience, or a turning point which was based on a personal or public crisis.

Presenting data on aidworkers

Core aspects of research ethics include informed consent, voluntary participation and the refusal to answer inappropriate questions as well as confidentiality and anonymity.[2] Confidentiality and anonymity are two separate but related issues, assuring that data obtained in research, for example, interviews, do not disclose the identity of an individual, usually by anonymizing those individuals and places in the dissemination of the study (Wiles et al. 2008). Anonymization has become the norm for social science (Tilley and Woodthorpe 2011). However, depending on the population that is studied, it may not be sufficient to assign pseudonyms, in particular when one reports on research on a particular organization or community. If real names of organizations or places are given, this is usually the case if they appear to be large enough or far enough away (Guenther 2009, p. 412). Anonymization raises a number of issues. On the one hand, not all research participants want their identities concealed (Wiles et al. 2008; Guenther 2009). On the other hand, attempts to disguise an organization or place may not go far enough and it is possible for insiders to identify the research site. Thus 'internal' (referring to the network) and 'external' confidentiality need to be distinguished (Sikes 2010). Furthermore, the wish of some respondents to be identified has consequences for those who prefer to stay anonymous as well as family members or work colleagues who have been mentioned in interviews but were not asked to give informed consent. It can therefore be quite a challenge for researchers to assure confidentiality by removing identifying information (for example, references to places, organizations or professions) and changing key characteristics (nationality, sexual orientation, number of children, gender) without raising questions concerning distortion of data. However, such strategies, namely of changing characteristics of research participants in order to disguise identities, and what consequences this has, for example, readers cannot know whether and what kinds of changes have been made, and are rarely addressed in ethical guidelines and methods textbooks (Wiles et al. 2008). What consequences does this have for the presentation of biographical data on people working in aid given the 'ethical significance of naming people, organizations and places' (Guenther 2009)? One of the paradoxes of aidwork is that the transnational community of people working in aid which spans the globe is actually a 'small world', a fact that is amplified by the use of social media. Those involved in aidwork belong to the 'humanitarian international' (De Waal 1997) and, as one of my respondents put it, 'are part of the family'. Not only does my sample (friendship network, participants on a training course, former colleagues) raise questions of internal confidentiality, but also the field itself which is a small world of aid professionals and volunteers who, as 'disaster gypsies' (Norris 2007) or 'development nomads' (Eyben 2007), move from one site to the next. When I showed an early draft based on this research to a friend, he told me that he thought he would be able to recognize some of the people I had described if he met them, even if I had changed their names and some characteristics. Therefore, in order to assure anonymity and confidentiality, in my publications based on this research I have removed identifying information such as nationality, organizations worked for and country of assignment. Instead, I provide information about the region (for example, Western Europe), type of organization (NGO or UN agency, faith-based or secular), region of assignment (for example, Middle East, Africa) and type of work (development, humanitarian, human rights). Furthermore, in order to stay close to the data without disclosing the identity of my respondents, rather than presenting biographies, in my presentation I focus on various stages in the life-courses of people working in aid. Rottenburg (2009) chose an alternative approach: he fictionalized his study employing experimental ethnographic writing and inventing the 'Normesian Development Bank', a fictional European country called 'Normland' and a fictionalized country in sub-Saharan Africa called 'Ruritania'.

Notes

1 In a few cases it was not possible to record the interview. Since I only had handwritten notes, these interviews could not be transcribed and therefore were not included in the analysis.
2 The study on which this book is based was submitted to an ethics review at the University of Pennsylvania, where I started this project, and several years later again at the University of Southampton, where I continued the research.

Acknowledgements

This book and the study on which it is based have been carried out with a lot of individual and some institutional support. First of all, I would like to thank the respondents who granted me insight into their lives. It was a great pleasure and privilege listening to them and I hope I did them justice. Equally, I am grateful to those who helped me identify and introduced me to potential participants in this study – Naomi Reich, Emmanuel D'Harcourt, Katy Thompson, Jens Matthes, Polly Truscott, Larry Hollingworth, Jonathan Potter, Christine Williamson, Yvonne Marshall and Valerie Gorin. The study was financially supported through small research grants from the University of Pennsylvania and the University of Southampton. The latter also granted me research semesters in autumn 2008 and autumn 2012, for which I am grateful. I thank Myra Marx Ferree and Aili Mari Tripp for inviting me to spend time at the Research Center for Gender and Women at the University of Wisconsin-Madison in autumn 2012. I greatly enjoyed and am grateful for the good company and hospitality of Myra, Don and Sophie. Parts of this study were presented at meetings of the German Sociological Association, the American Sociological Association, the British Sociological Association, the European Sociological Association, the International Sociological Association and the International Humanitarian Studies Association. Furthermore, I gave presentations at conferences, workshops and seminars at the University of Southampton, the University of Sussex, the University of East Anglia, the London School of Economics, the University of Munich, the Humboldt University Berlin and the University of Lyon, and am grateful to those who invited me and for all the helpful comments I received. I would also like to thank Heidi Armbruster, Ute Banerjea-Komers, Graham Crow, Anne-Meike Fechter, Myra Marx Ferree, François Guesnet, Bernard Harris, Hilde Jakobsen, Clare Saunders and Barbara Wolbert for reading the manuscript at various stages – in the case of Heidi, Bernard and Meike more than once! – and providing me with immensely useful comments. I am very grateful to Ellie Rivers for improving my writing and for her moral support. Thea Hilhorst has encouraged me over the years to pursue this project and I was delighted when she invited me to publish this book in Routledge's Humanitarian Studies Series. It has been a pleasure to collaborate with

Khanam Virjee, Helen Bell, Ann King, Siobhán Greaney, Megan Smith and Bethany Wright at Routledge. Finally, I would like to thank my parents and friends for their support, patience and understanding while I disappeared to write this book.

This book is dedicated to all the brave, compassionate and critical people who seek to contribute to social justice through various interventions.

Bibliography

Abbott, A. (1988) *The System of Professions: An Essay on the Division of Expert Labor*. Chicago, IL: University of Chicago Press.

Abu-Sada, C. (ed.) (2012) *In the Eyes of Others: How People in Crises Perceive Humanitarian Aid*. New York: MSF/NYU Center on International Cooperation.

Acemoglu, D., Johnson, S. and Robinson, J.A. (2001) 'The colonial origins of comparative development: an empirical investigation'. *American Economic Review* 91(5): 1365–1401.

Acker, J. (1990) 'Hierarchies, jobs, bodies: a theory of gendered organizations'. *Gender and Society* 4(2): 139–158.

Adams, R.G. (1998) The Demise of Territorial Determinism: Online Friendships. In *Placing Friendship in Context*. Ed. by R.G. Adams and G. Allan. Cambridge: Cambridge University Press, pp. 153–182.

Agger, B. (2004) *Speeding Up Fast Capitalism: Internet Culture, Work, Families, Food, Bodies*. Boulder, CO: Paradigm.

Ahmad, M.M. (2007) 'The careers of NGO field-workers in Bangladesh'. *Nonprofit Management and Leadership* 17(3): 349–365.

Allmendinger, J. and Hackman, J.R. (1995) 'The more, the better? A four-nation study of the inclusion of women in symphony orchestras'. *Social Forces* 74(2): 423–460.

Andonova, L.B. and Carbonnier, G. (2014) 'Business–humanitarian partnerships: processes of normative legitimation'. *Globalizations* 11(3): 349–367.

Andrews, M. (1991) *Lifetimes of Commitment: Aging, Politics, Psychology*. Cambridge: Cambridge University Press.

——(2007) *Shaping History: Narratives of Political Change*. Cambridge: Cambridge University Press.

Antares Foundation (2012) *Managing Stress in Humanitarian Workers: Guidelines for Good Practice*. Amsterdam: Antares Foundation.

Apthorpe, R. (2005) 'Postcards from Aidland', paper presented at the Institute of Development Studies, University of Sussex, Brighton, 10 June.

——(2011a) Coda. With Alice in Aidland: A Seriously Satirical Allegory. In *Adventures in Aidland: The Anthropology of Professionals in International Development*. Ed. by D. Mosse. New York and Oxford: Berghahn Books, pp. 199–219.

——(2011b) Who? Is International Aid: Some Personal Observations. In *Inside the Everyday Lives of Development Workers: The Challenges and Futures of Aidland*. Ed. by A-M. Fechter and H. Hindman. Bloomfield, CT: Kumarian, pp. 193–210.

——(2012) 'Effective aid: the poetics of some aid workers' angles on how humanitarian aid "works"'. *Third World Quarterly* 33(8): 1545–1559.

Arvidson, M. (2008) 'Contradictions and confusions in development work: exploring the realities of Bangladeshi NGOs'. *Journal of South Asian Development* 3(1): 109–134.

——(2009) Ideals, Contradiction and Confusion: NGO Development Workers at the Grassroots. In *Ethnographic Practice and Public Aid: Method and Meanings in Development Cooperation*. Ed. by S. Hagberg and C. Widmark. Uppsala: Uppsala University Library, 45, pp. 215–240.

Baker, C. (2010) 'The care and feeding of linguists: the working environment of interpreters, translators, and linguists during peacekeeping in Bosnia-Herzegovina'. *War and Society* 29(2): 154–175.

Balch, C.M., Freischlag, J.A. and Shanafelt, T.D. (2009) 'Stress and burnout among surgeons: understanding and managing the syndrome and avoiding the adverse consequences'. *Archives of Surgery* 144(4): 371–376.

Banks, M. and Milestone, K. (2011) 'Individualization, gender and cultural work'. *Gender, Work and Organization* 18(1): 73–89.

Barder, O. (2007) Reforming Development Assistance: Lessons from the UK Experience. In *Security by Other Means: Foreign Assistance, Global Poverty and American Leadership*. Ed. by L. Brainard. Washington, DC: Brookings Institute, pp. 277–320.

Barnett, M. (2011) *Empire of Humanity: A History of Humanitarianism*. Ithaca, NY: Cornell University Press.

Barnett, M. and Stein, J.G. (eds) (2012) *Sacred Aid: Faith and Humanitarianism*. Oxford: Oxford University Press.

Bauman, Z. (1998) *Globalization: The Human Consequences*. Cambridge: Blackwell.

Bebbington, A. and Kothari, U. (2006) 'Transnational development networks'. *Environment and Planning A* 38: 849–866.

Beck, U., Giddens, A. and Lash, S. (eds) (1994) *Reflexive Modernization: Politics, Tradition and Aesthetics in the Modern Social Order*. Cambridge: Polity Press.

Beech, N. (2011) 'Liminality and the practices of identity reconstruction'. *Human Relations* 64(2): 285–302.

Benedetti, C. (2006) 'Islamic and Christian inspired relief NGOs: between tactical collaboration and strategic diffidence?' *Journal of International Development* 18(6): 849–859.

Benthall, J. (2008) 'Have Islamic aid agencies a privileged relationship in majority Muslim Areas? The case of post-tsunami reconstruction in Aceh'. *Journal of Humanitarian Assistance*, 26 June 2008, http://sites.tufts.edu/jha/archives/153 (last accessed 13 September 2014).

——(2011) Islamic Humanitarianism in Adversarial Context. In *Forces of Compassion. Humanitarianism Between Ethics and Politics*. Ed. by E. Bornstein and P. Redfield. Santa Fe, NM: School for Advanced Research Press, pp. 99–121.

Bertaux, D. and Kohli, M. (1984) 'The life story approach: a continental view'. *Annual Review of Sociology* 10(1): 215–237.

Bhambra, G.K. (2007) Multiple Modernities or Global Interconnections: Understanding the Global Post the Colonial. In *Varieties of World-Making: Beyond Globalization*. Ed. by N. Karagiannis and P. Wagner. Liverpool: University of Liverpool, pp. 59–73.

——(2014) *Connected Sociologies*. London: Bloomsbury Academic.

Binder, A. and Witte, J.M. (2007) 'Business engagement in humanitarian relief: key trends and policy implications'. *Humanitarian Policy Group Background Paper*. London: Overseas Development Institute.

Binder, A., Meier, C. and Steets, J. (2010) 'Humanitarian assistance: truly universal? A mapping study of non-Western donors'. *GPPI Research Paper Series*. Berlin: Global Public Policy Institute, 12. http://www.gppi.net/fileadmin/gppi/Binder_Meier_Steets-2010-Truly_Universal-Mapping_Study._GPPi_RP_12.pdf (last accessed 13 September 2014).

Bird, D. (1998) *Never the Same Again: A History of VSO*. Cambridge: VSO.

Bjerneld, M., Lindmark, G., Diskett, P. and Garrett, M. (2004) 'Perceptions of work in humanitarian assistance: interviews with returning Swedish health professionals'. *Disaster Management and Response* 2(4): 101–108.

Bjerneld, M., Lindmark, G., McSpadden, S. and Garrett, M. (2006) 'Motivations, concerns and expectations of Scandinavian health professionals volunteering for humanitarian assignments'. *Disaster Management and Response* 4(2): 49–58.

Blanchet, K. and Martin, B. (eds) (2011) *Many Reasons to Intervene. French and British Approaches to Humanitarian Action*. London: Hurst & Company.

Bollettino, V. and Bruderlein, C. (2008) 'Training humanitarian professionals at a distance: testing the feasibility of distance learning with humanitarian professionals'. *Distance Education* 29(3): 269–287.

Boltanski, L. (1999) *Distant Suffering. Morality, Media and Politics*. Cambridge: Cambridge University Press.

Boltanski, L. and Chiapello, E. (2005) *The New Spirit of Capitalism*. London: Verso.

Borton, J. (2009) *The Future of the Humanitarian System. Impacts of Internal Changes*. Berkamsted, UK: John Borton Consulting.

Boserup, E. (2007) *Women's Role in Economic Development*. London: Earthscan.

Bourdieu, P. (1977) *Outline of a Theory of Practice*. Cambridge: Cambridge University Press.

——(1990) *The Logic of Practice*. Palo Alto, CA: Stanford University Press.

Bourdieu, P. and Wacquant, L.J.D. (1992) *An Invitation to Reflexive Sociology*. Chicago, IL: Chicago University Press.

Bradbury, M. and Kleinman, M. (2010) *Winning Hearts and Minds? Examining the Relationship Between Aid and Security in Kenya*. Medford, MA: Feinstein International Center/Tufts University.

Brauman, R. (2011) Preface. In *Many Reasons to Intervene: French and British Approaches to Humanitarian Action*. Ed. by K. Blanchet and B. Martin. London: Hurst and Company, pp. xiii–xvii.

Bronner, U. (2003) *Humanitäre Helfer in Krisengebieten. Motivation, Einsatzerleben, Konsequenzen – Eine psychologische Analyse*. Munster: Lit Verlag.

Bruckmüller, S. and Branscombe, N.R. (2010) 'The glass cliff: when and why women are selected as leaders in crisis contexts'. *British Journal of Social Psychology* 49(3): 433–451.

Bruderlein, C. and Gassmann, P. (2006) 'Managing security risks in hazardous missions: the challenge of securing United Nations access to vulnerable groups'. *Harvard Journal of Human Rights* 19: 63–93.

Buchanan-Smith, M. (2003) 'How the *Sphere* project came into being: a case study of policy making in the humanitarian aid sector and the relative influence of research'. *Working Paper 211*. London: Overseas Development Institute.

Budd, J. W. (2011) *The Thought of Work*. Ithaca, NY: ILR Press.

Burrell Storms, S.L., Labonte, M.T., Siscar, A.M.N. and Martin, S.F. (2014) 'Collaborative Learning and Innovative Assessment in Humanitarian Studies.' *International Studies Perspectives*, first view: http://onlinelibrary.wiley.com/doi/10.1111/insp.12081/full.

Cain, K., Postlewaite, H. and Thomson, A. (2004) *Emergency Sex and Other Desperate Measures: A True Story from Hell on Earth*. New York: Miramax Books.

Calhoun, C. (2010) The Idea of Emergency: Humanitarian Action and Global (Dis) Order. In *Contemporary States of Emergency*. Ed. by D. Fassin and M. Pandolfi. Boston, MA: MIT Press, pp. 29–58.

Cameron, J. and Haanstra, A. (2008) 'Development made sexy: how it happened and what it means'. *Third World Quarterly* 29(8): 1475–1489.

Campbell, C., Campbell, D., Krier, D., Kuehlthau, R. et al. (2009) 'Reduction in burnout may be a benefit for short-term medical mission volunteers'. *Mental Health, Religion and Culture* 12(7): 627–637.

Campbell, M.L. and Teghtsoonian, K. (2010) 'Aid effectiveness and women's empowerment: practices of governance in the funding of international development'. *Signs* 36(1): 177–202.

Cardozo, B.L. and Salama, P. (2002) Mental Health of Humanitarian Aid Workers in Complex Emergencies. In *Sharing the Front Lines and the Back Hills: Peacekeepers, Humanitarian Aid Workers and the Media in the Midst of Crisis*. Ed. by Y. Danieli. New York: Baywood, pp. 242–255.

Carr, S.C. (2000) 'Privilege, privation and proximity: "eternal triangle" for development?' *Psychology and Developing Societies* 12(2): 167–176.

Carr, S.C., McWha, I., MacLachlan, M. and Furnham, A. (2010) 'International–local remuneration differences across six countries: do they undermine poverty reduction work?' *International Journal of Psychology* 45(5): 321–340.

Carr, S.C., Rugimbana, R.O., Walkom, E. and Bolitho, F.H. (2001) 'Selecting expatriates in developing areas: "country-of-origin" effects in Tanzania?' *International Journal of Intercultural Relations* 25(4): 441–457.

Chamberlayne, P., Bornat, J. and Apitzsch, U. (eds) (2004) *Biographical Methods and Professional Practice: An International Perspective*. Bristol: Polity Press.

Chandler, D. (2012) 'Resilience and human security: the post-interventionist paradigm'. *Security Dialogue* 43(3): 213–229.

Charles, L.L. (2007) *Intimate Colonialism: Head, Heart and Body in West African Development Work*. Walnut Creek, CA: Left Coast Press.

Chirkowska-Smolak, T. (2012) 'Does work engagement burn out? The person–job fit and levels of burnout and engagement in work'. *Polish Psychological Bulletin* 43(2): 76–85.

Choo, H.Y. and Ferree, M.M. (2010) 'Practising intersectionality in sociological research: a critical analysis of inclusion, interaction and institutions in the study of inequalities'. *Sociological Theory* 28(2): 129–149.

Chouliaraki, L. (2010) 'Post-humanitarianism: humanitarian communication beyond a politics of pity'. *International Journal of Cultural Studies* 13(2): 107–126.

——(2013) *The Ironic Spectator: Solidarity in the Age of Post-Humanitarianism*. Cambridge: Polity Press.

Clarke, R. (1999) 'Institutions for training overseas administrators: the University of Manchester's contribution'. *Public Administration and Development* 19(5): 521–533.

Coles, A. (2007) Portrait of an Aid Donor: A Profile of DFID. In *Professional Identities. Policy and Practice in Business and Bureaucracy*. Ed. by S. Ardener and F. Moore. Oxford: Berghahn Books, pp. 125–141.

Cook, N. (2005) 'What to wear, what to wear? Western women and imperialism in Gilgit, Pakistan'. *Qualitative Sociology* 28(4): 351–369.

——(2007) *Gender, Identity and Imperialism: Women Development Workers in Pakistan*. Basingstoke: Palgrave Macmillan.

Cooke, B. (2003) 'A new continuity with colonial administration: participation in development management'. *Third World Quarterly* 24(1): 47–61.

Cornish, S. (2011) 'Negative capability and social work: insights from Keats, Bion and business'. *Journal of Social Work Practice: Psychotherapeutic Approaches in Health, Welfare and the Community* 25(2): 135–148.

Cornwall, A. (2007) 'Buzzwords and fuzzwords: deconstructing development discourse'. *Development in Practice* 17(4): 471–484.

Cornwall, A. and Brock, K. (2005) 'What do buzzwords do for development policy: a critical look at "participation", "empowerment" and "poverty reduction"'. *Third World Quarterly* 26(7): 1043–1060.

Corrigal-Brown, C. (2012) *Patterns of Protest: Trajectories of Participation in Social Movements*. Stanford, CA: Stanford University Press.

Coser, L.A. (1967) 'Greedy organisations'. *European Journal of Sociology/Archives Européennes de Sociologie* 8(2): 196–215.

Crack, A.M. (2014) 'Reversing the telescope: evaluating NGO peer regulation initiatives'. *Journal of International Development*, firstview http://dx.doi.org/10.1002/jid.3010.

Cresswell, T. (2006) *On the Move: Mobility in the Modern Western World*. New York, Oxford: Routledge.

Crewe, E. and Fernando, P. (2006) 'The elephant in the room: racism in representations, relationships and rituals'. *Progress in Development Studies* 6(1): 40–54.

Crewe, E. and Harrison, E. (1998) *Whose Development? An Ethnography of Aid*. London, New York: Zed Books.

Crush, E. (ed.) (1995) *Power of Development*. London: Routledge.

Cunningham, I., Hearne, G. and James, P. (2013) 'Voluntary organisations and marketisation: a dynamic of employment degradation'. *Industrial Relations Journal* 44(2): 171–188.

Damman, M., Heyse, L. and Mills, M. (2014) 'Gender, occupation, and promotion to management in the nonprofit sector. The critical case of Médecins sans Frontières Holland'. *Nonprofit Management and Leadership*, 25(2): 97–111.

DARA (2012) Humanitarian Response Index 2011/Addressing the Gender Challenge: 50–60. http://daraint.org/humanitarian-response-index/humanitarian-response-index-2011 (last accessed 13 September 2014).

Dauvergne, P. and LeBaron, G. (2014) *Protest, Inc. The Corporatization of Activism*. Cambridge: Polity Press.

Davey, E. (2012) *Beyond the 'French Doctors': The Evolution and Interpretation of Humanitarian Action in France*. London: Overseas Development Institute.

Davidson, S. and Raynard, P. (2001) *Ahead of the Field: Pilot Agencies and the People in Aid Code*. London: People in Aid.

Dawson, J. (2005) 'A history of vocation: tracing a keyword of work, meaning, and moral purpose'. *Adult Education Quarterly* 55(3): 220–231.

De Cooman, R., De Gieter, S., Petermans, R. and Jegers, M. (2011) 'A cross-sector comparison of motivation-related concepts in for-profit and not-for-profit service organizations'. *Nonprofit and Voluntary Sector Quarterly* 40(2): 296–317.

De Cordier, B. (2009) 'The "humanitarian frontline", development and relief, and religion: what context, which threats and which opportunities?'. *Third World Quarterly* 30(4): 663–684.

de Graaf, R., van Zessen, G. and Houweling, H. (1998) 'Underlying reasons for sexual conduct and condom use among expatriates posted in AIDS endemic areas'. *Aids Care* 10(6): 651–665.

de Jong, S. (2011) False Binaries: Altruism and Egoism in NGO Work. In *Inside the Everyday Lives of Development Workers: The Challenges and Futures of Aidland*. Ed. by A-M. Fechter and H. Hindman. Bloomfield, CT: Kumarian, pp. 21–40.

de Torrente, N. (2004) 'Humanitarian action under attack: reflections on the Iraq war'. *Harvard Human Rights Journal* 17: 1–29.

De Waal, A. (1997) *Famine Crimes: Politics and the Disaster Relief Industry in Africa*. Bloomington, IN: Indiana University Press.

Dederian, K., Stobbaerts, E., Shingh, I., Rocha, S. et al. (2007) 'UN humanitarian reforms: a view from the field'. *Humanitarian Practice Network* (39).

Dema, S. (2008) 'Gender and organizations: the (re)production of gender inequalities within development NGOs'. *Women's Studies International Forum* 31(6): 441–448.

Deutsch, F.M. (2007) 'Undoing gender'. *Gender and Society* 21(1): 106–127.

Development Initiatives, Global Humanitarian Assistance. GHA Report (2011) UK. http://www.globalhumanitarianassistance.org/report/gha-report-2011.

——(2013) UK. http://www.globalhumanitarianassistance.org/report/gha-report-2013.

Devereux, P. (2008) 'International volunteering for development and sustainability: outdated paternalism or a radical response to globalisation?' *Development in Practice* 18(3): 357–370.

Dijkzeul, D. and Moke, M. (2005) 'Public communication strategies of international humanitarian organizations'. *International Review of the Red Cross* 87(860): 673–691.

Dijkzeul, D. and Wakenge, C.I. (2010) 'Doing good, but looking bad? Local perceptions of two humanitarian organisations in eastern Democratic Republic of the Congo'. *Disasters* 34(4): 1139–1170.

Dik, B.J. and Duffy, R.D. (2009) 'Calling and vocation at work: Definitions and prospects for research and practice'. *The Counselling Psychologist* 37(3): 424–450.

Dik, B.J. and Hansen, J-I.C. (2008) 'Following passionate interests to well-being'. *Journal of Career Assessment* 16(1): 86–100.

Dogra, N. (2011) 'The mixed metaphor of "third world woman": gendered representations by international development NGOs'. *Third World Quarterly* 32(2): 333–348.

Donini, A. (1995) 'The bureaucracy and the free spirits: stagnation and innovation in the relationship between the UN and NGOs'. *Third World Quarterly* 16(3): 421–440.

——(ed.) (2013) *The Golden Fleece: Manipulation and Independence in Humanitarian Action*. Sterling, VA: Kumarian.

Driffield, N. and Jones, C. (2013) 'Impact of FDI, ODA and migrant remittances on economic growth in developing countries: a systems approach'. *European Journal for Development Research* 25(2): 173–196.

Duffield, M. (1997) 'NGO relief in war zones: towards an analysis of the new aid paradigm'. *Third World Quarterly* 18(3): 527–542.

——(2010) 'Risk-management and the fortified aid compound: everyday life in post-interventionary society'. *Journal of Intervention and Statebuilding* 4(4): 453–474.

Dufour, C., de Geoffroy, V., Maury, H. and Gruenewald, F. (2004) 'Rights, standards and quality in a complex humanitarian space: is *Sphere* the right tool?' *Disasters* 28(2): 124–141.

Duncan, S. and Phillips, M. (2010) 'People who live apart together (LATs) – how different are they?' *The Sociological Review* 58(1): 112–134.

Eddy, M.P. (2011) 'Freedom summer abroad: biographical pathways and cosmopolitanism among international human rights workers'. *Research in Social Movements, Conflict and Change* 31: 209–258.

Ehrenberg, A. (2009) *The Weariness of the Self: Diagnosing the History of Depression in the Contemporary Age*. Toronto: McGill University Press.

Ehrenreich, J.H., Reyes, G. and Jacobs, G.A. (2006) Managing Stress in Humanitarian Aid Workers: The Role of the Humanitarian Aid Organization. In *Handbook of International Disaster Psychology: Interventions with Special Needs Populations (Vol. 4)*. Westport, CT: Praeger Publishers/Greenwood Publishing Group, pp. 99–112.

Eidelson, R.J., D'Alessio, G.R. and Eidelson, J.I. (2003) 'The impact of September 11 on psychologists'. *Professional Psychology: Research and Practice* 34(2): 144–150.

Ekman, S. (2013) 'Work as limitless potential: how managers and employees seduce each other through dynamics of mutual recognition'. *Human Relations* 66(9): 1159–1181.

Escobar, A. (1995) *Encountering Development: The Making and Unmaking of the Third World*. Princeton, NJ: Princeton University Press.

Etherington, N. (2005a) Education and Medicine. In *Missions and Empire*. Ed. by N. Etherington. Oxford: Oxford University Press, pp. 261–284.

——(ed.) (2005b) *Missions and Empire*. Oxford: Oxford University Press.

Evans, S. (1979) *Personal Politics: The Roots of Women's Liberation in the Civil Rights Movement and the New Left*. New York: Alfred A. Knopf.

Eyben, R. (2003) 'Mainstreaming the social dimension into the overseas development administration: a partial history'. *Journal of International Development* 15(7): 879–892.

——(2006) Introduction. In *Relationships for Aid*. Ed. by R. Eyben. London: Earthscan, pp. 1–17.

——(2007) Becoming a Feminist in Aidland. In *Gender and Family among Transnational Professionals*. Ed. by A. Coles and A-M. Fechter. New York, London: Routledge, pp. 149–169.

——(2011) The Sociality of International Aid and Policy Convergence. In *Adventures in Aidland: The Anthropology of Professionals in International Development*. Ed. by D. Mosse. New York, Oxford: Berghahn Books, pp. 139–161.

——(2014) *International Aid and the Making of a Better World*. London: Routledge.

Farah, A.A. (2003) From the Other Side of the Fence: The Problems behind the Solutions. In *Basics of International Humanitarian Missions*. Ed. by K.M. Cahill. New York: Fordham University Press/The Center for International Health and Cooperation, pp. 241–268.

Fassin, D. (2012) *Humanitarian Reason: A Moral History of the Present*. Berkeley, CA: University of California Press.

Fast, L. (2014) *Aid in Danger: The Perils and Promise of Humanitarianism*. Philadelphia, PA: University of Pennsylvania Press.

Faulk, L., Edwards, L.H., Lewis, G.B. and McGinnis, J. (2013) 'An analysis of gender pay disparity in the nonprofit sector: an outcome of labor motivation or gendered jobs?' *Nonprofit and Voluntary Sector Quarterly* 42(6): 1268–1287.

Fearon, J.D. (2008) The Rise of Emergency Relief Aid. In *Humanitarianism in Question. Politics, Power, Ethics*. Ed. by M. Barnett and T.G. Weiss. Ithaca, NY, London: Cornell University Press, pp. 49–72.

Fechter, A-M. (2007) From 'Incorporated Wives' to 'Expat Girls'. A New Generation of Expatriate Women? In *Gender and Family among Transnational Professionals*. Ed. by A. Coles and A-M. Fechter. New York, London: Routledge, pp. 193–209.

——(2011) Anybody at home? The inhabitants of Aidland. In *Inside the Everyday Lives of Development Workers: The Challenges and Futures of Aidland*. Ed. by A-M. Fechter and H. Hindman. Bloomfield, CT: Kumarian.

——(2012) '"Living well" while "doing good"? (Missing) debates on altruism and professionalism in aid work'. *Third World Quarterly* 33(8): 1475–1491.

——(2013) Mobility as Enabling Gender Equality? The Case of International Aid Workers. In *Migration and Inequality*. Ed. by T. Bastia. London: Routledge, pp. 167–186.

——(2015) Development People: How Does Gender Matter? In: *Routledge Handbook of Gender and Development*. London: Routledge, pp. 550–559.

Fechter, A-M. and Hindman, H. (eds) (2011) *Inside the Everyday Lives of Development Workers: Challenges and Futures of Aidland*. Bloomfield, CT: Kumarian.

Fehr, B. (1996) *Friendship Processes*. Thousand Oaks, CA: Sage.

Ferguson, I. (2007) 'Neoliberalism, happiness and wellbeing'. *International Socialism* Issue 117, posted 18 December 2007, http://www.isj.org.uk/index.php4?id=400 (last accessed 13 September 2014).

Ferguson, J. (1990) *The Anti-Politics Machine: Development, Depoliticization and Bureaucratic Power in Lesotho*. Minneapolis, MN: University of Minnesota Press.

Fernando, U. and Hilhorst, D. (2006) 'Everyday practics of humanitarian aid: tsunami response in Sri Lanka'. *Development in Practice* 16(3 and 4): 292–302.

Ferree, M.M. (2009) Inequality, Intersectionality and the Politics of Discourse. Framing Feminist Alliances. In *The Discursive Politics of Gender Equality: Stretching, Bending and Policy-making*. Ed. by E. Lombardo, P. Meier and M. Verloo. London: Routledge, pp. 84–101.

Ferree, M.M. and McClurg Mueller, C. (2007) Feminism and the Women's Movement: A Global Perspective. In *The Blackwell Companion to Social Movements*. Ed. by D.A. Snow, S.A. Soule and H. Kriesi. Oxford: Blackwell, pp. 576–607.

Ferree, M.M. and Yancey, P. (eds) (1995) *Feminist Organizations: Harvest of the New Women's Movement*. Philadelphia, PA: Temple University Press.

Fluri, J. (2009) '"Foreign passports only": geographies of (post)conflict work in Kabul, Afghanistan'. *Annals of the Association of American Geographers* 99(5): 986–994.

——(2011) 'Armored peacocks and proxy bodies: gender geopolitics in aid/development spaces of Afghanistan'. *Gender, Place and Culture* 18(4): 519–536.

Forster, N. (1999) 'Another "glass ceiling"? The experiences of women professionals and managers on international assignments'. *Gender, Work and Organization* 6(2): 79–90.

Fox, R.C. (2014) *Doctors Without Borders: Humanitarian Quests, Impossible Dreams of Médecins Sans Frontières*. Baltimore, MD: Johns Hopkins University Press.

Frantz, C. (2005) *Karriere in NGOs: Politik als Beruf jenseits der Parteien*. Wiesbaden: VS Verlag.

Fraser, A.S. and Tinker, I. (eds) (2004) *Developing Power: How Women Transformed International Development*. New York: The Feminist Press.

Garcia, J.R., Reiber, C., Massey, S.G. and Merriwether, A.M. (2012) 'Sexual hookup culture: a review'. *Review of General Psychology* 16(2): 161–176.

Gardner, K. and Lewis, D. (2000) 'Dominant paradigms overturned or "business as usual"? Development discourse and the White Paper on international development'. *Critique of Anthropology* 20(1): 15–29.

Gerhard, J. and Hans, S. (2013) 'Transnational human capital, education, and social inequality: analyses of international student exchange'. *Zeitschrift für Soziologie* 42(2): 99–117.

Ghodsee, K. (2005) 'Examining "Eastern" aid: Muslim minorities and Islamic foundations in Bulgaria'. *Anthropology of East Europe Review* 23(2): 63–71.

Gilbert, J. (2005) '"Self-knowledge is the prerequisite of humanity": personal development and self-awareness for aid workers'. *Development in Practice* 15(1): 64–69.

Giugni, M.G. (2004) Personal and Biographical Consequences. In *The Blackwell Companion to Social Movements*. Ed. by D.A. Snow, S.A. Soule and H. Kriesi. Malden, MA: Blackwell, pp. 489–507.

Glanz, L. (2003) 'Expatriate stories: a vehicle of professional development abroad'. *Journal of Management Psychology* 18(3): 259–274.

Glucksmann, M. (1995) 'Why "work"? Gender and the "total social organization of labour"'. *Gender, Work and Organization* 2(2): 63–75.

——(2005) 'Shifting boundaries and interconnections: extending the "total social organisation of labour"'. *The Sociological Review* 53(s2): 19–36.

Go, J. (2008) 'Global fields and imperial forms: field theory and the British and American Empires'. *Sociological Theory* 26(3): 201–229.

——(2013) 'For a postcolonial sociology'. *Theory and Society* 42(1): 25–55.

Goffman, E. (1961) *Asylums: Essays on the Social Situation of Mental Patients and Other Inmates*. New York: Anchor Books.

Goldstone, J. and McAdam, D. (2001) Contention in Demographic and Life-Course Context. In *Silence and Voice in the Study of Contentious Politics*. R.R. Amizade, J. Goldstone, D. McAdam, E.J. Perry et al. Cambridge: Cambridge University Press, pp. 195–221.

Gonzalez, J., Loewenstein, W. and Malek, Mo. (eds) (1999) *Humanitarian Development Studies in Europe: Assessment of Universities' Training and NGO's Needs*. Bilbao: University of Deusto.

Gorman, E.H. and Sandefur, R.L. (2011) '"Golden age", quiescence, and revival: how the sociology of professions became the study of knowledge-based work'. *Work and Occupations* 38(3): 275–302.

Goudge, P. (2003) *The Whiteness of Power: Racism in Third World Development and Aid*. London: Lawrence and Wishart.

Grammig, T. (2002) *Technical Knowledge and Development: Observing Aid Projects and Processes*. London: Routledge.

Green, H. (2012) 'From paternalism to participation: the motivations and understandings of the "developers"'. *Development in Practice* 22(8): 1109–1121.

Grimm, S. and Harmer, A. (2005) *Diversity in Donorship: The Changing Landscape of Official Humanitarian Aid. Aid Donorship in Central Europe*. London: Overseas Development Institute.

Grimm, S., Humphrey, J., Lundsgaarde, E. and de Sousa, S-L.J. (2009) 'European Development Cooperation to 2020: Challenges by New Actors in International Development'. ED. Working Paper. http://isites.harvard.edu/fs/docs/icb.topic845 003.files/Session%205%20-%20Feb%208/Grimm%20et%20al_2009_EDC2020.pdf (last accessed 13 September 2014).

Grimshaw, P. and Sherlock, P. (2005) Women and Cultural Exchanges. In *Missions and Empires*. Ed. by N. Etherington. Oxford: Oxford University Press, pp. 173–193.

Grossrieder, P. (2003) Humanitarian Action in the Twenty-First Century: The Danger of a Setback. In *Basics of International Humanitarian Missions*. Ed. by K.M. Cahill. New York: Fordham University Press/The Center for International Health and Cooperation, pp. 3–17.

Groves, L. and Hinton, R. (eds) (2005) *Inclusive Aid: Changing Power and Relationships in International Development*. London: Earthscan.

Guenther, K.M. (2009) 'The politics of names: rethinking the methodological and ethical significance of naming people, organizations, and places'. *Qualitative Research* 9(4): 411–421.
Halford, S. and Leonard, P. (2001) *Gender, Power and Organisations*. Basingstoke: Palgrave.
Hall, D.T. (2004) 'The protean career: a quarter-century journey'. *Journal of Vocational Behavior* 65(1): 1–13.
Hall, D.T. and Chandler, D.E. (2005) 'Psychological success: when the career is a calling'. *Journal of Organizational Behavior* 26(2): 155–176.
Halrynjo, S. (2009) 'Men's work–life conflict. Career, care and self-realization: patterns of privileges and dilemmas'. *Gender, Work and Organization* 16(1): 98–125.
Hammond, L. (2008) The Power of Holding Humanitarianism Hostage and the Myth of Protective Principles. In *Humanitarianism in Question. Power, Politics and Ethics*. Ed. by M. Barnett and T.G. Weiss. Cornell, NY: Cornell University Press, pp. 172–195.
Hancock, G. (1989) *Lords of Poverty: The Power, Prestige, and Corruption of the International Aid Business*. New York: Atlantic Monthly Press.
Hannerz, U. (1996) *Transnational Connections: Culture, People, Places*. London: Routledge.
——(2004) *Foreign News: Exploring the World of Foreign Correspondencts*. Chicago, IL: University of Chicago Press.
Harrell-Bond, B. (2002) 'Can humanitarian work with refugees be humane?' *Human Rights Quarterly* 24(1): 51–85.
Harrison, E. (2013) 'Beyond the looking glass? "Aidland" reconsidered'. *Critique of Anthropology* 33(3): 263–279.
Hartmann, M. and Honneth, A. (2006) 'Paradoxes of capitalism'. *Constellations* 13(1): 41–58.
Harvey, P., Stoddard, A., Harmer, A., Taylor, G., DiDomenico, V. and Brander, L. (2010) *The State of the Humanitarian System: Assessing Performance and Progress*. A pilot study. London: ALNAP/ODI.
Haskell, T. (1985a) 'Capitalism and the origins of the humanitarian sensibility, Part 1'. *American Historical Review* 90(2): 339–361.
——(1985b) 'Capitalism and the origins of the humanitarian sensibility, Part 2'. *American Historical Review* 90(3): 547–566.
Heaton Shrestha, C. (2006) 'They Can't Mix Like We Can': Bracketing Differences and the Professionalization of NGOs in Nepal. In *Brokers and Translators: The Ethnography of Aid and Agencies*. Ed. by D. Lewis and D. Mosse. Bloomfield, CT: Kumarian, pp. 195–216.
Heldman, C. and Wade, L. (2010) 'Hook-up culture: setting a new research agenda'. *Sexuality Research and Social Policy* 7(4): 323–333.
Heron, B. (2005) 'Changes and challenges: preparing social work students for practicums in today's sub-Saharan African context'. *International Social Work* 48(6): 782–793.
——(2007) *Desire for Development: Whiteness, Gender, and the Helping Imperative*. Waterloo, Ontario: Wilfrid Laurier University Press.
Hesmondhalgh, D. (2010) 'Normativity and social justice in the analysis of creative labour'. *Journal for Cultural Research* 14(3): 231–249.
Hess, J.A. (2002) 'Distance regulation in personal relationships: the development of a conceptual model and a test of representational validity'. *Journal of Social and Personal Relationships* 19(5): 663–83.
Heyse, L. (2007). *Choosing the Lesser Evil: Understanding Decision Making in Humanitarian Aid NGOs*. Abingdon: Ashgate.

Hilhorst, D. (2002) 'Being good at doing good? Quality and accountability of humanitarian NGOs'. *Disasters* 26(3): 193–212.
——(2003) *The Real World of NGOs: Discourses, Diversity and Development*. London: Zed Books.
——(2005) 'Dead letter or living document? Ten years of the Code of Conduct for disaster relief'. *Disasters* 29(4): 351–369.
——(2013) Disaster, Conflict and Society in Crises: Everyday Politics of Crisis Response. In *Disaster, Conflict and Society in Crises: Everyday Politics of Crisis Response*. Ed. by D. Hilhorst. London: Routledge, pp. 1–15.
Hilhorst, D. and Schmiemann, N. (2002) 'Humanitarian principles and organisational culture: everyday practice in Médecins Sans Frontières-Holland'. *Development in Practice* 12(3 and 4): 490–500.
Hilhorst, D. and Serrano, M. (2010) 'The humanitarian arena in Angola, 1975–2008'. *Disasters* 34(s2): S183–S201.
Hilhorst, D., Andriessen, G., Kemkens, L. and Weijers, L. (2013) Doing Good/Being Nice? Aid Legitimacy and Mutual Imagining of Aid Workers and Aid Recipients. In *Disaster, Conflict and Society in Crisis*. Ed. by D. Hilhorst. London: Routledge, pp. 258–274.
Hindman, H. (2011) Hollow Aid: Subcontracting and the New Development Family in Nepal. In *Inside the Everyday Lives of Development Workers: The Challenges and Futures of Aidland*. Ed. by A-M. Fechter and H. Hindman. Bloomfield, CT: Kumarian.
Hoare, J., Smyth, I. and Sweetman, C. (2012) 'Introduction: post-disaster humanitarian work'. *Gender and Development* 20(2): 205–217.
Holmes, J. (2007) 'Humanitarian action: a Western-dominated enterprise in need of change'. *Forced Migration Review* 29: 4–5.
Honneth, A. (1996) *The Struggle for Recognition: The Moral Grammar of Social Conflicts*. Boston, MA: MIT Press.
——(2004) 'Organized self-realization: some paradoxes of individualization'. *European Journal of Social Theory* 7(4): 463–478.
Hopgood, S. (2006) *Keepers of the Flame: Understanding Amnesty International*. Ithaca, NY: Cornell University Press.
Howell, J. and Pearce, J. (2001) *Civil Society and Development: A Critical Exploration*. Boulder, CO and London: Lynne Rienner.
Humanitarian Exchange Magazine (2011) Humanitarian Partnerships, Issue 50, April 2011. http://www.odihpn.org/humanitarian-exchange-magazine/issue-50
Hunt, M.R., Schwartz, L., Sindig, C. and Elit, L. (2014) 'The ethics of engaged presence: a framework for health professionals in humanitarian assistance and development work'. *Developing World Bioethics* 14(1): 47–55.
Hunter, S. (2010) 'What a white shame: race, gender, and white shame in the relational economy of primary health care organizations in England'. *Social Politics: International Studies in Gender, State and Society* 17(4): 450–476.
Hyndman, J. (1998) 'Managing difference: gender and culture in humanitarian emergencies'. *Gender, Place and Culture* 5(3): 241–260.
——(2004) 'Mind the gap: bridging feminist and political geography through geopolitics'. *Political Geography* 23(3): 307–322.
Illich, I. (1977) *Disabling Professions*. London: Boyars.
Illouz, E. (2008) *Saving the Modern Soul: Therapy, Emotions, and the Culture of Self-help*. Berkeley, CA: University of California Press.
Inglehart, R. (1977) *The Silent Revolution*. Princeton, NJ: Princeton University Press.

Inkson, K., Gunz, H., Ganesh, S. and Roper, J. (2012) 'Boundaryless careers: bringing back boundaries'. *Organization Studies* 33(3): 323–340.
International Health Exchange and People in Aid (1997) *The Human Face of Aid: A Study of Recruitment by International Relief and Development Organisations in the UK*. London: International Health Exchange, People in Aid.
Jackson, C. and Pearson, R. (eds) (1998) *Feminist Visions of Development*. London: Routledge.
Jolly, S. (2011) 'Why is development work so straight? Heteronormativity in the international development industry'. *Development in Practice* 21(1): 18–28.
Jones, A. (2011) 'Theorising international youth volunteering: training for global (corporate) work?' *Transactions of the Institute of British Geographers* 36(4): 530–544.
Kamat, S. (2004) 'The privatization of public interest: theorizing NGO discourse in a neoliberal era'. *Review of International Political Economy* 11(1): 155–176.
Kamruzzaman, P. (2013) 'Civil society or "comprador class", participation or parroting?' *Progress in Development Studies* 13(1): 31–49.
Kapoor, I. (2013) *Celebrity Humanitarianism: Ideology of Global Charity*. London: Routledge.
Karam, A. (2000) 'Women in war and peace-building: the roads traversed, the challenges ahead'. *International Feminist Journal of Politics* 3(1): 2–25.
Kelman, I. (2007) 'Hurricane Katrina disaster diplomacy'. *Disasters* 31(3): 288–309.
Kennedy, D. (2004) *The Dark Sides of Virtue. Reassessing International Humanitarianism*. Princeton, NJ: Princeton University Press.
King, D. (2012) 'The new internationalists: World Vision and the revival of American evangelical humanitarianism, 1950–2010'. *Religions* 3(4): 922–949.
Kleinman, S. (1996) *Opposing Ambitions: Gender and Identity in an Alternative Organisation*. Chicago, IL: University of Chicago Press.
Knox Clarke, P. (2014) *Between Chaos and Control: Rethinking Operational Leadership*. ALNAP Study. London: ALNAP/Overseas Development Institute.
Korff, V.P. (2012) *Between Cause and Control. Management in a Humanitarian Organization*. Ph.D. Thesis. Rijksuniversiteit Groningen.
Kothari, U. (2005a) 'Authority and expertise: the professionalisation of international development and the ordering of dissent'. *Antipode* 37(3): 425–446.
——(2005b) A Radical History of Development Studies: Individuals, Institutions and Ideologies. In *A Radical History of Development Studies. Individuals, Institutions and Ideologies*. Ed. by U. Kothari. London: Zed Books, pp. 1–13.
——(2006a) 'Critiquing "race" and "racism" in development discourse and practice'. *Progress in Development Studies* 6(1): 1–7.
——(2006b) 'An agenda for thinking about "race" in development'. *Progress in Development Studies* 6(1): 9–23.
——(2006c) 'From colonialism to development: continuities and divergences'. *Journal of Commonwealth and Comparative Politics* 44(1): 118–136.
Krause, M. (2014) *The Good Project: Humanitarian Relief NGOs and the Fragmentation of Reason*. Chicago, IL: University of Chicago Press.
Kreutzer, F. and Roth, S. (eds) (2006) *Transnationale Karrieren: Biografien, Lebensführung und Mobilität*. Wiesbaden: VS Verlag.
Lang, S. (1997) The NGOization of Feminism: Institutionalization and Institution Building within the German Women's Movement. In *Transitions, Environments, Translations: Feminisms in International Politics*. Ed. by J. Scott, C. Kaplan and D. Keats. New York: Routledge, pp. 101–120.

Lange, M., Mahoney, J. and vom Hau, M. (2006) 'Colonialism and development: a comparative analysis of Spanish and British colonies'. *American Journal of Sociology* 111(5): 1412–1462.

Lee, Y-j. and Wilkins, V.M. (2011) 'More similarities or more differences? Comparing public and nonprofit managers' job motivations'. *Public Administration Review* 71(1): 45–56.

Leonard, P. (2010) *Expatriate Identities in Post-colonial Organizations: Working Whiteness.* Aldershot: Ashgate.

Lester, A. and Dussart, F. (2014) *Colonialization and the Origins of Humanitarian Governance: Protecting Aborigines across the Nineteenth-Century British Empire.* Cambridge: Cambridge University Press.

Lewis, D. (ed.) (1999) *International Perspectives on Voluntary Action: Reshaping the Third Sector.* London: Earthscan.

——(2006) 'Globalization and international service: a development perspective'. *Voluntary Action* 7(2): 13–26.

——(2008a) 'Using life histories in social policy research: the case of third sector/public sector boundary crossing'. *Journal of Social Policy* 37(4): 559–578.

——(2008b) 'Crossing the boundaries between "third sector" and state: life–work histories from the Philippines, Bangladesh and the UK'. *Third World Quarterly* 29(1): 125–141.

——(2014) 'Heading south: time to abandon the "parallel worlds" of international non-governmental organization (NGO) and domestic third sector scholarship?' *VOLUNTAS: International Journal of Voluntary and Nonprofit Organizations*, 25(5): 1132–1150.

Lewis, D. and Mosse, D. (eds) (2006) *Development Brokers and Translators: The Ethnography of Aid and Agencies.* Bloomfield, CT: Kumarian.

Lind, A. and Share, J. (2003) Queering Development: Institutionalized Heterosexuality in Development Theory, Practice and Politics in Latin America. In *Feminist Futures: Re-imagining Women, Culture and Development.* Ed. by K. Bhavnani, J. Foran and P. Kurian. New York: Zed Books, pp. 55–73.

Linehan, M. (2001) 'European female expatriate careers: critical success factors'. *Journal of European Industrial Training* 25(8): 392–418.

Linley, P.A. and Joseph, S. (2004) 'Positive change following trauma and adversity: a review'. *Journal of Traumatic Stress* 17(1): 11–21.

Long, N. (2001) *Development Sociology: Actor Perspectives.* London and New York: Routledge.

Loquercio, D., Hammersley, M. and Emmens, B. (2006) Understanding and addressing staff turnover in humanitarian agencies. *Network Paper.* Humanitarian Practitioners Network. London: Overseas Development Institute, 55.

Lorber, J. (1994) *Paradoxes of Gender.* New Haven, CT: Yale University Press.

Lyng, S. (1990) 'Edgework: a social psychological analysis of voluntary risk taking'. *American Journal of Sociology* 95(4): 851–886.

Lyons, K., Hanley, J., Wearing, S. and Neil, J. (2012) 'Gap year volunteer tourism: myths of global citizenship?' *Annals of Tourism Research* 39(1): 361–378.

Lyttle, A.D., Barker, G.G. and Cornwell, T.L. (2011) 'Adept through adaptation: third culture individuals' interpersonal sensitivity'. *International Journal of Intercultural Relations* 35(5): 686–694.

MacLachlan, M., Carr, S. and McAuliffe, E. (2010) *The Aid Triangle: Human Dynamics of Dominance, Justice and Identity.* London: Zed Books.

Macrae, J., Collinson, S., Buchanan-Smith, M., Reindorp, N. et al. (2002) Uncertain Power: The Changing Role of Official Donors in Humanitarian Action. *Humanitarian Practitioners Group Report*. London: Overseas Development Institute.

Mafessoli, M. (1996) *The Time of the Tribes*. Thousand Oaks, CA: Sage.

Mangold, K. (2012) '"Struggling to do the right thing": challenges during international volunteering'. *Third World Quarterly* 33(8): 1493–1509.

Manning, R. (2006) 'Will "emerging donors" change the face of international cooperation?' *Development Policy Review* 24(4): 371–385.

Manyena, S.B. (2006) 'The concept of resilience revisited'. *Disasters* 30(4): 434–450.

Maren, M. (1997) *The Road to Hell: The Ravaging Effects of Foreign Aid and International Charity*. New York: Free Press.

Martin, P.Y. (2003) '"Said and done" versus "saying and doing": gendering practices, practicing gender at work'. *Gender and Society* 17(3): 342–366.

Maslach, C., Schaufel, W.B. and Leiter, M.P. (1996) *Maslach Burnout Inventory Manual*. Mountain View, CA: CPP Inc. and Davies-Black.

——(2001) 'Job burnout'. *Annual Review of Psychology* 52(1): 397–422.

Maxwell, D. (2005) Decolonialization. In *Missions and Empire*. Ed. by N. Etherington. Oxford: Oxford University Press, pp. 285–306.

Maxwell, D.G. and Walker, P. (2008) *Shaping the Humanitarian World*. New York: Routledge.

McAdam, D. (1986) 'Recruitment to high risk activism'. *American Journal of Sociology* 92(1): 64–90.

——(1999) The Biographical Impact of Activism. In *How Social Movements Matter*. Ed. by M. Giugni, D. McAdam and C. Tilly. Minneapolis, MN: University of Minnesota Press, pp. 119–146.

McCoy, S.P. and Aamodt, M.G. (2010) 'A comparion of law enforcement divorce rates with those of other occupations'. *Journal of Police Criminal Psychology* 25(1): 1–16.

McDermott, A.M., Heffernan, M. and Beynon, M.J. (2012) 'When the nature of employment matters in the employment relationship: a cluster analysis of psychological contracts and organizational commitment in the non-profit sector'. *The International Journal of Human Resource Management* 24(7): 1490–1518.

McKinnon, K. (2007) 'Postdevelopment, professionalism, and the politics of participation'. *Annals of the Association of American Geographers* 97(4): 772–785.

McMaster, J. (2008) Direct Budget Support versus Project Aid. In *Interdisciplinary Research for Development: A Workbook on Content and Process Challenges*. Ed. by M. MacLachlan, S.C. Carr and I. McWha. New Dehli: Global Development Network.

McRobbie, A. (2002) 'Clubs to companies: notes on the decline of political culture in speeded up creative worlds'. *Cultural Studies* 16(4): 516–531.

McWha, I. (2011) 'The roles of, and relationships between, expatriates, volunteers, and local development workers'. *Development in Practice* 21(1): 29–40.

McWha, I. and MacLachlan, M. (2011) 'Measuring relationships between workers in poverty-focused organisations'. *Journal of Managerial Psychology* 26(6): 485–499.

Miethe, I. and Roth, S. (2005) Zum Verhältnis von Biographie-und Bewegungsforschung. In *Biographieforschung im Diskurs*. Ed. by B. Voelter, B. Dausien, H. Lutz and G. Rosenthal. Wiesbaden: VS Verlag, pp. 103–118.

Minear, L. (1988) *Helping People in an Age of Conflict: Toward a New Professionalism in US Voluntary Humanitarian Assistance*. New York and Washington, DC: Interaction.

——(2002) *The Humanitarian Enterprise: Dilemmas and Discoveries*. Bloomfield, CT: Kumarian.

Mizzi, R.C. (2013) '"There aren't any gays here": encountering heteroprofessionalism in an international development workplace'. *Journal of Homosexuality* 60(11): 1602–1624.

Momsen, J.H. (2008) *Gender and Development*. New York: Routledge.

Morse, N.C. and Weiss, R.S. (1955) 'The function and meaning of work and the job'. *American Sociological Review* 20(2): 191–198.

Mosse, D. (2005) *Cultivating Development: An Ethnography of Aid Policy and Practice*. London: Pluto.

——(ed.) (2011) *Adventures in Aidland: The Anthropology of Professionals in International Development*. New York and Oxford: Berghahn Books.

MSF International Movement (2011) *MSF Financial Report 2010*. Geneva: MSF International Office.

Muenz, R. (2007) *Im Zentrum der Katastrophe. Was es wirklich bedeutet, vor Ort zu helfen*. Frankfurt/M: Campus.

Muir, A. (2003) UK Higher Education in International Cooperation. In *University Development Cooperation Models of Good Practice*. Ed. by P. Beneitone, S. Hoivik, N. Molenaers, A. Obrecht and R. Renard. Bilbao: University of Deusto, pp. 157–171.

National Audit Office (2008) Department for International Development. 'Operating in insecure environments'. Report by the Comptroller and Auditor General.

Nepstad, S.E. and Smith, C.S. (1999) 'Rethinking recruitment to high-risk activism: the case of Nicaragua Exchange'. *Mobilization* 4(1): 40–51.

Newman, J. (2012) *Working the Spaces of Power: Activism, Neoliberalism and Gendered Labour*. London: Bloomsbury Academic.

Norris, J. (2007) *The Disaster Gypsies: Humanitarian Workers in the World's Deadliest Conflicts*. Westport, CT: Praeger Security International.

Nowicka, M. (2006) *Transnational Professionals and their Cosmopolitan Universes*. Frankfurt/M: Campus.

Nowicka, M. and Kaweh, R. (2009) Looking at the Practice of UN Professionals: Strategies for Managing Differences and the Emergence of a Cosmopolitan Identity. In *Cosmopolitanism in Practice*. Ed. by M. Nowicka and M. Rovisco. Farnham: Ashgate, pp. 51–71.

O'Dempsey, T. (2009) 'Fair training: a new direction in humanitarian assistance'. *Progress in Development Studies* 9(1): 81–86.

Ojelay-Surtees, B. (2004) 'Diversity in Oxfam GB: engaging the head and turning the heart'. *Gender and Development* 12(1): 56–67.

Olson, L. (1999) *A Cruel Paradise: Journals of an International Relief Worker*. Toronto: Insomniac Press.

Omi, M. and Winant, H. (1994) *Racial Formation in the United States. From the 1960 to the 1990s*. London and New York: Routledge.

O'Reilly, K. (2004) 'Developing contradictions: women's participation as a site of struggle within an Indian NGO'. *The Professional Geographer* 56(2): 174–184.

——(2006) 'Women fieldworkers and the politics of participation'. *Signs: Journal of Women in Culture and Society* 31(4): 1075–1098.

Osbaldiston, N. (2013) *Culture of the Slow: Social Deceleration in an Accelerated World*. Basingstoke: Palgrave Macmillan.

Owen, J.R. (2010) '"Listening to the rice grow": the local–expat interface in Lao-based international NGOs'. *Development in Practice* 20(1): 99–112.

Pahl, R. (ed.) (1988) *On Work: Historical, Comparative and Theoretical Approaches*. Oxford: Blackwell.

Pandolfini, M. (2011) Humanitarianism and its Discontents. In *Forces of Compassion. Humanitarianism Between Ethics and Politics.* Ed. by E. Bornstein and P. Redfield. Santa Fe, NM: School for Advanced Research Press, pp. 227–248.
Parkins, W. and Craig, G. (2006) *Slow Living.* Oxford: Berg.
Parment, A. (2011) *Generation Y in Consumer and Labour Markets.* London: Routledge.
Passy, F. and Giugni, M. (2000) 'Life-spheres, networks, and sustained participation in social movements: a phenomenological approach to political commitment'. *Sociological Forum* 15(1): 117–144.
Pérouse de Montclos, M-A. (2012) 'Humanitarian action in developing countries: who evaluates who?' *Evaluation and Program Planning* 35(1): 154–160.
Petersen, M. (2012a) 'Islamizing aid: transnational Muslim NGOs After 9.11'. *Voluntas: International Journal of Voluntary and Nonprofit Organizations* 23(1): 126.
——(2012b) 'Trajectories of transnational Muslim NGOs'. *Development in Practice* 22(5–6): 763–778.
Petras, J. and Veltmeyer, H. (2002) 'Age of reverse aid: neo-liberalism as catalyst of regression'. *Development and Change* 33(2): 281–293.
Pierce, J.L. (1995) *Gender Trials: Emotional Lives in Contemporary Law Firms.* Berkeley, CA: University of California Press.
Polman, L. (2010) *War Games: The Story of Aid and War in Modern Times.* London: Penguin.
Porter, B. and Emmens, B. (2009) *Approaches to Staff Care in International NGOs.* London: People in Aid/Interhealth.
Porter, F. and Sweetman, C. (eds) (2005) *Mainstreaming Gender in Development: A Critical Review.* Oxford: Oxfam.
Powell, C. (2001) Remarks to the National Foreign Policy Conference for Leaders of Nongovernmental Organizations. Washington, DC, 26 October, http://2001-9.state.gov/secretary/former/powell/remarks/2001/5762.htm (last accessed 15 September 2014).
Rai, S. (2008) *The Gender Politics of Development: Essays in Hope and Despair.* London, New York and New Delhi: Zed Books/Zubaan.
Rainhorn, J-D., Smailbegovic, A. and Jiekak, S. (2010) *Humanitarian Studies 2010: University Training and Education in Humanitarian Action.* Geneva: University of Geneva Graduate Institute.
Rajak, D. and Stirrat, J. (2011) Parochial Cosmopolitanism and the Power of Nostalgia. In *Adventures in Aidland: The Anthropology of Professionals in International Development.* Ed. by D. Mosse. New York and Oxford: Berghahn Books, pp. 161–176.
Ramalingam, B. (2013) *Aid on the Edge of Chaos.* Oxford: Oxford University Press.
Randel, J. and German, T. (eds) (1997) *The Reality of Aid. An Independent Review of Development Cooperation.* London: Earthscan.
Rebughini, P. (2011) 'Friendship dynamics between emotions and trials'. *Sociological Research Online* 16(1): 3.
Redfield, P. (2006) 'A less modest witness'. *American Ethnologist* 33(1): 3–26.
——(2008a) Doctors Without Borders and the Moral Economy of Pharmaceuticals. In *Human Rights in Crisis.* Ed. by A. Bullard. Aldershot: Ashgate Press, pp. 129–144.
——(2008b) Vital Mobility and the Humanitarian Kit. In *Biosecurity Interventions: Global Health and Security in Question.* Ed. by A. Lakoff and S. Collier. New York: Columbia University Press, pp. 147–171.
——(2010) The Verge of Crisis: Doctors Without Borders in Uganda. In *Contemporary States of Emergency: The Politics of Military and Humanitarian Interventions.* Ed. by D. Fassin and M. Pandolfini. London: Zone Books, pp. 173–195.

—— (2012) 'The unbearable lightness of ex-pats: double binds of humanitarian mobility'. *Cultural Anthropology* 27(2): 358–382.

—— (2013) *Life in Crisis. The Ethical Journey of Doctors Without Borders*. Berkeley, CA: University of California Press.

Redfield, P. and Bornstein, E. (2011) An Introduction to the Anthropology of Humanitarianism. In *The Forces of Compassion: Humanitarianism Between Ethics and Politics*. Ed. by E. Bornstein and P. Redfield. Santa Fe, NM: School of Advanced Research, pp. 3–30.

Rees, S. (1999) 'Managerialism in social welfare: proposals for a humanitarian alternative – an Australian perspective'. *European Journal of Social Work* 2(2): 193–202.

Rheingans, R. and Hollands, R. (2012) '"There is no alternative?": challenging dominant understandings of youth politics in late modernity through a case study of the 2010 UK student occupation movement'. *Journal of Youth Studies* 16(4): 546–564.

Rhoton, L.A. (2011) 'Distancing as a gendered barrier: understanding women scientists' gender practices'. *Gender and Society* 25(6): 696–716.

Richardson, F. (2006) 'Meeting the demand for skilled and experienced humanitarian workers'. *Development in Practice* 16(3): 334–341.

Richey, L.A. and Ponte, S. (2011) *Brand Aid: Shopping Well to Save the World*. Minneapolis, MN: University of Minnesota Press.

Ridde, V. (2010) 'Per diems undermine health interventions, systems and research in Africa: burying our heads in the sand'. *Tropical Medicine and International Health*: Early view, http://onlinelibrary.wiley.com/doi/10.1111/j.1365–3156.2010.02607.x/full (last accessed 13 September 2014).

Ridde, V., Goossens, S. and Shakir, S. (2012) 'Short-term consultancy and collaborative evaluation in a post-conflict and humanitarian setting: lessons from Afghanistan'. *Evaluation and Program Planning* 35(1): 180–188.

Riddell, R.C. (2007) *Does Foreign Aid Really Work?* Oxford: Oxford University Press.

Ridgeway, C.L. (2009) 'Framed before we know it: how gender shapes social relations'. *Gender and Society* 23(2): 145–160.

Rieff, D. (2002) *A Bed for the Night: Humanitarianism in Crisis*. London: Vintage.

Risman, B.J. (2009) 'From doing to undoing: gender as we know it'. *Gender and Society* 23(1): 81–84.

Robb, C. (2005) Changing Power Relations in the History of Aid. In *Inclusive Aid: Changing Power and Relationships in International Development*. Ed. by L. Groves and R. Hinton. London: Earthscan, pp. 21–41.

Rose, N. (1989) *Governing the Soul: The Shaping of the Modern Self*. London: Free Association Books.

Roseneil, S. (2006) 'On not living with a partner: unpicking coupledom and cohabitation'. *Sociological Research Online* 11(3).

Roth, S. (2006) Humanitäre Hilfe – Zugänge und Verläufe. In *Transnationale Karrieren. Biografien, Lebensführung und Identität*. Ed. by F. Kreutzer and S. Roth. Wiesbaden: VS Verlag, pp. 100–119.

—— (2010) Einsatz ohne Grenzen. Mobilitätserfahrungen in Entwicklungszusammenarbeit und humanitärer Hilfe. In *Mobilität und Mobilisierung. Arbeit im sozioökonomischen, politischen und kulturellen Wandel*. Ed. by I. Goetz, B. Lemberger, K. Lehner and A-C. Schondelmayer. Frankfurt/M: Campus, pp. 81–94.

—— (2011) Dealing with Danger: Risk and Security in the Everyday Lives of Aid Workers. In *Inside the Everyday Lives of Development Workers: The Challenges and*

Futures of Aidland. Ed. by A-M. Fechter and H. Hindman. Bloomfield, CT: Kumarian, pp. 151–168.
——(2012) 'Professionalisation trends and inequality: experiences and practices in aid relationships'. *Third World Quarterly* 33(8): 1459–1474.
——(2013) 'Alltag und Aktivismus – Schlüsselfiguren in Familie, Nachbarschaft und Arbeit.' *Forschungsjournal Soziale Bewegungen* 26(4): 43–51.
——(2014) 'Aid work as edgework – voluntary risk-taking and security in humanitarian assistance, development and human rights work'. *Journal of Risk Research.* first view http://dx.doi.org/10.1080/13669877.2013.875934 (last accessed 13 September 2014).
Rottenburg, R. (2009) *Far-Fetched Facts. A Parable of Development Aid.* Cambridge, MA: MIT Press.
Ruch, G. (2014) 'Beneficence in psycho-social research and the role of containment'. *Qualitative Social Work* 13(4): 522–538.
Ryfman, P. (2011) Crises of Maturity and Transformation in French NGOs. In *Many Reasons to Intervene. French and British Approaches to Humanitarian Action.* Ed. by K. Blanchet and B. Martin. London: Hurst and Company, pp. 9–25.
Sampson, S.D. and Moore, L.L. (2008) 'Is there a glass ceiling for women in development?' *Nonprofit Management and Leadership* 18(3): 321–339.
Saunders, C. (2009) NGOs in Contemporary Britain: Non-state Actors in Society and Politics Since 1945. In *NGOs in Contemporary Britain. Non-state Actors in Society and Politics Since 1945.* Ed. by N. Crowson, M. Hilton and J. McKay. Basingstoke: Palgrave Macmillan, pp. 38–57.
Schade, J. (2007) Neutralität humanitärer NGOs in Kriegs-und Nachkriegssituationen. Ein frommer Wunsch? In *NGOs im Spannungsfeld von Krisenprävention und Sicherheitspolitik.* Ed. by A. Klein and S. Roth. Wiesbaden: VS Verlag.
Schondelmayer, A-C. (2010) *Interkulturelle Handlungskompetenz: Entwicklungshelfer und Auslandskorrespondenten in Afrika. Eine narrative Studie.* Bielefeld: Transkript.
Schor, J. (2008) 'Tackling turbo consumption'. *Cultural Studies* 22(5): 588–598.
Scott-Smith, T. (2014) 'Control and biopower in contemporary humanitarian aid: the case of supplementary feeding'. *Journal of Refugee Studies,* firstview http://jrs.oxfordjournals.org/content/early/2014/06/28/jrs.feu018.abstract (last accessed 16 September 2014).
Selmer, J. and Leung, A.S.M. (2003) 'Expatriate career intentions of women on foreign assignments and their adjustment'. *Journal of Managerial Psychology* 18(3): 244–258.
Sharp, T.W., DeFraites, R.F., Thornton, S.A., Burans, J.A. et al. (1995) 'Illness in journalists and relief workers involved in international humanitarian assistance efforts in Somalia, 1992–93'. *Journal of Travel Medicine* 2(2): 70–76.
Shea, L., Thompson, L. and Blieszner, R. (1988) 'Resources in older adults' old and new friendships'. *Journal of Social and Personal Relationships* 5(1): 83–96.
Sheik, M. et al. (2000) 'Deaths among humanitarian workers'. *British Medical Journal* 321: 166–168.
Shepherd, L.J. (2011) 'Sex, security and superhero(in)es: from 1325 to 1820 and beyond'. *International Feminist Journal of Politics* 13(4): 504–521.
Shevchenko, O. and Fox, R.C. (2008) '"Nationals" and "expatriates": challenges of fulfilling "sans frontières" ("without borders") ideals in international humanitarian action'. *Health and Human Rights* 10(1): 109–122.
Shortland, S. and Cummins, S. (2007) 'Work–life balance: expatriates reflect the international dimension'. *Global Business and Organizational Excellence* 26(6): 28–42.

Shutt, C. (2012) 'A moral economy? Social interpretations of money in Aidland'. *Third World Quarterly* 33(8): 1527–1543.

Sikes, P. (2010) The Ethics of Writing Life Histories and Narratives in Educational Research. In *Exploring Learning, Identity and Power through Life History and Narrative Research*. Ed. by A-M. Bathmaker and P. Harnett. London: Routledge, pp. 11–24.

Simeant, J. (2005) 'What is going global? The Internationalization of French NGOs "without borders"'. *Review of International Political Economy* 12(5): 851–883.

Simon, D. (2009) 'From the Holocaust to development: reflections of surviving development pioneers'. *Third World Quarterly* 30(5): 849–884.

Simpson, K. (2004) '"Doing development": the gap year, volunteer-tourists and a popular practice of development'. *Journal of International Development* 16(5): 681–692.

——(2005) 'Dropping out or signing up? The professionalisation of youth travel'. *Antipode* 37(3): 447–469.

Six, C. (2009) 'The rise of postcolonial states as donors: a challenge to the development paradigm?' *Third World Quarterly* 30(6): 1103–1121.

Skocpol, T. (2003) *Diminished Democracy: From Membership to Management in American Civic Life/Theda Skocpol*. Norman, OK: University of Oklahoma Press.

Slim, H. (1995) 'The continuing metamorphosis of the humanitarian practitioner: some new colours for an endangered chameleon'. *Disasters* 19(2): 110–126.

——(1996) 'The stretcher and the drum: civil–military relations in peace support operations'. *International Peacekeeping* 3(2): 123–140.

——(1997) 'Doing the right thing: relief agencies, moral dilemmas and moral responsibility in political emergencies and war'. *Disasters* 21(3): 244–257.

——(2000) 'Dissolving the difference between humanitarianism and development: the mixing of a rights-based solution'. *Development in Practice* 10(3): 491–494.

——(2001) 'Violence and humanitarianism: moral paradox and the protection of civilians'. *Security Dialogue* 32(3): 325–339.

——(2005) *Idealism and Realism in Humanitarian Action*. Canberra: ACFID Humanitarian Forum.

——(2011) Establishment Radicals: An Historical Overview of British NGOs. In *Many Reasons to Intervene. French and British Approaches to Humanitarian Action*. Ed. by K. Blanchet and B. Martin. London: Hurst and Company, pp. 27–39.

——(2012a) 'Business actors in armed conflict: towards a new humanitarian agenda'. *International Review of the Red Cross* 94(887): 903–918.

——(2012b) Idealism and Realism in Humanitarian Action. In *Essays in Humanitarian Action*. Ed. by H. Slim. Kindle Book, Amazon.

——(2012c) *Essays in Humanitarian Action*. Kindle Book, Amazon.

——(2014). The Limits of Humanitarian Action. In *The Handbook of Global Health Policy*. Ed. by G.W. Brown, G. Yarney and S. Hoboken. Princeton, NJ: Wiley, pp. 341–353.

Smillie, I. and Minear, L. (2004) *The Charity of Nations: Humanitarian Action in a Calculating World*. Bloomfield, CT: Kumarian.

Smirl, L. (2012) The State We Are (n't) In: Liminal Subjectivity in Aid Worker Autobiographies. In *Statebuilding and State-formation: The Political Sociology of Intervention*. Ed. by B. Blieseman De Guevara. London: Routledge, pp. 230–245.

Smyser, W.R. (2003) *The Humanitarian Conscience: Caring for Others in the Age of Terror*. New York and Basingstoke: Palgrave Macmillan.

Sondorp, E. (2011) French or Anglo-Saxon: A Different Ethical Perspective? In *Many Reasons to Intervene: French and British Approaches to Humanitarian Action*. Ed. by K. Blanchet and B. Martin. London: Hurst and Company, pp. 41–47.

Srkribis, Z., Kendall, G. and Woodward, I. (2004) 'Locating cosmopolitanism: between humanist ideal and grounded social category'. *Theory, Culture and Society* 21(6): 115–136.
Stanley, B. (1990) *The Bible and the Flag: Protestant Missions and British Imperialism in the Nineteenth and Twentieth Centuries.* Leicester: Apollos.
Steger, M.F., Pickering, N.K. and Woodward, I. (2010) 'Calling in work: secular or sacred?'. *Journal of Career Assessment* 18(1): 82–96.
Steinmetz, G. (2013) Major Contributions to Sociological Theory and Research on Empire, 1830–Present. In *Sociology and Empire.* Ed. by G. Steinmetz. Durham, NC: Duke University Press, pp. 1–50.
Stirrat, J. (2006) 'Competitive humanitarianism: relief and the tsunami in Sri Lanka'. *Anthropology Today* 22(5): 11–16.
Stirrat, R.L. (2000) 'Cultures of consultancy'. *Critique of Anthropology* 20(1): 31–46.
——(2008) 'Mercenaries, missionaries and misfits: representations of development personnel'. *Critique of Anthropology* 28(4): 406–425.
Stoddard, A. (2003) 'Humanitarian NGOs: challenges and trends'. *HPG Briefing* (12).
——(2004) 'You say you want a devolution. Prospects of humanitarian assistance'. *Journal of Humanitarian Assistance*, www.jha.ac/articles/a154.pdf (posted November 2004).
Stoddard, A., Harmer, A. and Haver, A. (2006) Providing Aid in Insecure Environments: Trends in Policy and Operations. *HPG Report.* New York: Center on International Cooperation, New York University.
Stoddard, A., Harmer, A. and DiDomenico, V. (2009) Providing Aid in Insecure Environments: 2009 Update. Trends in Violence Against Aid Workers and the Operational Response: Why Violent Attacks on Aid Workers are on the Increase. *Policy Brief.* HP Group. London: Overseas Development Institute, 34.
Street, A. (2009) 'Humanitarian reform: a progress report'. *Humanitarian Exchange Magazine* (45).
Stride, H. and Higgs, M. (2014) 'An investigation into the relationship between values and commitment: a study of staff in the UK charity sector'. *Nonprofit and Voluntary Sector Quarterly* 43(3), 455–479.
Stroup, S.S. (2012) *Borders Among Activists: International NGOs in the United States, Britain, and France.* Ithaca, NY: Cornell University Press.
Stumpenhorst, M., Stumpenhorst, R. and Razum, O. (2011) 'The UN OCHA cluster approach: gaps between theory and practice'. *Journal of Public Health* 19(1): 587–592.
Subramaniam, G. (2006) 'Ruling continuities: colonial rule, social forces and path dependence in British India and Africa'. *Commonwealth and Comparative Politics* 44(1): 84–117.
Syed, J. and Ali, F. (2011) 'The white woman's burden: from colonial civilisation to third world development'. *Third World Quarterly* 32(2): 349–365.
Tadele, F. and Manyena, S.B. (2009) 'Building disaster resilience through capacity building in Ethiopia'. *Disaster Prevention and Management* 18(3): 317–326.
Taithe, B. (2004) 'Reinventing (French) universalism: religion, humanitarianism and the "French doctors"'. *Modern and Contemporary France* 12(2): 147–158.
Tanguy, J. (2003) The Sinews of Humanitarian Assistance: Funding Policies, Practices and Pitfalls. In *Basics of International Humanitarian Missions.* Ed. by K.M. Cahill. New York: Fordham University Press/The Center for International Health and Cooperation, pp. 200–240.
Tarrow, S. (2005) *The New Transnational Activism.* Cambridge: Cambridge University Press.

Taylor, R.F. (2004) 'Extending conceptual boundaries: work, voluntary work and employment'. *Work Employment Society* 18(1): 29–49.
——(2005) Rethinking Voluntary Work. A *New Sociology of Work?* Ed. by L. Pettinger, J. Parry, R. Taylor and M. Glucksmann. Oxford: Blackwell, pp. 119–35.
Taylor, S. and Littleton, K. (2012) *Contemporary Identities of Creativity and Creative Work*. Farnham: Ashgate.
Terry, F. (2002) *Condemned to Repeat? The Paradox of Humanitarian Action*. Ithaca, NY: Cornell University Press.
Thomas, R. (2005) Caring for Those Who Care. Aid Worker Safety and Security as a Source of Stress and Distress: A Case for Psychological Support? In *Workplace Violence: Issues, trends and strategies*. Ed. by V. Bowie, B.S. Fisher and C.L. Cooper. Portland, OR: Willan Publishing, pp. 121–140.
Thunman, E. (2012) 'Burnout as a social pathology of self-realization'. *Distinktion: Scandinavian Journal of Social Theory* 13(1): 43–60.
Tiessen, R. (2004) 'Re-inventing the gendered organization: staff attitudes towards women and gender mainstreaming in NGOs in Malawi'. *Gender, Work and Organization* 11(6): 689–708.
Tilley, L. and Woodthorpe, K. (2011) 'Is it the end for anonymity as we know it? A critical examination of the ethical principle of anonymity in the context of 21st century demands on the qualitative researcher'. *Qualitative Research* 11(2): 197–212.
Tomalin, E. (2012) 'Thinking about faith-based organisations in development: where have we got to and what next?' *Development in Practice* 22(5–6): 689–703.
Tong, J. (2004) 'Questionable accountability: MSF and *Sphere* in 2003'. *Disasters* 28(2): 176–189.
Torrey, C.L. and Duffy, R.D. (2012) 'Calling and well-being among adults: differential relations by employment status'. *Journal of Career Assessment* 20(4): 415–425.
Turner, V. (1987) Betwixt and Between: The Liminal Period in Rites of Passage. In *Betwixt and Between: Patterns of Masculine and Feminine Initiation*. Ed. by L.C. Mahdi, S. Foster and M. Little. Peru: Open Court, pp. 5–22.
UNDP (2008) *Capacity Development: Empowering People and Institutions*. Annual Report.
United Nations General Assembly (2008) *Improvement of the Status of Women in the United Nations System*. Report of the Secretary-General, United Nations.
UN-Women (2012) *UN System-wide Action Plan for Implementation of the CEB United Nations System-wide Policy on Gender Equality and the Empowerment of Women*. New York: UN-Women.
Urry, J. (2007) *Mobilities*. Cambridge: Polity Press.
Van Brabant, K. (2000) Operational Security Management in Violent Environments: A Field Manual for Aid Agencies. *Good Practice Review*. London: Humanitarian Policy Group, Overseas Development Institute.
——(2001) *Mainstreaming the Organisational Management of Safety and Security*. HP Group. London: Humanitarian Policy Group.
——(2010) Managing Aid Agency Security in an Evolving World: The Larger Challenge. *EISF Article Series*. London: European Interagency Security Forum.
Van Gennep, A. (1960) *The Rites of Passage*. Chicago, IL: University of Chicago Press.
van der Klis, M. (2008) 'Continuity and change in commuter partnerships: avoiding or postponing family migration'. *GeoJournal* 71(4): 233–247.
Vaux, T. (2001) *The Selfish Altruist: Relief Work in Famine and War*. London: Earthscan.

——(2006) 'Humanitarian trends and dilemmas'. *Development in Practice* 16(3): 240–254.
Verma, R. (2007) At Work and at Play in the 'Fishbowl'? Gender Relations and Social Reproduction among Development Expatriates in Madagascar. In *Gender and Family among Transnational Professionals*. Ed. by A. Coles and A-M. Fechter. New York and London: Routledge, pp. 171–191.
Vrasti, W. (2013) *Volunteer Tourism in the Global South: Giving Back in Neoliberal Times*. London and New York: Routledge.
Walker, E.T., McCarthy, J.D. and Baumgartner, F. (2011) 'Replacing members with managers? Mutualism among membership and nonmembership advocacy organizations in the United States'. *American Journal of Sociology* 116(4): 1284–1337.
Walker, P. (2004) 'What does it mean to be a professional humanitarian?' *Journal of Humanitarian Assistance*. http://jha.ac/2004/01/01/what-does-it-mean-to-be-a-professional-humanitarian.
——(2005) 'Cracking the code: the genesis, use and future of the Code of Conduct'. *Disasters* 29(4): 323–336.
Walker, P. and Russ, C. (2010) *Professionalising the Humanitarian Sector. A Scoping Study*. Cardiff: Enhancing Learning and Research for Humanitarian Assistance (ELHRA), Save the Children.
——(2011) 'Fit for purpose: the role of modern professionalism in evolving the humanitarian endeavour'. *International Review of the Red Cross* 93(884): 1193–1210.
Walkerdine, V. (2006) 'Workers in the new economy: transformation as border crossing'. *Ethos* 34(1): 10–41.
Ward, G.F. (2010) 'The humanitarian community needs a Foreign Service'. *The Review of Faith and International Affairs* 8(4): 59–64.
Watkins, S.C., Swidler, A. and Hannan, T. (2012) 'Outsourcing social transformation: development NGOs as organizations'. *Annual Review of Sociology* 38: 285–315.
Weiss, T.G. (2012) *What's Wrong with the United Nations and How to Fix It*. Cambridge: Polity Press.
Weiss, T.G. and Collins, C. (2000) *Humanitarian Challenges and Intervention*. Boulder, CO: Westview Press.
West, C. and Fenstermaker, S. (1995) 'Doing difference'. *Gender and Society* 9(1): 8–37.
West, C. and Zimmerman, D.H. (1987) 'Doing gender'. *Gender and Society* 1(2): 125–151.
White, S. (2002) 'Thinking race, thinking development'. *Third World Quarterly* 23: 407–419.
——(2006) 'The "gender lens": a racial blinder?' *Progress in Development Studies* 6(1): 55–67.
Wiles, R., Crow, G., Heath, S. and Charles, V. (2008) 'The management of confidentiality and anonymity in Social Research'. *International Journal of Social Research Methodology* 11(5): 417–428.
Williams, S. (2004) Mission Impossible: Gender, Conflict and Oxfam GB. In *Development, Women, and War: Feminist Perspectives*. Ed. by H. Afshar and D. Eade. Oxford: Oxfam GB: 315–336.
Willmott, P. (1987) *Friendship Networks and Social Support*. London: Policy Studies Institute.
Wilson, G. (2006) 'Beyond the technocrat? The professional expert in development practice'. *Development and Change* 37(3): 501–523.
Wilson, J. (2012) 'Volunteerism research: a review essay'. *Nonprofit and Voluntary Sector Quarterly* 41(2): 176–212.

Wolkowitz, C. (2009) 'Challenging boundaries: an autobiographical perspective on the sociology of work'. *Sociology* 43(5): 846–860.

Wood, A., Apthorpe, R. and Borton, J. (2001) *Evaluating International Humanitarian Action. Reflections from Practitioners*. London: Zed Books.

Yala, A. (2005) *Volontaire en ONG: l'aventure ambigue*. Paris: Editions Charles Leopold Mayer.

Yarrow, T. (2008) 'Life/history: personal narratives of development amongst NGO workers and activists in Ghana'. *Africa* 78(3): 334–358.

Index

abolitionism 18, 98
abuse 141
ActionAid 27, 130
Active Learning Network for Accountability in Humanitarian Action (ALNAP) 34, 85, 87
activism 10, 18, 41, 68–9
  corporatization of 2
advertising 6
advocacy 2, 5, 27–8, 39, 62, 71–2, 95, 120, 155
Afghanistan 30, 32, 39, 118, 174
aidworker memoirs 27, 103
altruism 43, 46, 51–2, 59, 61, 63, 70, 82, 93
Annan, K. 22
Antares Foundation 97, 169
apartheid 40
Arab Spring 171
Association pour la Taxation des Transactions pour l'Aide aux Citoyens (ATTAC) 2, 14
asylum seekers 9, 71, 170–1
audit cultures 5, 62
Australian Agency for International Development (AusAid) 21
Australian Development Agency (ADA) 21

Balkans 141
BandAid 41–2
Battle of Seattle 2
beneficiaries 2–4, 8, 31, 35–6, 43
best practice 36, 158
Biafra 27, 68
bilateral organizations 19–21, 24–6, 37, 40–1, 43
biographical approach 1, 3, 9–13, 16, 48, 57, 59, 66, 69, 176

biographical continuity 176–7
Bono 68
Bosnia 30, 39, 136, 144, 174
Boundary-crossing 12–13, 54–5, 63, 65–6, 73, 77, 82, 153
brain drain 77, 146, 157
Branding 2, 43, 52–3, 64
  Brand Aid 42
Bretton Woods 19
briefings 85–8, 120, 134, 146, 157
  de-briefing 61, 85–8, 91, 98, 164, 174
Britain 7, 18, 20, 26–7, 37, 48–9
bunkerization 138–9
bureaucracy 25, 34, 51, 94–5, 150–1
burnout 57–60, 97, 160, 166
buzzwords 38–40

calling 51–2, 70
capacity building 129–33, 145–6, 177
capitalism 7, 18, 50–1, 57
  new spirit of 58, 62
CARE 18, 26, 28, 34
Career 36, 38, 4347–52, 60–2, 67–75, 82,
  boundary-less 13, 54–5, 63, 65–6, 77
  patchwork 57, 77
  protean 54, 79
Catholics 26
celebrities 2, 7, 41–2, 67
celebrity humanitarianism 2, 7, 41–2, 67–8
Central Emergency Response Fund (CERF) 31
charisma 10, 27, 120
charities 18, 28–9, 68–9
Charity Commission 48
China 19, 40
Christians 17, 29–30, 69, 77, 140

206 *Index*

citizenship 47, 68, 154, 168, 170
  visa 56, 99, 103, 113
  work permit 56, 99, 103, 113
civil rights 41
civil society 5, 25, 29, 31
class 11–12, 17, 45–7, 53–4, 63
  (upper) middle class 7, 47, 54, 63, 66, 72
  working class 54, 69, 71
climate change 7, 43, 171–2
cluster approach 31, 89
codes of conduct 35–6, 53–4, 73, 81, 134, 158
Cold War 11, 16, 19, 30, 40
colonial administration 19–20
colonialism 4, 6, 12, 16–20, 27
Commonwealth 20, 40
communism 19, 29
competition 37, 47–8, 84, 88–91, 143, 150, 162
complex emergencies 30–1
compradore class 129
consultancy/consultants 2, 7, 11–12, 16, 21, 32, 37, 46, 49–50, 55, 72, 76–7, 87, 109, 126, 141, 149, 154, 160–6, 175
consumer culture 50, 63
Cooke, B. 39
cooperation 88–91
cosmopolitanism 56, 68, 136, 159
crisis situations 70–4, 115, 120, 135, 148, 169
Cuba 99
culture 124–5, 129, 131–5, 139–41, 144
curfews 138
curriculum issues 38

Dammam, M. 23
death rates of aidworkers 86
debt 19, 24–5, 42
decolonialization 16, 27, 168
Department for International Development (DFID) 8, 32
Department of Safety and Security 34
development 1, 3–6, 8–10, 12, 14
  celebrities 41–2
  gender 22–4, 111–13, 116–17, 119–20
  historical overview 16–22
  new donors 40–1
  NGOs 26–30
  professionalization 34–8, 52–4
Development Assistance Committee (DAC) 19–20, 26, 31, 40, 43, 130

development studies 4–5, 8, 36–7, 67, 75, 135, 162–3, 165, 168
diaspora 3, 29, 40, 119, 171–2
diplomatic corps 54
diplomats/diplomacy 70, 75, 82, 177
distance learning 38
distant suffering 6–7, 41, 43, 60, 71
divorce 70, 111, 113–16
  divorce rates 103
dominance 40, 61, 143
donors 1–2, 11, 19–20, 22, 25–6
  new 40–1
Dunant, H. 18, 27, 32

edgework 63–4, 91–2
education 74–6
Ekman, S. 90
Emergency Sex and Other Desperate Measures 103
emotional intelligence 60
employability 78
Engineers Without Borders 88
Enhancing Learning and Research for Humanitarian Assistance (ELHRA) 35
epiphany 66
ethics 41, 57, 70, 89, 164, 176, 178
  development ethics 61
ethnic minorities 18, 54, 69, 170–1
EU Volunteers 165
European Community Humanitarian Office (ECHO) 47
European Union (EU) 37, 47, 103, 153, 165
Eurostep 26
expatriates 2–4, 8, 11, 13–14, 23–4
  expatriate bubble 136–42
Eyben, R. 119

Failure Reports 88
Fair trade 7, 18, 155, 171
faith-based organizations 28–30, 43, 50–1, 62
family life 112–16, 127
  children 100, 103, 111, 113–16, 118, 150, 166, 178
  family planning 154–5, 162
Fast, L. 34
Fechter, A.-M. 134,
Feinstein International Center 87
feminism 25, 46, 112, 117
Ferree, M.M. 17, 48, 112,
financial crisis 135, 171
First World War 18–19

flexibility 54–7, 59, 63, 65–6, 79–81
  career decisions 148, 162, 166
  life-work balance 83–4, 99, 109
fuzzwords 38–40

gap years 42, 47, 55, 67
  gap year industry 42, 67
Gates, B. 18
Geldof, B. 68
gender 11, 13, 17, 22–4, 38
  and development 22–4, 43, 112
  gender differences 11, 100, 112–13, 115, 117–18, 122, 124–5, 133
  macho 111, 119–21, 123, 142
  (un)doing gender 111–27
  Women in Development 23, 43
General Assembly 23, 34
Generation Y 58
Geneva Conventions 18
genocide 16–17, 27
geopolitics 1, 46, 68–70
Ghodsee, K. 30
glass cliff 61
globalization 1, 29, 55–6, 161
Glucksmann, M. 46
graduates 9, 11, 21, 37, 54, 66–7, 69, 93
greedy organizations 109, 111
Gross Domestic Product (GDP) 171
Gross National Product (GNP) 20
guilt/guilty 50, 69, 92, 136, 156

Haiti 28, 88–9, 174
Hancock, G. 46
handbooks 35
Harrell-Bond, B. 54
Haskell, T. 18
head offices 6, 8, 11–12, 21, 50
healthcare professionals 51
hegemony 25
helping imperative 60–2
helping professions 51, 54, 60–1, 82, 103, 151, 171
Hepburn, A. 71
heteronormativity 61–2, 104
heteroprofessionalism 61
hierarchies 129–33
Hilhorst, D. 4–5, 8, 35, 48, 113, 130,
HIV/AIDS 27, 104
Holocaust 27
homosexuals 61, 104
hook-up cultures 102, 154
human rights 1, 5, 7, 11, 16–19
humanitarian arena 5, 71

Humanitarian Data Exchange (HDX) 87
Humanitarian Practice Network (HPN) 34, 158
humanitarian professional 53
humanitarian reason 2, 51, 62
humanitarian studies 5, 9, 14, 16, 35–8, 73, 82, 129, 134, 162, 164–5, 173, 176
humanitarianism 1–9, 12, 14, 16–18, 22
  complex emergencies 30–1
  professionalization 34–8, 52–4
Hunter, S. 61
Hurricane Katrina 51, 55
Hyndman, J. 127

ideology 112
Illich, I. 64
impact of aidwork 150–1
imperialism 16–17, 136
induction 85
industrialization 5, 17–18
information and communications technology (ICT) 87
International Humanitarian Studies Association (IHSA) 35
International Monetary Fund (IMF) 19, 22, 24–5
International Rescue Committee (IRC) 18
intersectionality 1, 13–14, 112, 119, 125, 129, 135, 176
introverts 101
Iraq 39, 111, 173–4
Islam 29–30

Jubilee Debt Campaign 25, 42

Kapoor, I. 7, 18
Keats, J. 60
Knowledge 4, 13, 42, 53, 66, 75, 96, 128–9, 132, 149
  academic knowledge 38
  expert knowledge 10, 20, 49, 53, 82, 87, 118, 134, 145, 153, 160–1, 166, 170
  knowledge transfer 170
  local knowledge 36, 131, 134, 145, 156, 169
  practical knowledge 74, 163, 165
  self knowledge 61
Knox Clarke, P. 116
Kosovo 23, 39, 174
Kouchner, B. 10, 27
Kuwait 40

lack of qualifications/experience 76–7
language/language skills 81, 132, 139, 141, 143, 146, 153, 155, 169
  Arabic 74, 175
  Asian 74
  English 38, 73–4, 98, 108, 131, 136–7, 140, 142, 145, 152, 173, 175
  French 74, 98, 142, 152, 175
  German 142, 175
  lingua franca 74, 137, 142, 145, 175
  non-European 74
  Oxbridge 14
  Spanish 74, 142, 175
  Swedish 142
leadership styles 120–4, 126–7
learning opportunities 151–4, 166
Lewis, D. 12
Libya 39
life-course/life-history perspective 9–10, 12, 14, 48, 55, 66, 69, 127, 168, 176–8
liminality 17, 66–73, 161, 174
LiveAid 41–2
living apart, together (LAT) 99, 104
locals 2–4, 128–47, 152–3, 156, 177
logistics 11, 32, 38, 53, 73, 76, 116, 120, 123–4, 153, 157
low-carbon economies 50

Mafessoli, M. 104
Make Poverty History 42
making a difference 92–6, 109, 129, 132, 144, 151, 161, 166–8
managerialism/managerial techniques 5, 25, 51–4
  middle manager 90
Manning, R. 40
marketization 5, 25
marriage 17, 48, 103–4, 113–15, 140–1, 154
Marshall Plan 19
Master's degrees 37–8, 65, 67, 78, 162–5
Maxwell, D.G. 26
MDM 26
Medair 29, 173
Médecins Sans Frontières (MSF) 6, 10, 23, 26–7, 35–6
media 4, 32, 41–3, 68, 71, 73–5, 81–2, 98, 165
  Access Campaign 27
mental health 57
  anxiety 59, 86
  depression 59, 158
mentoring 120–1, 145

Mexico 25
micro-credit 156
Middle East 10, 40, 81, 85–6, 96, 105, 119, 152, 169, 174
migrants 18, 56, 69, 71, 171
military 4, 24, 31–2, 38–9, 41
Millennium Development Goals 20, 25, 32
Minear, L. 5, 134
missionaries 4, 6, 17–19, 29–30, 62, 68, 77, 140
mobility 1, 54–7, 63, 69, 84, 109, 112–13, 141, 149, 162, 166
modernization 16–18, 168–72
multiculturality 36, 99, 159
multidisciplinarity 36–7
multilateral organizations 21–2, 25, 37, 40–1, 52–3, 72, 87
Muslims 29–30, 139

national aidworkers 2–4, 8–9, 11, 13, 24
National Health Service (NHS) 61
National Professional Officers 21
nationalism 18
Nazis 27
negative capability 60–2
neo-colonialism 4, 25, 62, 117
neo-liberalism 1–2, 5, 12, 21, 25–6
neo-tribalism 104
nepotism 80
Network on Humanitarian Assistance (NOHA) 37
networks 79–80, 85, 89, 91, 104
neutrality 6, 27, 31–2, 35, 83
Nobel Prize 27, 68
non-governmental organizations (NGOs) 2, 4–5, 10–12, 18, 21–6
  faith-based organizations 28–30
  professionalization 34–8, 52–4

Occupy 171
O'Dempsey, T. 39
Office for the Coordination of Humanitarian Affairs (OCHA) 21, 31, 87, 89
official development assistance (ODA) 19, 26, 31, 52–4
oil 24, 29
Ojelay-Surtees, B. 14
Omi, M. 14
OPEC 40
Organization for Economic Cooperation and Development (OECD) 19, 31, 40

Organization for European Economic
    Cooperation (OEEC) 19
Otherness 17, 61, 128–47
Oxfam 6, 18, 23, 26–8, 40, 48, 130, 173

Palestine/Palestinians 6, 97
parochialism 136
paternalism 61, 133, 146
patriarchy 117
Peace Corps 67
peacekeeping 22, 31–2, 38, 40, 141, 149
pensions 165
People in Aid 35–6, 158, 169
perception studies 134, 139
Pérouse de Montclos, M.-A. 87
persistence 79, 81
personal crises 70–3
personal growth 57–60, 62–3, 84, 97,
    129, 151, 166
Petersen, M. 30
Petras, J. 6
philanthrocapitalism 18
Pierce, J.L. 123
policies/policy-making 10, 19–21, 25, 27,
    32, 93, 120
political values 68–70
post-colonialism 17, 25, 40, 139, 168
post-Fordism 36
post-independence development 18–22
post-interventionism 39
post-modernism 56
post-traumatic stress disorder
    (PTSD) 97
poverty 6, 18, 20–1, 25–7, 36
Powell, C. 32
power relations 3–5, 8, 17–18, 39, 61
preparation 84–8
private sector 5, 12, 23, 38, 47
private sphere 46, 58, 101, 111,
    125, 138
privatization 5, 25
professionalization 9, 13, 26, 28–9, 43
Professionals in Humanitarian
    Assistance (PHAP) 35
profit 18, 171
promotion 84, 116–20, 145–6, 150,
    159, 170
prostitution 103, 141
Protestants 26
psychosocial support 96–8
public sector 23, 38, 47, 153, 157–8
public sphere 46, 101, 111, 125, 138

qualifications 73–7, 80, 84, 88, 117

race/racism 61–2, 69, 117, 141–3,
    168–70, 172
racial project 4, 14, 24
Rainhorn, J.-D. 37
Rajak, D. 56
re-evaluation of life 70–3
recession 159
recognition 58–9, 66, 90, 163
recruitment 116–20, 122
Red Crescent 2, 33, 35, 87
Red Cross 2, 16, 18, 27, 33–5, 75, 78,
    87, 111, 173
Redfield, P. 35
reflective practice 50, 60, 149,
    162, 174
refugees 5–6, 8–9, 11, 16, 18
relationships 102–6, 113, 115–16, 122,
    127, 133, 140–1, 176
ReliefWeb 85, 87
religious values 68–70
remittances 40, 171
resilience 3, 5–6, 8, 39, 54, 135,
    143–4
respect 129–35, 139
retirement 50, 55, 160, 165
reverse aid 6
risk/risk taking 60–3, 100, 126, 135,
    154, 156
  high-risk activism 10, 48
  putting at risk 86, 104, 114, 121, 133,
      138, 144, 146
  risk reduction 35, 135
romance 102–4
Rottenburg, R. 178
Russ, C. 37
Rwanda 16–17, 28, 34, 41, 173, 175

salaries 8, 10, 26, 47–50, 52–4, 73–4, 77,
    130–1, 135, 145
Salvation Army 18
Save the Children 18, 23, 26–7, 173
Second World War 18–19, 144
secondments 149, 152, 170
securitization 9
security 32, 38, 63
  financial security 13, 160
  human security 39
  job security 49, 100
  lack of security 31
  security advisers 34, 86
  security concerns 9
  security guards 7
  security incidents 84, 86, 91–2,
      121, 158

security management 83
security measures 33–4, 63, 92, 135
security situation 13, 86, 90, 92, 100, 113, 138
security threats 92
work-life balance 83, 86, 90–2, 98, 100
Security Council 22
segregation 138, 169, 171
self-governance 87, 162, 166
self-realization 57–60, 63, 73–4, 81, 84, 88, 92, 151
self-regulation 57
senior management 8, 22–4, 47
separate spheres 105–9
September 11 2001 2, 30–4, 51
sex 102–4, 109, 122, 133, 141
sexpatriates 103
sexual orientation 104, 176, 178
shared experiences 106–9
Simeant, J. 34
Simon, D. 19
Slim, H. 53, 60
slow culture 50, 63
Smilie, I. 5
social media 41, 178
social movements 9–10, 13–14, 46, 56, 59, 168
  new social movements 42, 48
  student movement 10
social work 55, 60, 69, 98, 168–9
Solferino, battle of 18
solidarity 4, 12, 29–30, 40–2, 46, 58, 68–9, 81, 159, 172
Somalia 29, 41, 173
South Africa 8, 28, 40, 130, 173
Soviet Union 30, 40
Sphere Handbook 35, 54, 89
Sri Lanka 28, 80, 173
Standards 22, 34, 36, 43–4, 53–4, 73, 81, 88–9, 114, 134, 139, 155–6, 158
  dissemination of 35
  Western standards 147
Stay-and-deliver 34
Steering Committee for Humanitarian Response 35
stereotypes 119, 121
Stirrat, J. 28, 56
stress 50–1, 58–9, 86, 90, 97
Stroup, S.S. 26, 28, 48
structural adjustment loans 25
sub-Saharan Africa 101, 169

Swedish International Development Cooperation Agency (SIDA) 20
Syria 41

Tearfund 29, 173
third culture individuals (TCIs) 140
third sector 23, 46–50, 55–6, 61, 158
third sex 124–5
Third World 40
Tobin Tax 2
total institution 101–2
total social organization of work (TSOL) 46
tourism 47, 98–9
  aid tourism 63
  disaster tourists 56
  humanitarian tourists 109
trade agreements/politics 6, 19, 40, 70, 155, 171–2
trade unions 19, 91
training 3, 5, 10, 18, 32, 35, 39–40, 47, 53, 72, 75–7, 166, 178
  academic training 74, 164–5
  as incentive 36, 152
  job training 13, 38, 66, 73, 153, 160
  resources for 28
  training opportunities 36, 54, 152, 159, 162
  training programmes 38, 54, 67, 73, 86, 131, 161, 163
transferable skills 54–5, 66, 72, 77, 82, 158, 169
transnational experiences 66–7
traumatic experiences 96–9, 101, 104, 106–7, 109, 135, 160, 168
tsunami 28, 51, 79
Tufts University, Massachusetts 87
Turkey 41
turning points 70, 168, 176–7

United Kingdom (UK) 26–7, 32, 37, 40, 48, 76, 171, 173, 175
United Nations Development Programme (UNDP) 21
United Nations Entity for Gender Equality and Empowerment of Women (UN Women) 23
United Nations High Commissioner for Refugees (UNHCR) 21, 23, 29, 97
United Nations Relief and Works Agency for Palestinian Refugees (UNWRA) 6

United Nations (UN) 2, 10–11, 16, 21–3, 25
  career decisions 149–54
  complex emergencies 30–1, 33–4
  entry requirements 67, 74, 77–80
  gender 116, 118–21, 126
  historical overview 29, 37, 43
  Joint Inspections Unit 22
  Secretary General 23
  UNICEF 23, 29
United Nations Volunteers (UNV) 22
United States (US) 19–20, 26–30, 37, 41, 49, 99, 173, 175
Urry, J. 55

values 1, 47, 49–53, 58–9, 63, 68–70, 101, 108, 134, 137, 148, 176–7
Vaux, T. 10
Veltmeyer, H. 6
Verma, R. 103
Vietnam War 41
violence 96–7, 168–9

vocation 51–2, 62–3
Voluntary Service Overseas (VSO) 165
volunteering/volunteer tourism 47, 56, 63, 78, 126

Walker, P. 26, 37, 53
War on Terror 16, 30–4
Ward, G.F. 64
Winant, H. 14
work experience 74–6, 78–80
work styles 120–4, 143
work-life balance 83–110, 113, 115
World Bank 19, 22, 25, 153
World Food Programme (WFP) 21, 23, 29–30, 173
World Health Organization (WHO) 23, 173
World Social Forum (WSF) 2
World Vision International (WVI) 26, 29, 173
World Wars 18–19, 144

Yarrow, T. 48

eBooks
from Taylor & Francis
Helping you to choose the right eBooks for your Library

Add to your library's digital collection today with Taylor & Francis eBooks. We have over 50,000 eBooks in the Humanities, Social Sciences, Behavioural Sciences, Built Environment and Law, from leading imprints, including Routledge, Focal Press and Psychology Press.

Choose from a range of subject packages or create your own!

Benefits for you
- Free MARC records
- COUNTER-compliant usage statistics
- Flexible purchase and pricing options
- 70% approx of our eBooks are now DRM-free.

Benefits for your user
- Off-site, anytime access via Athens or referring URL
- Print or copy pages or chapters
- Full content search
- Bookmark, highlight and annotate text
- Access to thousands of pages of quality research at the click of a button.

Free Trials Available

We offer free trials to qualifying academic, corporate and government customers.

eCollections
Choose from 20 different subject eCollections, including:

- Asian Studies
- Economics
- Health Studies
- Law
- Middle East Studies

eFocus
We have 16 cutting-edge interdisciplinary collections, including:

- Development Studies
- The Environment
- Islam
- Korea
- Urban Studies

For more information, pricing enquiries or to order a free trial, please contact your local sales team:

UK/Rest of World: **online.sales@tandf.co.uk**
USA/Canada/Latin America: **e-reference@taylorandfrancis.com**
East/Southeast Asia: **martin.jack@tandf.com.sg**
India: **journalsales@tandfindia.com**

www.tandfebooks.com

Lightning Source UK Ltd.
Milton Keynes UK
UKHW02f2328270718
326426UK00003B/80/P